Nutshell

of

WEST PUBLISHING COMPANY

P.O. Box 64526

St. Paul, Minnesota 55164–0526

Accounting—Law and, 1984, 377 pages, by E. McGruder Faris, Late Professor of Law, Stetson University.

Administrative Law and Process, 2nd Ed., 1981, 445 pages, by Ernest Gellhorn, Former Dean and Professor of Law, Case Western Reserve University and Barry B. Boyer, Professor of Law, SUNY, Buffalo.

Admiralty, 1983, 390 pages, by Frank L. Maraist, Professor of Law, Louisiana State University.

Agency-Partnership, 1977, 364 pages, by Roscoe T. Steffen, Late Professor of Law, University of Chicago.

American Indian Law, 1981, 288 pages, by William C. Canby, Jr., Adjunct Professor of Law, Arizona State University.

Antitrust Law and Economics, 3rd Ed., 1986, 472 pages, by Ernest Gellhorn, Former Dean and Professor of Law, Case Western Reserve University.

Appellate Advocacy, 1984, 325 pages, by Alan D. Hornstein, Professor of Law, University of Maryland.

Art Law, 1984, 335 pages, by Leonard D. DuBoff, Professor of Law, Lewis and Clark College, Northwestern School of Law.

Banking and Financial Institutions, 1984, 409 pages, by William A. Lovett, Professor of Law, Tulane University.

Church-State Relations—Law of, 1981, 305 pages, by Leonard F. Manning, Late Professor of Law, Fordham University.

Civil Procedure, 2nd Ed., 1986, 306 pages, by Mary Kay Kane, Professor of Law, University of California, Hastings College of the Law.

Civil Rights, 1978, 279 pages, by Norman Vieira, Professor of Law, Southern Illinois University.

Commercial Paper, 3rd Ed., 1982, 404 pages, by Charles M. Weber, Professor of Business Law, University of Arizona and Richard E. Speidel, Professor of Law, Northwestern University.

Community Property, 1982, 447 pages, by Robert L. Mennell, Former Professor of Law, Hamline University.

Comparative Legal Traditions, 1982, 402 pages, by Mary Ann Glendon, Professor of Law, Harvard University, Michael Wallace Gordon, Professor of Law, University of Florida and Christopher Osakwe, Professor of Law, Tulane University.

Conflicts, 1982, 470 pages, by David D. Siegel, Professor of Law, St. John's University.

Constitutional Analysis, 1979, 388 pages, by Jerre S. Williams, Professor of Law Emeritus, University of Texas.

Constitutional Federalism, 2nd Ed., 1987, 411 pages, by David E. Engdahl, Professor of Law, University of Puget Sound.

Constitutional Law, 1986, 389 pages, by Jerome A. Barron, Dean and Professor of Law, George Washington University and C. Thomas Dienes, Professor of Law, George Washington University.

Consumer Law, 2nd Ed., 1981, 418 pages, by David G. Epstein, Dean and Professor of Law, Emory University and Steve H. Nickles, Professor of Law, University of Minnesota.

Contract Remedies, 1981, 323 pages, by Jane M. Friedman, Professor of Law, Wayne State University.

Contracts, 2nd Ed., 1984, 425 pages, by Gordon D. Schaber, Dean and Professor of Law, McGeorge School of Law and Claude D. Rohwer, Professor of Law, McGeorge School of Law.

Corporations—Law of, 2nd Ed., 1987, 515 pages, by Robert W. Hamilton, Professor of Law, University of Texas.

Corrections and Prisoners' Rights—Law of, 2nd Ed., 1983, 386 pages, by Sheldon Krantz, Dean and Professor of Law, University of San Diego.

Criminal Law, 2nd Ed., 1987, 321 pages, by Arnold H. Loewy, Professor of Law, University of North Carolina.

Criminal Procedure—Constitutional Limitations, 3rd Ed., 1980, 438 pages, by Jerold H. Israel, Professor of Law, University of Michigan and Wayne R. LaFave, Professor of Law, University of Illinois.

Debtor-Creditor Law, 3rd Ed., 1986, 383 pages, by David G. Epstein, Dean and Professor of Law, Emory University.

Employment Discrimination—Federal Law of, 2nd Ed., 1981, 402 pages, by Mack A. Player, Professor of Law, University of Georgia.

Energy Law, 1981, 338 pages, by Joseph P. Tomain, Professor of Law, University of Cincinnatti.

Environmental Law, 1983, 343 pages by Roger W. Findley, Professor of Law, University of Illinois and Daniel A. Farber, Professor of Law, University of Minnesota.

Estate and Gift Taxation, Federal, 3rd Ed., 1983, 509 pages, by John K. McNulty, Professor of Law, University of California, Berkeley.

Estate Planning—Introduction to, 3rd Ed., 1983, 370 pages, by Robert J. Lynn, Professor of Law, Ohio State University.

Evidence, Federal Rules of, 2nd Ed., 1987, 473 pages, by Michael H. Graham, Professor of Law, University of Miami.

Evidence, State and Federal Rules, 2nd Ed., 1981, 514 pages, by Paul F. Rothstein, Professor of Law, Georgetown University.

Family Law, 2nd Ed., 1986, 444 pages, by Harry D. Krause, Professor of Law, University of Illinois.

Federal Jurisdiction, 2nd Ed., 1981, 258 pages, by David P. Currie, Professor of Law, University of Chicago.

Future Interests, 1981, 361 pages, by Lawrence W. Waggoner, Professor of Law, University of Michigan.

Government Contracts, 1979, 423 pages, by W. Noel Keyes, Professor of Law, Pepperdine University.

Historical Introduction to Anglo-American Law, 2nd Ed., 1973, 280 pages, by Frederick G. Kempin, Jr., Professor of Business Law, Wharton School of Finance and Commerce, University of Pennsylvania.

Immigration Law and Procedure, 1984, 345 pages, by David Weissbrodt, Professor of Law, University of Minnesota.

Injunctions, 1974, 264 pages, by John F. Dobbyn, Professor of Law, Villanova University.

Insurance Law, 1981, 281 pages, by John F. Dobbyn, Professor of Law, Villanova University.

Intellectual Property—Patents, Trademarks and Copyright, 1983, 428 pages, by Arthur R. Miller, Professor of Law, Harvard University, and Michael H. Davis, Professor of Law, Cleveland State University, Cleveland-Marshall College of Law.

International Business Transactions, 2nd Ed., 1984, 476 pages, by Donald T. Wilson, Late Professor of Law, Loyola University, Los Angeles.

International Law (Public), 1985, 262 pages, by Thomas Buergenthal, Professor of Law, Emory University and Harold G. Maier, Professor of Law, Vanderbilt University.

Introduction to the Study and Practice of Law, 1983, 418 pages, by Kenney F. Hegland, Professor of Law, University of Arizona.

Judicial Process, 1980, 292 pages, by William L. Reynolds, Professor of Law, University of Maryland.

Jurisdiction, 4th Ed., 1980, 232 pages, by Albert A. Ehrenzweig, Late Professor of Law, University of California, Berkeley, David W. Louisell, Late Professor of Law, University of California, Berkeley and Geoffrey C. Hazard, Jr., Professor of Law, Yale Law School.

Juvenile Courts, 3rd Ed., 1984, 291 pages, by Sanford J. Fox, Professor of Law, Boston College.

Labor Arbitration Law and Practice, 1979, 358 pages, by Dennis R. Nolan, Professor of Law, University of South Carolina.

Labor Law, 2nd Ed., 1986, 397 pages, by Douglas L. Leslie, Professor of Law, University of Virginia.

Land Use, 2nd Ed., 1985, 356 pages, by Robert R. Wright, Professor of Law, University of Arkansas, Little Rock and Susan Webber Wright, Professor of Law, University of Arkansas, Little Rock.

Landlord and Tenant Law, 2nd Ed., 1986, 311 pages, by David S. Hill, Professor of Law, University of Colorado.

Law Study and Law Examinations—Introduction to, 1971, 389 pages, by Stanley V. Kinyon, Late Professor of Law, University of Minnesota.

Legal Interviewing and Counseling, 2nd Ed., 1987, 487 pages, by Thomas L. Shaffer, Professor of Law, Washington and Lee University and James R. Elkins, Professor of Law, West Virginia University.

Legal Research, 4th Ed., 1985, 452 pages, by Morris L. Cohen, Professor of Law and Law Librarian, Yale University.

Legal Writing, 1982, 294 pages, by Lynn B. Squires and Marjorie Dick Rombauer, Professor of Law, University of Washington.

Legislative Law and Process, 2nd Ed., 1986, 346 pages, by Jack Davies, Professor of Law, William Mitchell College of Law.

Local Government Law, 2nd Ed., 1983, 404 pages, by David J. McCarthy, Jr., Professor of Law, Georgetown University.

Mass Communications Law, 2nd Ed., 1983, 473 pages, by Harvey L. Zuckman, Professor of Law, Catholic University and Martin J. Gaynes, Lecturer in Law, Temple University.

Medical Malpractice—The Law of, 2nd Ed., 1986, 342 pages, by Joseph H. King, Professor of Law, University of Tennessee.

Military Law, 1980, 378 pages, by Charles A. Shanor, Professor of Law, Emory University and Timothy P. Terrell, Professor of Law, Emory University.

Oil and Gas Law, 1983, 443 pages, by John S. Lowe, Professor of Law, University of Tulsa.

Personal Property, 1983, 322 pages, by Barlow Burke, Jr., Professor of Law, American University.

Post-Conviction Remedies, 1978, 360 pages, by Robert Popper, Dean and Professor of Law, University of Missouri, Kansas City.

Presidential Power, 1977, 328 pages, by Arthur Selwyn Miller, Professor of Law Emeritus, George Washington University.

Products Liability, 2nd Ed., 1981, 341 pages, by Dix W. Noel, Late Professor of Law, University of Tennessee and Jerry J. Phillips, Professor of Law, University of Tennessee.

Professional Responsibility, 1980, 399 pages, by Robert H. Aronson, Professor of Law, University of Washington, and Donald T. Weckstein, Professor of Law, University of San Diego.

Real Estate Finance, 2nd Ed., 1985, 262 pages, by Jon W. Bruce, Professor of Law, Vanderbilt University.

Real Property, 2nd Ed., 1981, 448 pages, by Roger H. Bernhardt, Professor of Law, Golden Gate University.

Regulated Industries, 2nd Ed., 1987, 389 pages, by Ernest Gellhorn, Former Dean and Professor of Law, Case Western Reserve University, and Richard J. Pierce, Professor of Law, Southern Methodist University.

Remedies, 2nd Ed., 1985, 320 pages, by John F. O'Connell, Professor of Law, University of La Verne College of Law.

Res Judicata, 1976, 310 pages, by Robert C. Casad, Professor of Law, University of Kansas.

Sales, 2nd Ed., 1981, 370 pages, by John M. Stockton, Professor of Business Law, Wharton School of Finance and Commerce, University of Pennsylvania.

Schools, Students and Teachers—Law of, 1984, 409 pages, by Kern Alexander, President, Western Kentucky University and M. David Alexander, Professor, Virginia Tech University.

Sea—Law of, 1984, 264 pages, by Louis B. Sohn, Professor of Law, University of Georgia and Kristen Gustafson.

Secured Transactions, 2nd Ed., 1981, 391 pages, by Henry J. Bailey, Professor of Law Emeritus, Willamette University.

Securities Regulation, 2nd Ed., 1982, 322 pages, by David L. Ratner, Dean and Professor of Law, University of San Francisco.

Sex Discrimination, 1982, 399 pages, by Claire Sherman Thomas, Lecturer, University of Washington, Women's Studies Department.

Taxation and Finance, State and Local, 1986, 309 pages, by M. David Gelfand, Professor of Law, Tulane University and Peter W. Salsich, Professor of Law, St. Louis University.

Taxation of Corporations and Stockholders, Federal Income, 2nd Ed., 1981, 362 pages, by Jonathan Sobeloff, Late Professor of Law, Georgetown University and Peter P. Weidenbruch, Jr., Professor of Law, Georgetown University.

Taxation of Individuals, Federal Income, 3rd Ed., 1983, 487 pages, by John K. McNulty, Professor of Law, University of California, Berkeley.

Torts—Injuries to Persons and Property, 1977, 434 pages, by Edward J. Kionka, Professor of Law, Southern Illinois University.

Torts—Injuries to Family, Social and Trade Relations, 1979, 358 pages, by Wex S. Malone, Professor of Law Emeritus, Louisiana State University.

Trial Advocacy, 1979, 402 pages, by Paul B. Bergman, Adjunct Professor of Law, University of California, Los Angeles.

Trial and Practice Skills, 1978, 346 pages, by Kenney F. Hegland, Professor of Law, University of Arizona.

Trial, The First—Where Do I Sit? What Do I Say?, 1982, 396 pages, by Steven H. Goldberg, Professor of Law, University of Minnesota.

Unfair Trade Practices, 1982, 445 pages, by Charles R. McManis, Professor of Law, Washington University.

Uniform Commercial Code, 2nd Ed., 1984, 516 pages, by Bradford Stone, Professor of Law, Stetson University.

Uniform Probate Code, 2nd Ed., 1987, 454 pages, by Lawrence H. Averill, Jr., Dean and Professor of Law, University of Arkansas, Little Rock.

Water Law, 1984, 439 pages, by David H. Getches, Professor of Law, University of Colorado.

Welfare Law—Structure and Entitlement, 1979, 455 pages, by Arthur B. LaFrance, Professor of Law, Lewis and Clark College, Northwestern School of Law.

Wills and Trusts, 1979, 392 pages, by Robert L. Mennell, Former Professor of Law, Hamline University.

Workers' Compensation and Employee Protection Laws, 1984, 274 pages, by Jack B. Hood, Former Professor of Law, Cumberland School of Law, Samford University and Benjamin A. Hardy, Former Professor of Law, Cumberland School of Law, Samford University.

Hornbook Series

and

Basic Legal Texts

of

WEST PUBLISHING COMPANY

P.O. Box 64526

St. Paul, Minnesota 55164–0526

Admiralty and Maritime Law, Schoenbaum's Hornbook on, 1987, about 550 pages, by Thomas J. Schoenbaum, Professor of Law, University of Georgia.

Agency and Partnership, Reuschlein & Gregory's Hornbook on the Law of, 1979 with 1981 Pocket Part, 625 pages, by Harold Gill Reuschlein, Professor of Law Emeritus, Villanova University and William A. Gregory, Professor of Law, Georgia State University.

Antitrust, Sullivan's Hornbook on the Law of, 1977, 886 pages, by Lawrence A. Sullivan, Professor of Law, University of California, Berkeley.

Civil Procedure, Friedenthal, Kane and Miller's Hornbook on, 1985, 876 pages, by Jack H. Friedental, Professor of Law, Stanford University, Mary Kay Kane, Professor of Law, University of California, Hastings College of the Law and Arthur R. Miller, Professor of Law, Harvard University.

Common Law Pleading, Koffler and Reppy's Hornbook on, 1969, 663 pages, by Joseph H. Koffler, Professor of Law, New York Law School and Alison Reppy, Late Dean and Professor of Law, New York Law School.

Conflict of Laws, Scoles and Hay's Hornbook on, 1982, with 1986 Pocket Part, 1085 pages, by Eugene F. Scoles, Professor of Law, University of Illinois and Peter Hay, Dean and Professor of Law, University of Illinois.

Constitutional Law, Nowak, Rotunda and Young's Hornbook on, 3rd Ed., 1986, 1191 pages, by John E. Nowak, Professor of Law, University of Illinois, Ronald D. Rotunda, Professor of Law, University of Illinois, and J. Nelson Young, Late Professor of Law, University of North Carolina.

Contracts, Calamari and Perillo's Hornbook on, 3rd Ed., 1987, 1049 pages, by John D. Calamari, Professor of Law, Fordham University and Joseph M. Perillo, Professor of Law, Fordham University.

Contracts, Corbin's One Volume Student Ed., 1952, 1224 pages, by Arthur L. Corbin, Late Professor of Law, Yale University.

Corporations, Henn and Alexander's Hornbook on, 3rd Ed., 1983, with 1986 Pocket Part, 1371 pages, by Harry G. Henn, Professor of Law Emeritus, Cornell University and John R. Alexander.

Criminal Law, LaFave and Scott's Hornbook on, 2nd Ed., 1986, 918 pages, by Wayne R. LaFave, Professor of Law, University of Illinois, and Austin Scott, Jr., Late Professor of Law, University of Colorado.

Criminal Procedure, LaFave and Israel's Hornbook on, 1985 with 1986 pocket part, 1142 pages, by Wayne R. LaFave, Professor of Law, University of Illinois and Jerold H. Israel, Professor of Law University of Michigan.

Damages, McCormick's Hornbook on, 1935, 811 pages, by Charles T. McCormick, Late Dean and Professor of Law, University of Texas.

Domestic Relations, Clark's Hornbook on, 2nd Ed., 1988, about 900 pages, by Homer H. Clark, Jr., Professor of Law, University of Colorado.

Economics and Federal Antitrust Law, Hovenkamp's Hornbook on, 1985, 414 pages, by Herbert Hovenkamp, Professor of Law, University of Iowa.

Employment Discrimination Law, Player's Hornbook on, about 600 pages, 1987, by Mack A. Player, Professor of Law, University of Georgia.

Environmental Law, Rodgers' Hornbook on, 1977 with 1984 Pocket Part, 956 pages, by William H. Rodgers, Jr., Professor of Law, University of Washington.

Evidence, Lilly's Introduction to, 2nd Ed., 1987, about 550 pages, by Graham C. Lilly, Professor of Law, University of Virginia.

Evidence, McCormick's Hornbook on, 3rd Ed., 1984 with 1987 Pocket Part, 1156 pages, General Editor, Edward W. Cleary, Professor of Law Emeritus, Arizona State University.

Federal Courts, Wright's Hornbook on, 4th Ed., 1983, 870 pages, by Charles Alan Wright, Professor of Law, University of Texas.

Federal Income Taxation of Individuals, Posin's Hornbook on, 1983 with 1987 Pocket Part, 491 pages, by Daniel Q. Posin, Jr., Professor of Law, Catholic University.

Future Interest, Simes' Hornbook on, 2nd Ed., 1966, 355 pages, by Lewis M. Simes, Late Professor of Law, University of Michigan.

Insurance, Keeton and Widiss' Basic Text on, 2nd Ed., 1988, about 800 pages, by Robert E. Keeton, Professor of Law Emeritus, Harvard University and Alan I. Widiss, Professor of Law, University of Iowa.

Labor Law, Gorman's Basic Text on, 1976, 914 pages, by Robert A. Gorman, Professor of Law, University of Pennsylvania.

Law Problems, Ballentine's, 5th Ed., 1975, 767 pages, General Editor, William E. Burby, Late Professor of Law, University of Southern California.

Legal Ethics, Wolfram's Hornbook on, 1986, 1120 pages, by Charles W. Wolfram, Professor of Law, Cornell University.

Legal Writing Style, Weihofen's, 2nd Ed., 1980, 332 pages, by Henry Weihofen, Professor of Law Emeritus, University of New Mexico.

Local Government Law, Reynolds' Hornbook on, 1982 with 1987 Pocket Part, 860 pages, by Osborne M. Reynolds, Professor of Law, University of Oklahoma.

New York Estate Administration, Turano and Radigan's Hornbook on, 1986, 676 pages, by Margaret V. Turano, Professor of Law, St. John's University and Raymond Radigan.

New York Practice, Siegel's Hornbook on, 1978 with 1987 Pocket Part, 1011 pages, by David D. Siegel, Professor of Law, St. John's University.

Oil and Gas Law, Hemingway's Hornbook on, 2nd Ed., 1983, with 1986 Pocket Part, 543 pages, by Richard W. Hemingway, Professor of Law, University of Oklahoma.

Property, Boyer's Survey of, 3rd Ed., 1981, 766 pages, by Ralph E. Boyer, Professor of Law Emeritus, University of Miami.

Property, Law of, Cunningham, Whitman and Stoebuck's Hornbook on, 1984, with 1987 Pocket Part, 916 pages, by Roger A. Cunningham, Professor of Law, University of Michigan, Dale A. Whitman, Dean and Professor of Law, University of Missouri, Columbia and William B. Stoebuck, Professor of Law, University of Washington.

Real Estate Finance Law, Nelson and Whitman's Hornbook on, 1985, 941 pages, by Grant S. Nelson, Professor of Law, University of Missouri, Columbia and Dale A. Whitman, Dean and Professor of Law, University of Missouri, Columbia.

Real Property, Moynihan's Introduction to, 2nd Ed., 1987, about 250 pages, by Cornelius J. Moynihan, Late Professor of Law, Suffolk University.

Remedies, Dobb's Hornbook on, 1973, 1067 pages, by Dan B. Dobbs, Professor of Law, University of Arizona.

Secured Transactions under the U.C.C., Henson's Hornbook on, 2nd Ed., 1979 with 1979 Pocket Part, 504 pages, by Ray D. Henson, Professor of Law, University of California, Hastings College of the Law.

Securities Regulation, Hazen's Hornbook on the Law of, 1985, with 1987 Pocket Part, 739 pages, by Thomas Lee Hazen, Professor of Law, University of North Carolina.

Sports Law, Schubert, Smith and Trentadue's, 1986, 395 pages, by George W. Schubert, Dean of University College, University of North Dakota, Rodney K. Smith, Professor of Law, Delaware Law School, Widener University, and Jesse C.

Trentadue, Former Professor of Law, University of North Dakota.

Torts, Prosser and Keeton's Hornbook on, 5th Ed., 1984 with 1987 Pocket Part, 1286 pages, by William L. Prosser, Late Dean and Professor of Law, University of California, Berkeley, Page Keeton, Professor of Law Emeritus, University of Texas, Dan B. Dobbs, Professor of Law, University of Arizona, Robert E. Keeton, Professor of Law Emeritus, Harvard University and David G. Owen, Professor of Law, University of South Carolina.

Trial Advocacy, Jeans' Handbook on, Soft cover, 1975, 473 pages, by James W. Jeans, Professor of Law, University of Missouri, Kansas City.

Trusts, Bogert's Hornbook on, 6th Ed., 1987, 794 pages, by George T. Bogert.

Uniform Commercial Code, White and Summers' Hornbook on, 2nd Ed., 1980, 1250 pages, by James J. White, Professor of Law, University of Michigan and Robert S. Summers, Professor of Law, Cornell University.

Urban Planning and Land Development Control Law, Hagman and Juergensmeyer's Hornbook on, 2nd Ed., 1986, 680 pages, by Donald G. Hagman, Late Professor of Law, University of California, Los Angeles and Julian C. Juergensmeyer, Professor of Law, University of Florida.

Wills, Atkinson's Hornbook on, 2nd Ed., 1953, 975 pages, by Thomas E. Atkinson, Late Professor of Law, New York University.

Advisory Board

INTRODUCTION

TO THE

STUDY and PRACTICE OF LAW

IN A NUTSHELL

By

KENNEY HEGLAND
Professor of Law
University of Arizona

ST. PAUL, MINN.
WEST PUBLISHING CO.
1983

Other Nutshells by the author:
  Trial and Practice Skills 1978

Library of Congress Cataloging in Publication Data

Hegland, Kenney F., 1940–
  Introduction to the study and practice of law in a
nutshell.

  (Nutshell series)
  Includes index.
  1. Law—Study and teaching—United States. 2. Practice
of law—United States. I. Title. II. Series.
KF273.H4 1983   349.73'07'11   83–10474
                      347.300711

ISBN 0–314–73632–8

Hegland Study & Practice of Law NS
  2nd Reprint—1987

For

    Robert, Alex and Caleb

Who, be they law students or no,
Will someday read this book
And share a laugh with someone
Who loves them

*

ACKNOWLEDGEMENTS

But for the help of many, this book would have been lousy.

My parents, Edwina and Sheridan, and my wife, Barbara toiled with countless drafts and made critical stylistic and substantive suggestions. And they encouraged. Bill Boyd, Liz Dworkin, Peter Gross, Elizabeth Hite, Dale Luciano, Mike Sacken and Andy Silverman read most of the manuscript. I thank them for their time and insight; most of all, I thank them for their courage to point out my errors—to tell me where I was garbled, where I was wrong, and where I was simply crude. Joe Livermore, as always, played the tough and constructive critic. Others read parts of the manuscript and provided valuable review and encouragement—Chuck Ares, Dan Dobbs, Michele Martin, Pat Luciano, Thornton Robison, Anita Royal, Anne Ryan, David Wexler and Winton Woods. I thank these good folks for a much finer book.

Others contributed substantially but indirectly. The faculty of Boalt Hall introduced me to the joys and terrors of law study; much of this book is merely recollection. Law students at Arizona, U.C.L.A. and Harvard have also introduced me to joys and terrors—those of law teaching. I thank them for contributing so much to my education and, indeed, to my life. I also thank Tom Hall, mentor extraordinaire, for encouraging me to follow my own style. Jack Himmelstein and the Devil's

Thumb crowd have undoubtedly made their imprint on these pages. So too, Sylvia, who first encouraged and supported my writing.

I also thank those who typed and prepared the manuscript—Barbara Clelland, Julie Acedo, Maria Campos, Pam Hagan and Debbie Stahl. They put up with me and my continued revisions with humor, grace, and efficiency. (Or should that read "efficiency, grace and humor"?). And, speaking of graceful toleration of last minute revisions, I must thank the staff at West. They have done an excellent job with the manuscript.

I wish to thank the authors and publishers who have given permission to reprint copyrighted material:

Turow, *One L.* Excerpts reprinted with permission of G. G. Putman's Sons.

Bellow and Moulton, *The Lawyering Process.* Excerpt reprinted with permission of Foundation Press.

Mueller and Rosett, *Contract Law and Its Applications.* Excerpt reprinted with permission of Foundation Press.

Dworkin *et al, On Becoming a Lawyer.* Excerpt reprinted with permission of author and the West Publishing Company.

Noonan, *Persons and Masks of the Law.* Excerpt reprinted with permission of author and Farrar, Straus and Giroux.

ACKNOWLEDGEMENTS

Last I would like to say hello to my good friend Paul Bergman. Hello Paul.

KENNEY F. HEGLAND

June, 1983

*

SUMMARY OF CONTENTS

OUTLINE

PART TWO. LAW SCHOOL SKILLS

PART THREE. BEYOND SKILLS

INTRODUCTION
TO THE
STUDY and PRACTICE OF LAW
IN A NUTSHELL

*

CHAPTER 1

LAW SCHOOL
WHAT TO EXPECT AND HOW
TO COPE

It is the best of schools, it is the worst of schools. It is law school and it won't be the same.

Legal education is different from undergraduate education. As an undergraduate you sat and took notes while the professor lectured. You left, often inspired, occasionally depressed, but generally with the feeling that you *learned* something:

"That Sartre believed essence precedes existence."

"That the Second Law of Thermodynamics suggests that the universe will eventually run out of energy."

"That Sartre, had he known of the Second Law of Thermodynamics, would have been even more depressed."

In law classes you naturally expect to *learn* the law.

"That murder is the unlawful killing of a human being."

"That minors don't have contractual capacity."

"That torts are not English muffins."

Your experience of law school will be quite different from your expectation. Not only do you not "learn" any law in class, often it will seem that

[*1*]

you are considerably worse off for having attended it. ("Now I don't even know what a human being is!") In law school professors generally make no attempt to explain the assigned reading nor do they attempt to supplement it. Their mission, you will discover, is something quite different.

In law school you don't just sit and take notes; you are expected to participate. Well and good, this sounds like an undergraduate seminar. However, you will find a critical distinction in the kind of dialogue that occurs. In an undergraduate seminar you participate by offering and defending your opinion on the issue at hand. In law school your opinion, by itself, counts for little; what you say must be reasoned and justified in the context of law. At first it is very difficult to do this.

Preparing for class is also different. You don't skim the material looking for central ideas nor do you sit long hours attempting to memorize key points. In law school you struggle with the ideas—expect, at first, to be whipped by a two page case.

Finally, law exams are unlike tests you have taken in the past. You will not be asked to merely recite what you have learned ("Define murder.") nor will you be given broad essay questions such as "Is Law Just?" Law exams require you to apply the law you have learned to new factual situations.

You will find all of these differences bewildering and threatening. You will also find them challenging and exhilarating. It is the best of schools, it is the worst of schools. Welcome.

This book introduces you to the study and practice of law. You can't understand legal education without knowing something of what lawyers do. Part One of this book tells you what lawyers do and shows the relationship between law practice and law study. Part Two deals with the skills you will need as a law student. Part Three moves beyond skills, first to explore the psychological side of the first year, second, to describe the second and third years of law school, and, finally, to look at law careers. This first chapter will preview the other chapters and suggest when and in what order to read them. Then it will suggest one way to cope with the intensity and confusion of the first year: *Keep a Journal.* Law school is too significant merely to attend. The chapter will close with some thoughts on law and humor. Silent somber soliloquies help; so do jokes.

A striking aspect of American legal education is its uniformity. No matter where you go to law school you will learn much the same thing. In your first year the odds are overwhelming that you will take courses in Contracts, Torts, Property, Constitutional Law, and Civil Procedure. Given the relatively few number of casebooks in each area, it is likely that you will be using the same books to study these subjects as are students in Maine, South Carolina and Oregon. The method of study will also be the same. You will read and analyze appellate court decisions. Go to the "best" law school in the country or go to the "worst" and sit in on a first year class. You won't be able to tell at which school you are. There will be many students and on their desks large casebooks colored brown, blue or red. And the professor will ask, "Mr. Fell, please recite the facts of MacPherson v. Buick Motor Company."

This uniformity should solace those who were unable to attend their "first choice" of law schools; it should humble those who did. The question here, however, is what does the standard method of teaching law have to do with the actual practice of law? It is self-evident that lawyers will need to know the rules of law in the areas they study: contracts, torts, property. But what of the method of instruction? Why not have students read books stating the legal rules rather than forcing them to extract those very same rules from judicial opinions? In short, what does the case method have to do with the practice of law?

Part One deals with what lawyers do and attempts to show how needed skills and competencies are learned in reading and analyzing appellate court decisions. What do lawyers do? One popular image is that of the lawyer standing before the jury casting a spell of logic and rhetoric. The other popular image is that of the lawyer standing before the Supreme Court, using wit and wisdom to fashion a rule of law to make a more just society. (*My* favorite image is that of a bound and gagged Woody Allen cross-examining a hostile witness in the movie *Bananas*. Needless to say, the witness breaks and confesses all after being subjected to a series of well put mumbles.) In Part One, you will learn something of how to try a lawsuit and something of how to make an appellate argument. This knowledge will help you understand the cases you will read in your courses. Read Part One early in the first semester. Knowing what lawyers do all day will help you understand what you should do all day.

Part Two deals with skills you will need as a law student. Chapter 5, *Studying Law*, should be read soon. Chapter 8, *Writing Law School Exams*, is *central* and should be read as soon as you have two or three hours to devote to it. It will provide practice in writing an exam. First you will be given some rules of law to study and then you will be given a typical exam question based on those rules. Write an answer and then compare it to two answers that are provided. To get the most out of the chapter, you must work your way through it, and this should take at least *two hours*. The earlier you tackle the chapter, the better. Once you know what is expected of you in terms of exams, you will know better how to study. A well written exam is not a particular art form; it is an instance of good legal writing and analysis and reflects what it is to "think like a lawyer." The chapter explores legal reasoning and analysis.

The other chapters in Part 2, *Legal Writing* and *Moot Court,* are less pressing. Read the chapter on Moot Court when you are engaged in that program and read the chapter on writing just before your first writing assignment. However, read the chapter on writing before your first exams. It should help.

Part Three moves beyond skills to explore some of the human dimensions of law study. Read early *Fear and Loathing in the First Year.* You will discover you are not alone.

The lockstep of the first year—where you are assigned your classes and professors (at some schools, even your seats)—gives way to chaos in the second and third. *The Second and Third Years* will help you make difficult decisions. What courses should you take? Should you go on law review? Should you clerk? The chapter also suggests some "fun and games" activities for your last two years: teaching law in high school, law school film forums and law and literature groups. The chapter discusses some interesting issues of jurisprudence and tells you some of the history of the American law school. It is important to consider these matters in your first year and I recommend the chapter for semester break.

The last two chapters of the book, *Career Choices* and *Lawyers Talk About Their Jobs,* can

also wait, but not for too long. What's it like to
work in a large firm? What skills does it take to
do trial work? What are the joys and frustrations of working for the government? What are
the risks and satisfactions of solo practice? And
what of law teaching? The last two chapters address these concerns. In the first I have described career options in human terms, in terms
of joys, risks, frustrations and satisfactions. In
the second I have asked lawyer friends to write
briefly of their jobs. Lawyers in large firms and
small, lawyers prosecuting and defending, lawyers teaching and those judging, lawyers working for legal aid and those working for the government have graciously responded.

Career decisions may seem a long way off but
it is wise to consider them early. As you will see
there are things you can do in law school which
will help you select a meaningful career.

To recap what to read when:

Read early:

All of Part One: Chapters 2–4

Chapter 5: Studying Law

Chapter 8: Writing Law School Exams

Because these chapters describe essential law
study skills, you should plan to *reread* them after
a few months in law school. You will get much
more out of them at that point. The more you
know the more you learn.

Chapter 9: Fear and Loathing

Read at your leisure:

This book is about your future, what you will become, first as a "law student" and then as a "lawyer." But what of you right now, the person standing at the shore? Know this: Law study is turbulent and overwhelming. The powerful tides can take you far to sea, to drift without aspiration and without sense of self. You need an anchor; you need to occasionally quit the hurly-burly and step out of role to reflect on what is happening to you. Many law students achieve calm by a secret, intensely personal method. In a journal they write: to themselves, of themselves and for themselves. I recommend that you keep a journal and take 20 to 30 minutes several days a week to be with yourself and your thoughts.

Talk to lawyers of all ages and callings and they will recall the intensity of the first year. Talk to law students at any school and they will tell you of the profound effects of the first year, some students finding the effects beneficial, others devastating. Talk with yourself and you will find that much more is going on than merely "learning law." *Write* your thoughts, because until you write them you really don't know what they are. In your head they are just vague impressions and fragments of ideas; on paper they take shape and content. Write your thoughts *now* while you are experiencing what will be an intense and highly significant period in your life. Next year it will be too late; then you will have only memories.

If your soul is not sufficient warrant, keeping a journal will help you write better. Expressing yourself in writing is an essential lawyering skill. The more difficult and complicated your thoughts, the more beneficial will be the process of reducing them to writing. Think big to write big.

Good lawyers not only *do*, they also reflect on what they have *done*. After the verdict, for example, good trial lawyers do not immediately celebrate. They first reflect on the trial process: What went right? What went wrong? What was going on with the jurors? With the judge? With me? The habit of stepping back and reflecting upon experience is a critical part of your self-education. By keeping a journal you will develop a more profound understanding of the law school experience, of the law, and of lawyers. Of equal importance, you will come to know yourself better because writing requires a silent dialogue about what you think and feel.

As to the specific content of your journal, many entries will simply involve random reflections on the events of the day. Occasionally force yourself to attempt something in the nature of an es-

say. Throughout this book issues of jurisprudence and issues of role are raised which should
trigger your thoughts. Here are some additional
themes to consider:

- *Reflections on a particular case or legal doctrine.* Did you find it just? Placed in the position of judge would you have decided things differently? Does the rule satisfactorily take into
  account what you believe to be the important considerations? Were there certain aspects of the
  case that you found of special interest which
  your classmates and professor did not?

- *Reflections on law school.* How is it affecting
  you? How does it conform to what you thought
  it would be? How does it compare with undergraduate education? How do you feel about the
  issues of competition and cooperation as they influence your relations with your fellow students?
  What of male/female reactions in the classroom?
  Do the males tend to dominate discussions? Do
  you participate in class? Why or why not?

- *Reflections on lawyering.* Based on what you
  see, what do you think the practice of law will be
  like? What do you think the lawyers who handled a particular case were feeling? Were thinking? Could they have done something to avoid
  litigation?

Consider how fascinating it will be, in two or
three years, to learn what you thought and felt
as a first year law student. Will you have
changed? If so, how and why? What do you
think you would like to know about yourself in

two or three years? Write yourself a letter. Here are some specific suggestions.

1. "Why I came to law school."

Forget the quick one-liners—"Because I couldn't get into medical school" and forget that self-serving rhetoric you wrote on your law school application. Try to be honest with yourself in stating your aspirations, however "corny" or impossibly lofty those aspirations sound even to you. In two or three years, when you are considering what kind of job to take, it will be well to recall why you came to law school. Is your career choice coherent with your initial motivation?

2. "Do lawyers make a difference?"

What do you conceive the role of the lawyer in our complex society to be? Can they make positive and significant contributions? Do you think you will?

3. "Time letter."

What would you like to say to yourself when you are a third year student? Congratulations will obviously be in order. I imagine you will say a great deal more once you get started.

Finally, as to journals, what if you find it difficult writing one? Write an essay: "Why I find it difficult writing a journal." And what if you think keeping a journal would be a waste of time? Write: "Why keeping a journal is a waste of time." Writing's the thing!

Enough of journals and enough of introducing the contents of this book. Now a few final words on the style of this book, more particularly its hu-

mor. I crack jokes. I tell you this because the
joke not got is far worse than no joke at all. For
example, Chapter 8 is entitled "Writing School
Exams: The Only Skill Worth Having." A very
intelligent and sensitive colleague, in critiquing a
draft of this book, thought me serious and castigated me for suggesting such a limited view of
life. I don't believe writing exams is the only
skill worth having. I used a satirically exagger-
ated title because many law students come to believe that grades mean everything; they forget
their prior accomplishments and lose sense of
their uniqueness—they come to judge their worth
solely in terms of law school grades. This is ridiculous and tragic. My hope was to bring the
matter of grades and exams into perspective by
humor and wild overstatement. Humor, alas,
sometimes misses the mark.

That I occasionally treat the law lightly does
not mean that I don't take it seriously. I do. I
share the views of Oliver Wendell Holmes that
"the law is one of the vastest products of the
human mind," and that it is "possible to live
greatly in the law." The law is rich and legal careers can be quite profound. My point, simply, is
that neither need be pompous.

Let's get on with it.

PART ONE

WHAT DO LAWYERS DO ALL DAY? AND WHAT DOES IT HAVE TO DO WITH LAW SCHOOL?

CHAPTER 2

LEARNING LAWYERING SKILLS BY READING CASES

The first year of law school is devoted mostly to reading and analyzing appellate court decisions. What does this have to do with the practice of law? Can you learn anything about trying lawsuits, advising clients and drafting documents sitting in a library reading cases? The answer is "yes" and, if you read the cases the right way, you can learn a great deal about the practical day-to-day tasks lawyers perform. The argument is this. Although lawyering involves many skills the primary skill is the ability to *analyze the interplay of law and fact.* Reading cases develops this skill.

1. Questions of Fact

Let's jump ahead a few years to your first day on the job as a lawyer. You are nervous but ready. Enter First Client. Her name, Ms. K, and her tale, woeful.

> Several months ago I fell down the back stairs of my apartment house and was badly injured. It was my landlord's fault because the top stair was loose.

From the dark recesses of your mind come two rules of law you learned in your first year torts class: (1) that landlords have a duty to maintain common areas in apartment houses and (2) that a person is negligent if he fails to act reasonably. As lawyer your job is to *analyze how these legal rules would apply in the client's particular fact situation.* Did her injury occur in a "common area" and, if so, was it the result of the landlord's "negligence"? You begin to develop the relevant facts:

You: Did other tenants use the stairs?

Ms. K: Yes. It is the backstairs and people use it to take out the garbage.

You: These stairs are for common use?

Ms. K: Yes.

You: You said the landlord was at fault. Why do you say that?

Ms. K: Well, the top stair was loose and that's what caused me to fall.

You: Did the landlord know about the stair being loose before you fell?

Ms. K: I don't know.

You: Do you know how long the stair had been in that condition?

Ms. K: No.

[*14*]

It looks like it might be a rough day. Your client, Ms. K, has sustained real life injuries and she needs to know if she can successfully sue for the harm she has suffered. Was the landlord negligent? If the case is pursued by Ms. K and is not settled out of court, ultimately a jury will decide the issue. It will be your job to stand before the jury, swallow once and with great conviction begin your closing argument:

> Ladies and Gentlemen of the Jury, the first issue I will address is that of the landlord's neglect. The judge will instruct you that, Ms. K, my client, has the burden of proving, by a preponderance of the evidence, that the landlord failed to act as would an ordinarily careful person. We have met this burden. Let us review the evidence that supports that conclusion.

Closing argument is that last step in trying a lawsuit. Let's begin with the first.

1. You read appellate court decisions involving suits for the negligent maintenance of common areas. From those cases you learn the law which shall be applied in your case. That law will be given to the jury in the form of jury instructions. Reading the cases you decide what the judge will likely instruct the jury as to the landlord's liability.

2. Given the probable jury instruction, next you decide what you would want to argue to the jury. It would be nice to argue, for example, that the landlord knew of the condition for a long time but did nothing about it. An "ordinarily careful person" would have fixed the stairs.

3. Knowing what you want to argue to the jury, you determine what kinds of evidence you will need to introduce at trial. You cannot argue the landlord's prior knowledge unless there was some evidence of it introduced at trial.

4. Knowing the evidence you want before the jury, you next determine what specific witnesses you must call to produce that evidence and what specific questions you must ask them.

Note the progression: *From abstract rule of law to specific facts. This is what trials are all about.* Reading and analyzing appellate decisions in law school develops a sensitivity to how legal rules play out in particular fact situations. Hence it is not fanciful to suggest that in reading those dusty volumes you are learning something of trying lawsuits.

2. Questions of Law

Applying legal rules to facts will not be your only task. Often the task is to decide *what* legal rule will apply in a particular factual situation. To illustrate, let's return to that memorable morning, the morning of the First Client.

You: Did you sign a lease?

Ms. K: Yes, here it is.

You: Let me have a minute to read it.

You begin reading the lease, thinking how professional you must seem. You are also quite excited. Your first case and it seems like a good one!

Doesn't specify if landlord is negligent or not

Suddenly there *it* is, buried among the enumeration of conditions on the second page of the lease:

13. The Landlord shall in no event be held liable for any loss or damage which may occur to the tenant.

Bonkers. Professional veneer crumbles. Your chest tightens and your mind races: "Lost, all lost. How can I tell her? A loser. My first case a tragic loser! Why did I do this? Why wasn't I satisfied as simply another unemployed college graduate? Lost! *But wait!* Perhaps this clause is unenforceable. I remember something in Contracts about clauses like this. Oh why didn't I study more in law school?"

Breathe deeply and regain composure. Calmly, you tell your client, "There is a clause that seems to bar your suit. However, the clause may be unenforceable. This is a very complicated matter. I will research the point and get back to you."

Your task here is different than it is in considering whether, *as a matter of fact*, the landlord was negligent. Here you must determine, *as a matter of law*, whether the clause is enforceable. To answer this question you will research the law, a skill you will learn in law school. Ideally you will find a case in your jurisdiction which is on "all fours" and which clearly and flatly states that such clauses are unenforceable. Most likely, however, you will find no cases directly on point in your state but will find cases in other states, some striking such clauses, others upholding

[*17*]

them. You likely will also find cases in your state which involve analogous fact situations and contain language suggestive of how the issue might be resolved. If Ms. K's case is not settled out of court, it will be your job to stand before the judge, swallow hard and, with great conviction, begin:

You: Your Honor, the landlord asserts that he cannot be sued for negligence because a clause in the lease provides that he shall not be held liable. Our position is that such clauses are unenforceable, both as a matter of public policy and as a matter of unconscionability.

Judge: Say what? Do you have any cases in this jurisdiction striking these clauses?

You: No, Your Honor, I have found no cases. However, there are no cases in this state upholding the validity of the clauses and hence this case seems to be one of first impression.

Judge: You don't say. Why shouldn't the clause be enforced? Your client signed the lease, didn't she?

You: Very good question Your Honor. My first argument is . . . .

Reading cases in law school you learn how to make legal arguments. Hence it is not fanciful to suggest that in reading those dusty volumes you are learning how to argue before the Supreme Court.

[*18*]

Consider the twin assertions of this chapter. First, the primary lawyering skill is *analyzing the interplay of law and fact.* Second, *the case method teaches this skill.*

All lawyering tasks, advising clients, drafting documents, trying lawsuits, involve the same basic skill. Sometimes the question will be *how* a legal rule applies in a given situation, other times *whether* the legal rule will apply. In either event the skill is the same, analyzing the interplay of law and fact. To say that this is the primary skill is not to say it is the only necessary skill. It is critical to be sensitive to clients, bold in their behalf, and creative and flexible in solving their problems. There are many skills which go to successful lawyering; analytical ability is simply *necessary* if not sufficient.

Can reading and analyzing appellate cases teach this skill? Absolutely. Read cases as do lawyers and judges. Lawyers and judges don't read cases to *discover* the rules of law. They read cases to *use* the rules of law. Trial lawyers read cases to determine what they must prove at trial. Appellate lawyers read cases to find arguments supporting their positions. Judges read cases to decide controversies before them.

Don't read cases merely to learn black letter law. *Dissect* cases rather than simply understand them. Read as a practitioner.

1. After reading a decision, take it apart to understand how it was put together. Each appellate

decision came after the competing lawyers made their arguments. Reconstruct those arguments.

2. After reading case, pretend it is the only case in the world and assume you are a judge confronted with a similar, but not identical, fact pattern. Should you apply the rule of the only case in the world or does the difference in facts mean a different rule?

3. After reading a case, assume you are a trial lawyer. Given the rule of the case, what will the jury be instructed? Given the instruction, what would you want to argue as plaintiff? As defendant? What evidence would you need to support your argument?

How to read cases these ways will be explained in the next two chapters. Understanding these methods you can do more than read cases, you can *do law*.

"Thinking like a lawyer" means the ability to analyze the interplay of law and fact. When the emphasis is on "law" the usual forum is the appellate courtroom; when the emphasis is on "fact" the usual forum is the trial courtroom. The next chapters explore the dynamics involved:

Chapter 3: Questions of Law—Arguing and Distinguishing Cases

Chapter 4: Questions of Fact—The Trial Process

CHAPTER 3

QUESTIONS OF LAW: THE ART OF ARGUING AND DISTINGUISHING CASES

Lawyers advise clients, negotiate controversies, and draft documents. To take intelligent legal action it is necessary to know both the factual context in which you act and the law which governs it. Often the legal standard will be unclear:

Is a clause in an apartment house lease exempting the landlord from liability enforceable?

Does a farmer who uses a spring gun to defend his property have a valid claim of self-defense?

Does a statute which imposes a tariff on imported "animals" apply to the importation of canaries?

These are all questions of law. They will be decided by a judge. Juries, on the other hand, decide questions of *fact*:

Was the landlord negligent in maintaining the common stairway?

Did the defendant murder the canary?

The next chapter deals with questions of fact; here we deal with questions of law.

Under our system of justice, judges, when asked to decide questions of law, are to follow *precedent*. They are to look to previous decisions to determine whether the issue has been already decided and, if not, to see if there are analogous cases to guide their current decision. This

chapter concerns that process. You will learn
something of how lawyers argue and distinguish
cases, something of how judges decide.

The chapter opens with a short introduction to
the key notion that like cases should be treated
alike. Then it will restate a legal argument and
introduce a valuable learning technique—viewing
legal argument as ping pong. Next comes a discussion of some of the theory behind the dictate
that judges should follow precedent. It is not
self-evident. The chapter will close on a very important matter. Often cases raise compelling issues of lawyer ethics and role, issues you should
consider even though they may not be on the final.

1. Treating Like Cases Alike

At the core of our jurisprudence is the belief
that like cases should be treated alike. There is
something quite fundamental about it. Children
pick up on it early.

> My eldest, then 4, was resisting eating his vegeta-
> bles. He finally came up with a winner: "Well, it's
> my body!" Good arguments should be rewarded, so
> we backed off. The next day his two year old broth-
> er was marking the walls with his crayons. "Stop
> it!" was the command. "Well," he retorted, "it's my
> body!"

The basic idea was there; who can fault a two-
year-old for less than elegant execution?

"Following precedence" and *stare decisis* embody the basic notion. The key is knowing what's "alike." Much of the lawyer's art lies in making this determination.

Assume Paradise. People mind their own business and everyone is happy. There is *no* litigation. Think of it. Not one single judicial opinion; not one, anywhere. Suddenly someone overreaches and The First Case arises! To make matters worse, far worse, the West Publishing Company is founded and The First Case is published and distributed throughout Paradise. In the First Case, (1 *Paradise Reporter 1st* 1), the court applied Rule of Law X. Present in that case were Facts 1, 2 and 3.

More trouble in Paradise (except, of course, for the West Publishing Company). Case Two arises. In that case there are Facts 1 & 2, but *no* Fact 3. Should the court in Case Two follow Case One and apply Legal Rule X? It should if Case Two is "like" Case One. The side wishing to avoid the imposition of Rule X will argue:

> Your Honor, the presence of Fact 3 was critical to the court in Case One. Without it, the court never would have adopted Rule X. Therefore you need not follow Case One because it is *distinguishable.* The cases are not alike!

The lawyer wanting Rule X to be applied in Case Two will argue:

> Your Honor, Fact 3 is not important. It was not key to the previous decision. What was important in Case One was the presence of Facts 1 and 2. Facts

[*23*]

1 and 2 are present in this case as well. The decision of Case One *controls;* under the doctrine of *stare decisis*, you must apply Rule X because this case is *indistinguishable!* Besides, it's my body!

And what happens when Paradise really starts to fall apart with Case Three? Case Three has Facts 1, 2, 3, & 4.

Your Honor, Case One does not control Case Three because of the presence of Fact 4. Had that fact been in Case One, the court never would have adopted Rule X.

And so it goes.

To give some content to the process of arguing and distinguishing cases, assume that the second case in Paradise stems from the following events. A tenant trips and falls on a common stairway in the apartment house where she lives. She sues the landlord, alleging that he negligently maintained the stairway. By way of defense the landlord claims she cannot sue him for negligence because of a clause in the lease which reads:

The Landlord shall in no event be liable for any loss or damage which may occur to the Tenant.

This is known as an "exculpatory" clause and, if the court enforces it, the tenant will be out of luck. Should the court enforce the clause? To decide the issue, the court, quite rightly, will look for guidance from the First Case in Paradise. Sure enough that case, aptly called the *Globe* case, involved an "exculpatory" clause. There the court enforced the clause and barred a plaintiff from suing for negligence. In writing its

[24]

opinion, the *Globe* court said "In Paradise exculpatory clauses are valid."

Should the rule of *Globe* be applied to the Landlord/Tenant case? It should *if* the cases are alike. Are they? We need to know more about the *Globe*. We need to know the *factual context* in which the rule was announced. We also need to know the *reasoning* the court used. We read *Globe* carefully, noting its *Facts, Rule* and *Rationale*.

Globe, 1 *Para.* 1

Facts:	Plaintiff sues a credit bureau for negligently omitting a mortgage from a report it made to plaintiff. Because of the omission, plaintiff suffered an economic loss. The contract between plaintiff and defendant provided that defendant should not be liable for negligence. The court enforced the clause.
Rule:	In Paradise, exculpatory clauses are valid. Plaintiff's suit is barred.
Rationale:	The Court stressed the importance of freedom of contract. The court wrote that if parties who make ordinary contracts cannot agree to limit the extent of liability, it is difficult to see where such a ruling would lead.

Knowing something of the facts and rationale of *Globe*, should its rule be applied to the Landlord/Tenant case? Before reading further, take a few minutes to think, if you represented the

[*25*]

tenant, how you would *distinguish Globe?* You must argue *not only* that the two cases are different, but also that the differences are so critical that a court would be justified in ignoring the rule of *Globe.* After you have done that, put yourself in the role of lawyer for the landlord. How would you meet tenant's arguments?

Imagine a courtroom. The judge sits behind the bench, a court reporter takes notes and a bored bailiff works a crossword puzzle. Lawyers for the tenant and landlord sit at counsel table.

Judge:

This is the case of Tenant versus Landlord. Landlord has moved to dismiss Tenant's case on the basis of an exculpatory clause in the lease. I have read the *Globe* case and it seems to me that it clearly stands for the proposition that exculpatory clauses are enforceable. What do you have to say to that, Tenant's Lawyer?

Tenant's Lawyer:

Your Honor. My client has serious injuries here. It isn't fair to let the Landlord off the hook simply because he snuck some clause into the lease. How would you feel if it was your mother?

Stop! That, while satisfying, is not a legal argument. Basic notions of fairness are reflected in legal doctrines. However legal arguments are not emotional broadsides nor are they philosophic

[*26*]

tracts. Emotion and philosophy must always be grounded in principles of law.

Tenant's Lawyer:

The rule of *Globe* should not apply in this case because the facts of that case are quite different. That case involved a purely *financial loss*. This case involves a *personal injury*. This is an essential difference.

In a purely commercial contract, it makes sense to allow the parties to shift the risk of loss between themselves. It does not make sense in contracts between landlords and tenants. The law should not allow landlords to escape liability for negligence because otherwise they will be less careful. More tenants will suffer grave personal injuries.

Your Honor, *Globe should be limited to its facts!*

Judge:

I do see a distinction between financial losses and personal injuries. What do you have to say to that, Landlord Attorney?

Landlord's Attorney:

Our position is that *Globe* is *controlling*. Admittedly there are some differences in the facts. There will always be some differences in the facts. These differences are

not pivotal, however. What
is pivotal is the notion of
freedom of contract. The
Globe case protects freedom
of contract by enforcing the
terms the parties agreed to.
Globe should not be limited
to its facts. You should *follow its rationale* and hence
apply its rule.

What's the answer? Should cases be "limited to
their facts" or should their "rationale", their spirit, be followed? Sometimes one, sometimes the
other. That's why legal arguments can be so exciting and creative.

With this short introduction to legal argument,
a more full treatment.

2. A Legal Argument Restaged: The Ping Pong of the Law

In many ways, legal argument is like ping
pong. Typically it proceeds something like this:

Plaintiff: You promised to do it! You didn't do
it! Therefore pay me big bucks!

Defendant: Oh yeah! I did too do it!

Plaintiff: So sorry, many people were there and
they'll testify you didn't!

Defendant: Oh yeah! Then I never promised to do
it in the first place!

Plaintiff: So sorry, I got it in writing.

Defendant: Oh yeah! Then the Devil made me do
it!

Plaintiff: So sorry, the Devil was out of town.

Defendant: Oh yeah! Then I was drunk! And joking! And insane! Besides the promise was crude and the courts don't enforce crude promises!

Plaintiff: Oh yeah! Your mom wears combat boots!

Each appellate decision is the product of legal ping pong. To effectively learn legal argument, restage the game. In their opinions, courts refer to other cases and make certain arguments to justify their decision. The judges didn't find those cases or create those arguments. *The lawyers did.* To restage the game means to pull the case apart by asking which side cited a particular case or made a particular argument. Is the argument a main argument or merely a supporting one? Is it an offensive argument or a defensive argument, one offered to rebut a point made by the other side?

Let's play. We'll use the facts of the Second Case in Paradise involving a tenant's suit for her landlord's negligence. Here we'll give her a name, Ms. Kuzmiak. The issue is whether exculpatory clauses are enforceable. The actual case arose in New Jersey, whether Paradise or not, I leave to you. In reading the decision, consider the questions I will raise in the opinion.

KUZMIAK v. BROOKCHESTER, INC.

New Jersey Superior Court, App.Div., 1955.
33 N.J.Super. 575, 111 A.2d 425.

Freund, J.A.D. (after stating the facts): The question here is whether the provision does immunize the landlord from liability to his tenants for negligence
. . .

Generally, the law does not favor a contract exempting a person from liability for his own negligence, as it induces a want of care. Although in disfavor, a promise not to sue for future damage caused by simple negligence may be valid . . . .

It is clear that private parties to a transaction lacking public interest are bound by their agreements relieving against liability for negligence. *Globe Home Improvement Co. v. Perth Amboy, etc., Inc.,* (citation omitted) was a suit against a credit bureau for negligently omitting a mortgage from its report. The defendant asserted an agreement releasing it from liability. In upholding the contract, Judge WolfsKeil said:

> "If parties who make ordinary contracts cannot agree to limit the extent of liability, it is difficult to see where such a ruling would lead us
> . . . ."

Question: Which side cited *Globe* and for what purpose? Before continuing, try making the argument.

In these times, an exculpation clause in a credit information contract is not to be compared with an exculpatory clause in a lease for an apartment in an apartment building. The duties and rights of parties to a contract, as in the Globe case, are created by

[*30*]

and arise solely from the contract. The State has no
interest in it. On the other hand, the State, because
of its interest in the welfare of its citizens, regulates
and supervises apartment buildings through the
Board of Tenement House Supervision. Additionally, the landlord is under a common law duty for the
maintenance of the premises under his control.
Hence, the principle stated in the *Globe* case has no
application to the facts in the instant case.

Which side made these arguments? Do they
stand alone or are they in response to a point
made by the other side?

The first reported case in this State involving an
exculpatory clause in an apartment house lease is
the recent case of *Wade v. Park View, Inc.* (citation
omitted) There, suit was brought by a tenant to recover for injuries sustained from a fall upon snow
and ice on the sidewalk which constituted the common approach to the apartment building, and the
cause of action was based on the landlord's failure
to remove the snow and ice. The court sustained
the validity of the clause relying on the *Globe* case
and held that was no distinction between the exculpatory clause in the *Globe* case and one in an apartment building lease . . . . In reaching that decision, the court relied on a New York case
Kirshenbaum v. General Outdoor Adv. Co. (citation omitted). However, it may not have been
brought to the attention of the court that the *Kirshenbaum* case was expressly overruled [by the
New York Legislature] by legislative enactment,
providing that any clause in a lease whereby a landlord attempts to exonerate himself from liability to a
tenant because of the landlord's negligence is void
and against public policy, and wholly unenforceable.
We must, therefore, reexamine the question of the

validity of exculpatory clauses in apartment house leases. Indeed, a comprehensive article, entitled Exculpatory Clauses in Leases reported in 15 *Georgia Bar Journal*, 389 (1953), states at page 402:

> "A large majority of the courts continue to approach the subject *de novo* each time a case involving an exculpatory clause becomes a subject of litigation."

Which side brought up *Wade?* Which side argued *Kirshenbaum* and for what purpose? Which side cited the Georgia Bar Journal and to what argument was it responding?

Some jurisdictions adhere strictly to the freedom of contract concept, holding that a lease is a matter of private agreement with which the general public is not concerned and that if a tenant enters into a contract releasing the lessor from liability for negligence, the law must give effect to and enforce such a contract . . . .

Other jurisdictions, particularly New Hampshire, have held that "one may not by contract relieve himself from the consequences of the future non-performance of his common-law duty to exercise ordinary care." *Papkalos v. Shaka* (citation omitted) . . . .

Although it may be primarily a prerogative of the Legislature to declare exculpatory contracts in landlord and tenant relationships to the contrary to public policy, the courts may also do so.

Which side made the "primary prerogative" argument?

(The court proceeds to decide the case).

PING PONG IN *KUZMIAK*

Before a judge the ping pong format is not actually followed—rather one side gets up and makes all of its points, then the other side responds, and finally the first lawyer rebuts. Analyzing the argument in terms of ping pong, however, forces you to see how each argument fits and responds. Try it with *Kuzmiak*. Speak out the dialogue something like this:

Landlord's Lawyer:	Your honor, in this case my client is being sued for negligent maintenance in an apartment house. The plaintiff signed a lease. A clause in that lease releases my client from liability for negligence. The only question before this court is the validity of that lease provision. Plaintiff, quite naturally, claims that it is void. However, under the case law that I will relate, it is clear that such clauses, freely entered into, are valid.
	Turning to that law, the first case I want to discuss is *Globe Home Improvement v. Perth*. In that case it was held _____. This court should follow that case. If it does, the result would be _____.
Tenant's Lawyer:	Bananas! The *Globe* case should not apply to this case because . . . .

> Landlord's Lawyer: Oh yeah!

Before reading my rendition, try yours.   In mine
I have noted some matters of strategy as well.

> Landlord's Lawyer: In the case of *Globe Home* it
> was held that private parties
> are bound by agreements re-
> lieving against liability for
> negligence. Admittedly the
> facts of *Globe* are different
> than the facts here. The
> *Globe* case did not involve a
> landlord/tenant agreement.

Admit to your weak points—it is very unlikely
your opponent will miss them. Admit them and
then deal with them, showing you're a winner
anyway!

> Landlord's Lawyer: Even though *Globe* is factually
> (continuing)   distinguishable, this court
> should follow it because that
> case is grounded in the notion
> of freedom of contract. Free-
> dom of contract means that
> the clause should be enforced
> here as well as in *Globe*.
>
> Following *Globe* would mean
> barring the tenant's suit.

The lawyer is quite *explicit* as to why he is bringing up *Globe*.

> Tenant's Lawyer: Bananas!

You can't actually shout such things in court, no
matter how good it would feel!

Tenant's Lawyer: (continuing)

Your Honor, you should not follow the *Globe* case because it is clearly distinguishable. It involved an exculpation clause in a credit information contract and cannot be compared with an exculpatory clause in a lease for an apartment. The duties in a simple contract relationship, as in *Globe*, arise only from the contract and the state has no interest in such contracts. However, the state has an interest in apartment leases because of its interest in the welfare of its citizens. This interest is shown by the laws creating the Board of Tenement House Supervision which regulates and supervises apartment buildings. This interest of the state in the landlord/tenant relationship is also shown in the common law duty of the landlord to maintain premises under his control. Therefore, your Honor, the *Globe* case should not apply to this case (and my distinguished opponent should apologize for bringing it up in the first place!).

The *Globe* decision, if it applies, is binding on the court because it is the decision of a higher court in that state. Thus tenant's counsel, to avoid instantaneous death, must convince the court that the *Globe* case does *not apply* because it is *distinguishable.* Distinguishing cases is a central lawyering skill and you will, I promise, get plenty of practice. Observe that by distinguishing *Globe*, counsel has avoided only automatic execution: If the court is convinced that *Globe* is distinguishable, all this means is that the court *need not* follow it; it can still apply the rule of *Globe*, enforcing these clauses, if it thinks the rule best.

> Landlord's Lawyer: OK, so you want to play hardball, do you! I've got a case right on point, *Wade v. Park View*. It is a New Jersey case and is binding on this court. It involved an exculpatory clause in an apartment house lease. There were personal injuries. The court held the clause valid and dismissed the tenant's suit. And that case was decided only two years ago. So there!

Tenant's counsel cannot *distinguish* the *Wade* case as she did the *Globe* case because she can't point out that the facts are so different that the rule applied should also be different. *Wade* seems to be on "all fours". What to do in this situation? Steel yourself and make the much more difficult argument that the previous case is simply wrong.

> Tenant's Lawyer: Your Honor, the *Wade* case should not be followed because it was improperly decided. The

court in *Wade* seemed to be influenced by a decision from our sister state, New York, *Kirshenbaum v. General Outdoor.* However it probably was not brought to the attention of the *Wade* court that the *Kirshenbaum* case was expressly overruled by legislative enactment. New York statute now declares that a clause exonerating a landlord from liability for negligence is void and against public policy.

Here the argument is not that the judges in *Wade* were dumb but rather misinformed, an easier pill for the new court to swallow. Sometimes, however, one must argue, flat out, that a case was wrongly decided. To continue with Landlord's response:

Landlord's Lawyer: Now that's a pretty weak argument, suggesting that the court in this state would have changed its mind if it knew that a decision in another state had been overruled. Your Honor, the *Wade* case has been decided, it holds that such clauses are valid and that should be the end of it. Courts shouldn't change the rules all the time. What's settled is settled!

Tenant's Lawyer: Sounds to me like my opponent hasn't been reading the

[*37*]

1953 *Georgia Bar Journal* which states: "A large majority of courts continue to approach the subject *de novo* each time a case involving an exculpatory clause becomes a subject of litigation."

Landlord's Lawyer: The *Georgia Bar Journal?* You gotta be kidding! There are authorities and there are authorities. This court is obligated to follow decisions of the United States Supreme Court and all higher courts of this state. It can look to the decisions of courts in other states for guidance but it need not follow them. It can seek similar guidance from such things as Restatements and texts of leading academics. But the *Georgia Bar Journal?* Your Honor, would you like to know what my barber thinks?

More seriously, your Honor, I think the New York experience supports our case. There the *legislature* made such clauses void. The legislature in New Jersey has not done so. If these clauses are to be invalidated, it should be the legislature that does so, not the courts.

[*38*]

Tenant's Lawyer: Oh yeah! Although it may be primarily a prerogative of the legislature to declare exculpatory contracts in landlord and tenant relationships to the contrary to public policy, the courts may also do so.

Here our little play ends. As a first nighter, however, you may feel somewhat at loose ends: "Who won?" Although that question is central to Ms. Kuzmiak and her landlord, it is at best tangential to the law student. While it might be nice to know what the New Jersey court decided, this is not essential information. It is clear that some states enforce exculpatory clauses while others do not. As a law student what you need to know is that there is a *legal issue* concerning whether people can contractually agree not to sue one another for negligence. In law practice, or on the exam, you may see this very issue presented. More likely, you will confront an analogous situation—perhaps a lease in which the tenant waives his legal right to be given 30-day notice before eviction. Having read *Kuzmiak* you know that some clauses are subject to legal attack and know some of the policy issues involved—the freedom of contract versus the interest of the state in the well-being of its citizens. With this knowledge you can begin to analyze whether the waiver of notice clause would be enforced.

Having some feel for legal ping pong and the art of arguing and distinguishing cases, we can

[*39*]

focus on the key to common law adjudication, the concept of "case".

3. What Is a "Case"?

What is this thing judges are to follow according to the doctrine of *stare decisis?* A case is the enunciation of a *principle of law in a specific factual context.* It is error to overlook this relationship in applying the doctrine. It is error to put too great an emphasis on *factual similarity,* to say simply "Well *Globe* and *Kuzmiak* are different factually and therefore the rule of *Globe* need not govern *Kuzmiak.*" There will always be factual differences between cases and to insist upon near identity would defeat one rationale of *stare decisis,* which is to insure some predictability in the law by controlling individual whim. A judge, in reaching a decision, should consider and account for decisions other judges have made. He is not free to impose his own standards of fairness. He should not ignore prior decisions simply by pointing out factual differences. *Stare decisis* would neither be a check nor a guide if it could be avoided that easily.

Conversely, it is error to place too much emphasis on a case's *legal principle* and overlook the factual context. To do so defeats another rationale of *stare decisis.* Courts follow a prior decision because of a belief that the judges in the previous case thought long and hard on the issue and hence probably came to a wise decision. It is inappropriate to apply the legal doctrine of the case outside its factual context because it was in that factual context that the previous judges thought long and hard. Would the judges that decided *Globe* have reached the same decision had it involved an apartment house lease and a broken leg?

Arguing precedent and testing the limits of a legal doctrine are skills of central import to the lawyer. Much of the first year of law school is devoted to teaching you this skill. "Now, Students, let's change the facts of that case a little and see what happens. Assume that it was Hansel and Gretal's *natural* mother rather than stepmother. Would you then feel more sympathetic to the witch?"

A good study device is to play this game yourself. Change the facts of a case and then ask if the rule of the case would still apply. Use the adversary approach. First argue, as lawyer, that the factual change means the rule would not apply; then put on the other hat and argue that the change makes no real difference. Make your arguments lawyerlike: refer to specific facts and language of the opinion. Keep the judge's mother out of it.

4. Should Like Cases Be Treated Alike?

Ms. Kuzmiak tumbles. She sues. She is confronted with the lease. There are legal arguments. Eventually the court decides and that de-

cision settles the matter between Ms. Kuzmiak
and her landlord. Under the common law method
of adjudication, however, that is *not* the end of
the story. A case not only settles the controversy between the parties but also becomes part of
the general law which will be applied in the future. Under the doctrine of *stare decisis* the
rule of *Kuzmiak v. Brookchester* (perhaps
"clauses in apartment house leases exonerating a
landlord from liability for negligence are unenforceable") will be applied to all future cases involving similar facts in that jurisdiction. Like
cases should be treated alike.

Should past decisions be *precedent* for future
decisions? There is nothing inevitable about it.
It would be quite possible and rational to have a
system in which cases only settle controversies
between the actual parties and have no implications for the future. The judge in *Kuzmiak*
could decide the case before the court and that
would be that. In the next landlord/tenant case
involving a similar clause, the matter would be
resolved without reference to what the judge did
in *Kuzmiak.*

If the doctrine of *stare decisis* is not inevitable,
is it justified because it leads to more just decisions? Is it well to caution the judge:

> "You can't just decide upon the basis of what you
> think the law is or should be between Ms. Kuzmiak
> and her landlord. You must also decide upon what
> you think the law is or should be between all land-

lords and tenants because, whatever rule you adopt, it will be applied to them as well!"

Does this admonishment lead to a more just resolution of the *particular* case? Perhaps it will force the judge to approach this real life situation too abstractly by forcing him to treat Ms. Kuzmiak and her landlord as "representative parties" rather than as the living individuals they actually are. Occasionally you will read cases where the judge explicitly states "I know that the result of my decision will be unfair to the parties before me; however, to rule otherwise would create bad law." Note that *if* the judge were not "making law," he would not have to sacrifice the few for the many.

Stare decisis can be justified by the argument that, even if it sometimes produces injustice, it is needed to assure predictability in the law. While predictability is a very important goal, there are serious objections as to whether *stare decisis* (1) is needed to achieve it and (2) even if it is needed, whether it can actually achieve it. Is it true that different judges would decide the enforceability of the exculpatory clauses differently if they were freed from the restraints of *stare decisis?* Would the clauses be enforceable in Judge A's Court while unenforceable in Judge B's? And even if judicial decisions would be unpredictable without *stare decisis*, how predictable are decisions following that doctrine? Given the flexibility in reading cases, can courts pretty much come out where they want to? Recall the landlord's position in *Kuzmiak*. When he drafted the lease, there was a controlling decision, *Wade*, which had upheld an exculpatory clause in an apartment house lease. Lo and behold it now looks like the court in *Kuzmiak* is about to toss *Wade*, and the landlord's carefully drafted lease, into the ash can.

Consider the implications of the doctrine of *stare decisis* during your legal education. Does it seem to produce justice? Does it control judicial whim and thus lead to predictability? There are definite costs to the doctrine. First, it makes the law mystical and very much the estate of legal "experts". Judges do not decide cases by applying a basic legal standard to the facts. Rather they apply that basic legal standard only as *refined and interpreted* by other judges in previous cases. And, of course, only legal experts can find, analyze and argue previous cases. Second, the doctrine, to the degree it controls decision making, tends to freeze the law. Rules that made sense years ago are followed even though times and values have changed.

5. A Final Word: Consider Ethics

This chapter has introduced legal argument. It has suggested two ways you can use the cases you read to develop the art of arguing and of distinguishing cases. The first is to take the case apart and restage the ping pong game. The second way is to play "The Only Case in the World

Game" and change some of the facts in the case and argue whether or not the rule of the case should still apply.

There is another important learning which can come from reading cases. Some raise compelling issues of lawyers' ethics and role. *Kuzmiak* is such a case. Consider:

1. If a landlord comes and asks you to draft a form lease, do you automatically include an exculpatory clause (assuming they are legal in your jurisdiction)? Should you discuss the issue with the landlord, expressing your feelings about the propriety of the clauses?

2. Assuming exculpatory clauses have been held nonenforceable in your state, what if the landlord says "Draft one anyway. Maybe the courts will change their minds; in any event most of my tenants don't know the law and won't sue."

3. Assume that exculpatory clauses are valid in your state. A landlord who has been quite negligent and whose negligence has seriously injured a tenant seeks your representation. Reviewing the store-bought lease, you find an exculpatory clause buried on the second page. Would it be proper for you not to raise the defense? If you do raise it, should you tell your not-too-bright opponent that similar clauses have been found invalid in other states?

4. Should you decide these issues yourself or should you do whatever the official lawyer ethics dictate?

Consider questions of role and ethics. Discuss them with your classmates; write of them in your Journal. While they may not be on the final, they will be "on your career."

CHAPTER 4

QUESTIONS OF FACT: THE TRIAL PROCESS

Knowing something of trials will deepen your understanding of law. Announced in the cool of appellate courtrooms, legal doctrines ultimately must be tested in the hectic of trial courtrooms. How will they fare? Take, for example, a doctrine of Contract Law which basically states that jokes do not become contracts:

> It is not every loose conversation that is to be turned into a contract, although the parties may seem to agree. A man is not to be snapped up for an unintended proposition made when he has no reason to suppose anyone wants to accept what he proposes.

So sayest the appellate court. Well and good. We read the statement, mark it with our yellow highlighter and move on. But wait! What does that doctrine mean in practice? Think in terms of a lawyer preparing for trial. You represent, as it happens, the prankster.

How will the jury be instructed? If the judge instructs "A person is not bound by an offer he never intended" then the prankster will win if he can convince the jury he was joking *no matter* how serious he appeared to others. The judge may instruct, however, as to a more objective standard: "If a reasonable third party would have concluded that prankster was making a seri-

[47]

ous offer, then prankster is bound." If this objective test is used, then the case must be tried differently. Indeed under that test, the prankster's testimony that he was joking may be *inadmissible:* A reasonable third party would know only what prankster did, not what he intended or thought.

Who will have the burden of proof? Must prankster prove himself the fool or must his opponent prove him the sage? Representing the prankster, you would hope that the burden would fall on your opponent for it is a *burden.* If the evidence on an issue is evenly divided, he who has the burden loses.

What evidence can and must be introduced? Thinking in terms of proof adds substance to abstract doctrines. To say, as we do in torts, that people must act with "due care," what exactly do we mean? What do people acting with due care do? And what do they do when they don't?

Convert legal doctrines into jury instructions, closing arguments, burdens of proof and matters of evidence. This is one way to analyze the propriety of the doctrine itself. Some legal doctrines make sense only when considering problems of proof. Take the doctrine that minors do not have contractual capacity. The reason behind this policy is that *most* minors are not mature enough to enter into contracts, contracts which will bind them, and their earnings, in the future. But isn't it arbitrary to draw the line precisely at one's

[*48*]

18th birthday? So it seems. But consider how difficult a contrary rule would be in terms of proof. How can you prove someone mature enough or too immature? "Arbitrary" rules occasionally make very good sense when one considers the world of practice.

Appellate courts must always keep an eye on the world of practice in formulating legal doctrine:

> Will the doctrine encourage perjury in situations where it would be difficult to detect?

> Will the doctrine require complicated matters of proof, so complicated that the expense and time devoted to it would not be justified?

> Will the doctrine lead the trial into lengthy collateral matters which would confuse the real issues of the dispute?

> Will the doctrine be so complicated as to confuse the jury?

It is always permissible to argue to an appellate court "Your Honors, the rule you are considering seems to be quite fair but it would not work in practice. It would require juries to make determinations they really cannot." In arguing that prankster's *subjective* state of mind should not be the legal test, you could argue:

> Your Honors, to have the matter turn on prankster's subjective intent, as opposed to how he appeared to others, would make all contracts vulnerable. Any time you wanted to get out of a contract you could simply claim you were joking when you entered it, no matter how serious you appeared at the time.

[49]

This argument raises a key issue: How much do we trust juries? If we believe that juries are good at discovering liars, then we might let them "try" prankster's state of mind. A jury will be able to distinguish the truth from recent fabrication. Indeed, if we believe juries make good decisions, we might allow them to decide whether someone is "mature enough" to enter contracts. The more we trust juries, the more power we will give them. To assess how much juries can be trusted, to determine whether they can ferret out the clever liar, you must know something of trials. This is the topic of this chapter.

We will begin with a very short overview of the trial process. This is necessary to put the next topic, jury instructions, in context. At trial, jury instructions come last; in planning a trial, they come first. After the instructions, we will consider pretrial preparation. Among other things, you will learn that *complaint* is a piece of paper. You will also get a feel for how the lawyer funnels facts into recognized legal categories and learn some of the procedural devices designed to challenge the legal sufficiency and relevancy of fact. The final part of the chapter deals with the trial itself. You will see how the most esoteric of legal doctrines becomes, in the hands of a trial lawyer, a series of questions on direct examination.

1. A Short Overview of the Trial Process

Jury trials go something like this.

1. *Jury selection.* In some jurisdictions, the lawyers question ("voir dire") prospective jurors. Where the lawyers don't, the judge does.

> Do you know any of the parties to this action?

> This case involves a suit for personal injuries growing out of an automobile accident. Have you been in such an accident yourself? Is there anything about the case that makes you think you could not try it fairly? The plaintiff is asking for damages for pain and suffering. The law allows for such damages. If you believed the evidence warranted damages for pain and suffering, would you award them?

> This is a criminal case involving burglary. Have you been the victim of a crime? Do you have any relatives in law enforcement? If I instruct you that you should not consider what will happen to the defendant if she is convicted, will you follow that instruction?

The purpose of voir dire is to impanel a jury which will render a fair verdict. Each side can challenge potential jurors for cause and each has a limited number of peremptory challenges—those are exercised when the lawyer feels, for whatever reason, it would be best not to have the person on the jury.

2. *Plaintiff's opening statement.* Opening statements relate what will be proven and how it will be proven. "We will then call Dr. Dread who examined the plaintiff shortly after the accident.

[*51*]

He will testify as to her injuries and as to the great pain she was in."

3. *Defendant's opening statement.*

4. *Plaintiff's case-in-chief.* Plaintiff presents the evidence needed to make out the case. In a typical personal injury case, the following elements must be proved.
  a. That the defendant was negligent
  b. That the negligence caused plaintiff's injuries
  c. The extent of those injuries

The evidence can consist of exhibits (X-rays showing plaintiff's broken bones, photographs of the victim's injuries and photographs of the accident scene), documents (doctor bills) and, of course, witnesses. When the lawyer calls his witnesses, he takes the witness on *direct* examination.

Mr. Plaintiff, tell the jury of the injuries you received in the accident.

A lawyer cannot *lead* his own witness; that is, cannot suggest answers to him as does the following:

Mr. Plaintiff, isn't it a fact that you received severe back injuries in the accident?

The reason for the prohibition against leading is that the witness is to testify, not the lawyer. A witness does not testify simply by saying "yes" every now and then.

[*52*]

After each witness, the defense lawyer has the opportunity to *cross-examine*.

Mr. Plaintiff, you testified on direct that you injured your back in the accident. Now isn't it a fact that you had injured your back several weeks prior to the accident?

On cross-examination the lawyer can, and usually does, lead the witness.

5. *Plaintiff rests* after presenting all the evidence supporting the claim. Quite likely, out of the jury's hearing, the defense will move for a *nonsuit* or a *directed verdict*. Although the precise name of the motion may vary from jurisdiction to jurisdiction, the basic notion is the same: "Plaintiff has failed to present enough evidence to win." In the auto accident case, for example, the defendant could make such a motion on the basis that, even though the plaintiff proved injuries, there was insufficient evidence to prove the defendant negligent. If there is enough evidence to go to the jury on *all elements* the plaintiff must prove, the judge will deny the motion. The ball is now in the defendant's court.

6. *Defendant's case-in-chief.*

7. *Defendant rests.*

8. *Plaintiff's rebuttal.* Certain things may come out during the defendant's case that plaintiff feels he can prove wrong. Rebuttal is his opportunity. Suppose defendant calls a witness who testifies he saw the accident. Plaintiff, during rebuttal, can call witnesses to rebut the de-

fense witness by testifying that they were vacationing with the witness in Nova Scotia at the time of the wreck.

9. *Defendant's rebuttal.* Quite infrequent. Perhaps witnesses could testify that plaintiff's rebuttal witnesses don't even know where Nova Scotia is.

10. *Plaintiff's closing argument.* Here the task is to marshal the evidence and convince the jury.

11. *Defendant's closing argument.* The job is to expose plaintiff's errors.

12. *Plaintiff's rebuttal argument.* This is to answer *only* points raised in defendant's closing. It is not to bring up new arguments. The defendant had a chance to respond to plaintiff's closing argument and it is only fair to allow the plaintiff to respond to the defendant's closing argument.

In criminal cases, the prosecution is the plaintiff and hence gets last shot at the jury.

13. *Jury instructions,* finally.

14. *Jury Deliberation and Verdict.*

15. *The Joy of Victory, The Agony of Defeat!*

2. Jury Instructions: Defining the Legal Relevance of Fact

Jury instructions cover many crucial matters: the allocation of responsibility between judge and jury, the factfinding process, burden and standard of proof, and the substantive law of the case. To give you some feel for them, I will quote *in toto* the instructions that might be given in a simple negligence action. Reading them, put yourself in the role of juror who only *hears* them.

Ladies and Gentlemen of the jury:

It is my duty to instruct you in the law that applies to this case. It is your duty to apply the law as I state it to you.

It is your exclusive duty as jurors to decide all questions of fact submitted to you and for that purpose to determine the effect and value of the evidence.

You must not be influenced by sympathy, prejudice or passion.

Statements made by the attorneys during the trial are not evidence.

Concerning any question to which an objection was sustained, you must not try to guess what the answer might have been or speculate about the reason for the objection.

You must never assume to be true any insinuation suggested by a question asked a witness. A question is not evidence and may be considered only as it supplies meaning to the answer.

Every person who testifies under oath is a witness. You are the sole judges of the believability of a witness and the weight to be given his testimony.

In determining the believability of a witness you may consider anything that has a tendency in reason to prove or disprove the truthfulness of that testimony, including but not limited to any of the following:

The extent of his opportunity and ability to see or hear [or otherwise become aware of]; to remember or to communicate any matter about which he testified;

The character and quality of his testimony;

The demeanor of the witness while testifying and the manner in which he testifies; and

The existence or nonexistence of a bias, interest, or other motive.

I will now tell you the rules of law which you must follow to decide this case. (1) If you find that the defendant was **not** negligent or that the defendant's negligence did **not** cause plaintiff's injuries, your verdict must be *for* the defendant. (2) If you find that the defendant **was** negligent, and that his negligence caused the plaintiff's injuries, then your verdict must be *for* the plaintiff.

Plaintiff claims that defendant was negligent.

Negligence is the failure to use reasonable care. Negligence may consist of action or inaction. A person is negligent if he fails to act as an ordinarily careful person would act under the circumstances.

Before you can find the defendant liable, you must find that the defendant's negligence caused the plaintiff's injury. Negligence causes an injury if it helps produce the injury, and if the injury would not have happened without the negligence.

If you decide *for* the plaintiff on the question of liability, you must then fix the amount of money which will reasonably and fairly compensate for any of the following damages proved by the evidence to have resulted from the defendant's negligence:

(1) The nature, extent and duration of the injury;

(2) The pain, discomfort, suffering, [disfigurement], [disability] and anxiety experienced [and (rea-

sonably) to be experienced in the future] as a result
of the injury;

(3) Reasonable expenses of necessary medical
care, treatment, and services rendered [and reasonably probable to be incurred in the future]; and

(4) Earnings which were lost by the plaintiff to
date, and any decrease in earning power or capacity
by the plaintiff in the future.

(5) If you find that before the accident the plaintiff had a physical [or emotional] subnormal condition, and if you find that because of the defendant's
negligence, this condition was aggravated so as to
cause additional suffering, disability or pain, then
the plaintiff is entitled to recover for any additional
suffering, disability or pain resulting from such ag-
gravation.

The plaintiff has the burden of proving by a preponderance of the evidence:

(1) That the defendant was negligent;

(2) That the plaintiff was injured [and plaintiff's
property was damaged];

(3) That the defendant's negligence was a cause
of the injury to the plaintiff [and the damage to
plaintiff's property]; and

(4) The amount of money that will compensate the
plaintiff for his injury [and the damage to his prop-
erty].

I will now tell you the standard of proof in this case.
Preponderance of the evidence means such evidence as, when weighed with that opposed to it, has
more convincing force and the greater probability of
truth. In the event that the evidence is evenly bal-
anced, so that you are unable to say that the evidence on either side of an issue preponderates, then

your finding upon that issue *must be against the party who had the burden of proving it.*

When you go to the jury room, it is your duty to discuss the case for the purpose of reaching an agreement if you can do so.

Each of you must decide the case for yourself, but should do so only after a consideration of the case with the other jurors.

You should not hesitate to change an opinion if you are convinced it is erroneous. However, you should not be influenced to decide any question in a particular way simply because a majority of the jurors, or any of them, favor a decision.

The attitude and conduct of jurors at the outset of their deliberations are matters of considerable importance. It is rarely productive or good for a juror, upon entering the jury room, to make an emphatic expression of his opinion on the case or to announce a determination to stand for a certain verdict. When one does that at the outset, his sense of pride may be aroused, and he may hesitate to recede from an announced position if shown that it is wrong. Remember that you are not partisans or advocates in this matter, but are judges.

For you Criminal Law fans:

A defendant in a criminal action is presumed to be innocent until the contrary is proved, and in case of a *reasonable doubt* whether his guilt is satisfactorily shown, he is entitled to a verdict of not guilty. This presumption places upon the State the burden of proving him guilty beyond a reasonable doubt.

Reasonable doubt is defined as follows: It is not a mere *possible doubt*, because everything relating to human affairs is open to some possible or imaginary doubt. *Reasonable doubt* is that state of the case which, after the entire comparison and consideration of all the evidence, leaves the minds of the jurors in that condition that they cannot say they feel an abiding conviction, to a moral certainty, of the truth of the charge.

Where does the Judge come up with all that good stuff? Is he "just one smart dude?" No! Standard jury instructions are found in books. (Take some time to look through one at the law library. They often provide a good review of legal principles). Ultimately, however, jury instructions come from appellate cases and statutes. For example, what constitutes "reasonable doubt" has been the subject of many legal arguments, some insisting it means "sure thing" while others would be happy with "strong hunch." The language quoted above came from an appellate court deciding what reasonable doubt means.

3. Pretrial Preparation: Finding and Funneling Fact

Ms. K tumbles on the stairs of her apartment house and is injured. She consults an attorney, Ms. Darrow. She describes her fall and injuries. Darrow advises that there is a good case against the landlord, Larry Landlord. They discuss fee arrangements. Rather than an hourly fee or a flat fee, they agree, as is usual in personal injury cases, that Darrow will work on a contingency fee basis. If the matter is settled prior to trial, she will receive 25% of the recovery, if the matter is litigated, she will receive 35%. If there is no recovery, Darrow gets nothing. Ms. K must, however, pay the *costs* of litigation, filing fees, reporter's fees for depositions, juror fees. Depending on the complexity of the case and the extent of discovery, these costs can run into thousands of dollars. If Ms. K prevails on the case, however, most likely the defendant will be ordered to pay these costs.

At trial Darrow will have to prove that Larry Landlord was negligent in maintaining the stairs and that his negligence caused Ms. K's injuries. She must also prove how much damage Ms. K suffered due to her fall. As a result of her fall Ms. K broke her leg, hurt her back and incurred hospital and doctor's bills. She also missed 10 days of work. Darrow knows that it will be relatively easy to prove the amount of the "reasonable expenses of necessary medical care" by simply introducing the bills at trial. She can easily prove "lost earnings" by having Ms. K testify as to their amount. The difficult matter will be convincing the jury to put a high monetary value on the "pain, discomfort, suffering and anxiety experienced" by Ms. K.

It will be difficult to prove Larry Landlord negligent. Ms. K says she fell because the step at the top of the stairs was loose. Darrow and her photographer visit the scene and inspect the stair-

[*60*]

case. They find that the top step, made of wood, is cracked so that, when one steps on its outside edge, it gives. Neither Darrow nor her photographer can tell how long the step has been cracked. Has Larry Landlord been negligent? Has he "failed to act as an ordinarily careful person would act under the circumstances?" If Darrow can't prove this by a "preponderance of the evidence," no cigar. How can she? What would you like to argue to a jury to convince it that Larry was not acting reasonably?

Ideally you would like to argue that Larry knew of the defective stair for months prior to Ms. K's accident, knew that many people used the stairs and knew that it was only a matter of time before someone was seriously injured. Fat chance Larry will admit it. So how might you prove it?

Unfortunately Ms. K never told Larry of the defective stair prior to her fall. She was unaware of it because she very infrequently used those stairs. (Conversely, the fact that Ms. K didn't know of the defect in the stairs is helpful; otherwise Larry might argue that she was contributorily negligent in using them.) To prove Larry knew of the defect before the accident, Darrow sends an investigator to talk to other tenants. Did they ever report the condition to Larry? Were there other accidents on the stairs? Does Larry himself use the stairway, thus possibly having firsthand knowledge?

If you can't prove Larry actually knew of the condition, how can you stand before a jury and argue, with a straight face, that Larry "failed to act as an ordinarily careful person?" Well, it seems like an ordinary landlord would periodically inspect the premises to see if they are safe. The argument would be that if Larry had periodically inspected the stairs, he *would have known* of the defect. To make that argument fly, however, it seems that the defective condition must have existed some time before the accident; otherwise no inspection would have disclosed it. How to prove that the stair had been cracked for a long time? Perhaps an expert could make that determination. An expert need not have special degrees; an expert is simply someone who has special knowledge that will help the jury understand the facts of the case. Darrow calls a carpenter to inspect the stairs.

Meanwhile, while this investigation is going on, Darrow has contacted Larry Landlord's lawyer, Big Jim Owens. Her initial overtures to settle the case meet with sullen rejection:

"Larry Landlord wasn't negligent. Ms. K wasn't injured. Besides, there is a clause in the lease releasing the landlord from all liability."

If that's the way it is going to be, the only thing left to do is sue. Darrow drafts a complaint using, as a model, one in a legal form book.

IN THE SUPERIOR COURT
IN AND FOR THE COUNTY OF KERN
STATE OF CONTENTION

Ms. K	Civil Action Number
Plaintiff	———
vs.	COMPLAINT FOR NEG-
Larry Landlord	LIGENCE AND STRICT
Defendant	LIABILITY

Comes now plaintiff and complains of the defendant as follows:

Count I

1. The court has jurisdiction of this matter as all events complained of herein occurred in this county and both Ms. K and Larry Landlord are residents thereof.

2. At the times herein mentioned defendant owned the Owl Apartment Building, at 1112 4th Street, McFarland.

3. At the times herein mentioned defendant retained control in the Owl Apartment Building of the halls, lobbies and stairways used in common by all tenants of the building and others lawfully coming onto the premises.

4. On Nov. 17, 1983, plaintiff was a tenant of defendant.

5. On that date, while plaintiff was proceeding down the common stairway provided by defendant for the use of all tenants, plaintiff was tripped by a defective stair on the stairway, thrown violently down the stairway,

[*63*]

and in falling sustained injuries to her back and a broken leg.

6. As a result of such injuries, plaintiff sustained damages in the amount of $20,000.

7. Defendant knew, or with the exercise of reasonable care should have known, of the defective condition of the stairway, but negligently failed to correct, remove or repair such defective condition, and such negligence by defendant was a proximate cause of plaintiff's injuries and the damages incidental thereto.

Count II

1. Plaintiff realleges 1-6 of her first cause of action.

2. Defendant was strictly liable for defective conditions in the stairway and said defective conditions were a direct cause of plaintiff's injuries.

WHEREFORE, plaintiff prays judgment against the defendant for $20,000, for costs of suit, and for such other and further relief as the court deems proper.

_____

C. Darrow
Attorney for
Plaintiff
10 Wall Street

Proud of her work, Darrow takes it down to the County Courthouse, pays the County Clerk the filing fee, and files the complaint. The clerk gives it a case number and we're off to the races. Darrow gives a copy of the complaint and a summons to a process server who thereupon serves it on Larry Landlord.

Now it is time for Big Jim to go scurrying to the law library. He has but 20 days to "answer."

Ms. K	
Plaintiff	Civil Action Number
vs.	1066
Larry Landlord	ANSWER
Defendant	

Comes now defendant to answer plaintiff's complaint as follows:

1. Admits allegations 1–4 inclusive.

2. Denies allegations 5, 6 and 7.

3. As to count two, denies all matters not admitted to in number 1 hereof.

AFFIRMATIVE DEFENSE

As an affirmative defense to both counts, defendant alleges

1. That the lease between Ms. K and Larry Landlord which Ms. K signed, provides: ''The Landlord shall in no event be liable for any loss or damage which may occur to the Tenant.''

2. Said clause bars plaintiff's suit.

WHEREFORE, defendant prays

1. That plaintiff take nothing on her complaint.

2. That the court order plaintiff to pay defendant's costs of suit and order

[*65*]

such other further relief as the court
deems proper.

Love and Kisses

_____

Big Jim Owens
Lawyer for
Defendant

With the Complaint and Answer filed, things
are likely to sit quite some time. The lawyers
will engage in *discovery*. Big Jim will *depose*
Ms. K. On the day noticed, Ms. K and Darrow
will arrive at Big Jim's office. A court reporter
will transcribe the questions and answers. Ms. K
will be sworn and Big Jim will try to pin her
down, both as to the cause of her accident and to
the extent of her injuries. If Ms. K changes her
story at trial, she can be *impeached* by these pri-
or statements. Suppose, for example, she testifies at trial that she hurt her left arm quite badly
during the fall. As to this point, the cross would
look something like this:

Cross Examination: by Big Jim Owens

Q: (by Big Jim) Ms. K you testified on direct that
you injured your arm during the
fall, is that correct?

A: Yes.

Q: Do you remember coming to my office for your deposition?

A: Yes.

Q: Wasn't your attorney with you?
[*66*]

A: Yes.

Q: And you were sworn to tell the truth on that occasion?

A: Yes.

Q: And I told you before we began not to answer any question you didn't understand, isn't that a fact?

A: Yes, I remember. You seemed like such a nice man at the time.

Q: During the deposition I asked you to describe your injuries. You told me of your back pains and your broken leg, isn't that right?

A: Yes, my back was quite painful. And my leg was really smashed up. It was terrible.

Q: I appreciate your injuries. Please just answer my questions. Now, after you indicated your problems with your back and leg, didn't I ask you whether you were injured in any other way?

A: Yes, you asked me that.

Q: And didn't you tell me, "No, I had no other injuries." Weren't those your precise words?

A: Yes, but . . . .

Q: Thank you, nothing further.

If Ms. K has a good explanation for her inconsistency, Darrow can bring it out during redirect. In the jargon of the trial bar, this is known as *rehabilitation*.

Redirect by C. Darrow

Q: Before you were cut off by Big Jim, I believe
you were about to explain your inconsistency.

A: Yes. During the deposition I was in pain and
my back and leg hurt so much that I simply forgot about the injuries to my arm.

Trial lawyers will tell you that some rehabilitation is better than others.

Darrow will be engaged in her own discovery.
One of the goals of discovery is to narrow and
define the factual disputes for trial. Recall that
Darrow alleged in her complaint that the defendant "owned the Owl Apartment Building," that
the plaintiff "was a tenant of the defendant," and
that the defendant maintained control over "common stairways." She alleged all these things because as a matter of substantive tort law she
must prove all of them before she can recover.
In all likelihood these facts will not be contested
by the landlord and indeed Big Jim admitted them
in his answer. But what if Big Jim was playing
it petty and filed as an answer what is known as
a *general denial,* one which denies everything?
Must then Ms. K call witnesses at trial to prove
Larry Landlord owned the building? No. She
can, before trial, force Big Jim's hand to see what
he is really contesting. She sends the following
to Big Jim:

Ms. K
        Plaintiff
      vs.
Larry Landlord
        Defendant

Civil Action Number 1066
DEMAND FOR ADMISSIONS

You are requested to admit the truth of the following statements, pursuant to the Rules of Civil Procedure which provide that these matters will be deemed admitted unless, as to each, you serve within 30 days an answer, or an objection thereto, stating the reasons why you cannot truthfully admit or deny the matter. You may not give lack of information or knowledge as a reason for failure to admit or deny unless you state you have made reasonable inquiry and that you still lack sufficient information to admit or deny. The statements are as follows:

1. That on November 17, 1983, and for several months previous thereto, Larry Landlord was the owner of the Owl Apartment Building.

2. That on November 17, 1983, and for several months previous thereto, Ms. K was a tenant of Larry Landlord.

3. That on November 17, 1983, and for several months previous thereto, the back staircase in the Owl Apartment Building was for the common use of the tenants of said building and was in the control of Larry Landlord.

                  Date: February 1, 1984

              _____

        C. Darrow

If Big Jim admits to these matters, then C. Darrow can introduce the admissions at trial to prove those aspects of her case. What happens if Big Jim denies them? Then C. Darrow will have to prove them at trial. So why should Big Jim admit them? Because if C. Darrow is forced to prove them at trial she may, under many discovery statutes, "apply to the court for an order requiring the other party to pay the reasonable expenses incurred in making that proof, including reasonable attorney fees." Best to admit what you must.

Darrow will undoubtedly depose Larry Landlord, hoping to find that he either knew of the condition or failed to make ordinary inspections of the stairs. All is going per usual when suddenly Big Jim makes a move designed *to end it all.*

	Civil Action Number 1066
Ms. K	
Plaintiff	DEFENDANT'S MOTION TO DISMISS COUNT 2
vs.	OF PLAINTIFF'S COMPLAINT
Larry Landlord	
Defendant	DEFENDANT'S MOTION FOR SUMMARY JUDGMENT

TAKE NOTICE THAT at 8:30 a.m. or as soon thereafter as the matter can be heard, on April 6, 1984, in Courtroom 4 of the Superior Court of the County of Kern, defendant will move the court to dismiss

[*70*]

Count 2 in plaintiff's complaint as it
fails to state a claim upon which relief
can be granted. DEFENDANT WILL FURTHER
MOVE that summary judgment be granted it
as to both counts on the basis that there
is no triable issue of fact in this case.

```
                              Big Jim
```

What's going on? Will Big Jim, Big Bad Jim,
get away with it? Stay tuned. [If the matter
was to be tried under the Federal Rules of Procedure, Big Jim has made a bad mistake. He
should have filed his Motion to Dismiss before filing his Answer. Not to worry; you will learn all
about this in Civil Procedure. Note here simply
that the drafters of the Federal Rules apparently
had no sense of dramatic moment.]

4. Pretrial Devices to Test the Legal Effect and Sufficiency of Fact

Why have a lengthy and expensive trial if it is
clear that one of the parties is a sure loser? Procedural law allows for various moves to abort
cases without trial if there really isn't a true factual dispute. ("Procedural law" refers to the
rules which govern the *method* by which disputes
are resolved, such as rules governing which court
should decide the controversy—jurisdiction—
what issues may be joined in the same lawsuit,
and how long one has to answer a complaint.
"Substantive law" refers to rules which determine the *outcome* of the dispute, the rules of con-

[71]

tract, property, and dog bite.   Another way of looking at substantive rules is to see them as the rules governing our daily lives and those of our dogs.)

The two most common procedural devices to test the legal effect and sufficiency of fact are *motions to dismiss* and *motions for a summary judgment.*

a. Motions to dismiss a pleading as insufficient as a matter of law

The plaintiff files a complaint, the defendant an answer, each making certain factual allegations. A motion to dismiss basically says "no soap"— what is alleged doesn't make it as a matter of substantive law.

In this case defendant is moving to dismiss plaintiff's second count. Plaintiff alleged that the defendant landlord should be liable on a theory of strict liability, that he should be liable even though the plaintiff cannot prove his negligence. Darrow wanted a fallback position in the event she could not prove negligence. Clever idea. Defendant's motion to dismiss is saying "Without showing negligence, there is no cause of action as a matter of law and hence the count should be dismissed. No need to have a trial on it."

Motions to dismiss can be used to test the legal sufficiency of answers as well as complaints. Darrow could have moved to dismiss the affirmative defense by arguing that exoneration clauses are void. If that motion was granted, then the defendant could not even introduce evidence of the clause at trial: You can introduce evidence only in support of what you have alleged (or evidence

[*72*]

which contradicts what your opponent has alleged).

In olden days, days of grace and style, motions to dismiss were called "demurrers." You will find that term in some opinions you read. It is still used in our more romantic states, such as California.

b. Motions for summary judgments

A motion to dismiss is solely defensive in that it can only attack the sufficiency of the facts alleged by the opposition in his complaint or answer. But what if there is an important fact not alleged by the opposition that would abort the case? How can you get it before the court? By a motion for Summary Judgment. You file an affidavit setting forth additional "fact." Unless the opposing party denies it, the court deems it admitted and rules. Admitted that Ms. K signed an exoneration clause, does that, as a matter of law, bar her suit?

Come 8:30, April 6, 1984. C. Darrow and Big Jim arrive in Courtroom 4. Most likely they have previously submitted *Memorandums of Points and Authorities* arguing their respective positions. The parties will argue, quoting precedent, arguing policies and distinguishing cases. No doubt the judge will "take the matter under advisement." After a short interval the judge will enter judgment, in all likelihood striking the plaintiff's second count (nice try Darrow) and denying Big Jim's motion for summary judgment, holding exoneration clauses unenforceable.

The matter is set for trial of plaintiff's remaining count, the one alleging negligence. Can Darrow make it out *factually?*

5. Trial

We have already reviewed the overall structure of trials. This part is to give you some flavor for the litigation process. In terms of *lessons* it is designed to show how *objections to evidence* fulfill the same role as motions to dismiss (demurrers without poetry) and motions for summary judgment: They force a legal determination of the legal relevance and effect of fact. Again the interplay of law and fact. After the lesson, a quick look at closing argument because, well, because it is the most artistic of the lawyer's craft.

Darrow, for the plaintiff, has the burden of proof. She goes first. She plans to call Ms. K to testify to her fall and injuries. She plans to call Dr. Dread to establish the extent of those injuries. To establish Larry Landlord's negligence, she will call Joseph Ham, an ex-tenant of the apartment house who will testify that he complained of the loose stairs to Larry Landlord two weeks before the unfortunate accident. Darrow will also call a carpenter, with the unlikely name of Woody Nails, who inspected the stairs shortly after the accident and concluded that they had been in a dangerous condition for at least two months. The defense, at the pretrial hearing, indicated to the judge that it would call only two witnesses, Larry Landlord and Chuck Pile, a tenant who will testify that weekly he takes out the garbage by way of the back stair and has not once tumbled.

Darrow can call her witnesses in any order she pleases. Knowing that the first and last positions are key, she decides to put Ms. K on first and to put on Dr. Dread last. She wants to leave the jury with a powerful presentation of her client's suffering. The weak part of her case, that of Larry's negligence, she plans to sandwich in between high points, the fall and the suffering. As to each witness, Darrow knows she can develop the testimony in any order she selects. With Ms. K, for example, she plans to develop four main points. First she plans to use Ms. K to prove up medical bills and loss of earnings. These matters are not controversial and lack emotional impact; they should go in the middle of the testimony. Second, Darrow wants Ms. K to testify she was being careful at the time of her fall. Although defense did not, in its pleadings, raise the issue of contributory negligence, Darrow is concerned that some juror during deliberations might remark "If she had been looking where she was going, this would never have happened." Third, Ms. K will testify as to the accident itself and, fourth, to the pain and suffering she experienced. Darrow decides on the following order:

1. Introduction and personalization of Ms. K.

2. Description of the accident and its terror.

3. Testimony showing Ms. K was not negligent.

4. The amount of medical bills and loss of earnings.

5. The pain and suffering; the fear she would never walk again.

Let's pick up the testimony at point three:

Q: (by Ms. Darrow)	Prior to the accident, did you know the step was loose?
A:	No, I seldom use the back stairs. I hadn't used them before my fall for at least two months.
Q:	Now as you approached the top of the stairs, were you distracted in any way?
A:	No, I was looking where I was going.
Q:	Then why did you step on a step that was loose?
A:	Well when you walk you look ahead, not at your feet. I had no idea that the step was going to give away like it did.
Q:	After the accident, did you have occasion to inspect the top step?
A:	Yes.
Q:	Is it your opinion that Larry Landlord was negligent?
Q: (by Big Jim)	Objection! That question is clearly improper as it calls for an opinion of a lay witness. Darrow knows better than that.
Court:	Sustained.

[76]

Darrow does know better than that. She knows that the question is improper. She also knows that it is unethical to ask an improper question to sneak impermissible material before the jury. You can't ask "When did you stop beating your wife?" unless you have a good faith belief that the witness did at one time beat his wife. But before you get too upset with Darrow's questionable behavior, let me come to her defense. I, as puppeteer extraordinaire, urged her to ask that question, indeed I insisted that she ask it. I wanted to introduce a very important rule of evidence, the "opinion rule." One statement of the rule is found in the Federal Rules of Evidence:

OPINION TESTIMONY BY LAY WITNESSES

If the witness is not testifying as an expert, his testimony in the form of opinions or inferences is limited to those opinions or inferences which are (a) rationally based on the perception of the witness and (b) helpful to a clear understanding of his testimony or the determination of a fact in issue.

The rule forces witnesses to testify about the raw data of experience, what they saw, heard, smelled, tasted and felt, not what they concluded from those experiences. Drawing conclusions is the job of the jury. A witness cannot testify "Landlord was negligent." That opinion is neither "rationally based on perception"—the witness didn't *see* the landlord being negligent—nor is it helpful to a "clear understanding of his testimony." A witness can testify:

> I stepped on the stair and *felt* it give. I *looked* at the stair and found a crack about 6 inches long and a quarter of an inch wide. I told landlord about it and *heard* him say "That sounds dangerous. I will fix it immediately." A week later I *looked* at the stair and *saw* nothing had been done.

From the facts perceived by witnesses, the jury concludes whether the landlord was negligent.

Note how the opinion rule fits into the lawyer's main task of analyzing the interplay of law and fact. By emphasizing specific facts, rather than factual conclusions, we deepen our understanding of the law. As a lawyer, you can never be satisfied with vague factual conclusions. Say you represent a man charged with murder and the defense is self-defense. You cannot be satisfied by "I shot him because he had a knife and was approaching me in a threatening manner." You must insist on specific facts. "What exactly about his manner did you find threatening?"

Some witnesses can testify as to their opinions—experts. For example, the Federal Rules provide:

TESTIMONY BY EXPERTS

If scientific, technical, or other specialized knowledge will assist the trier of fact to understand the evidence or to determine a fact in issue, a witness qualified as an expert by knowledge, skill, experience, training, or education, may testify thereto in the form of an opinion or otherwise.

Darrow plans to call two experts. Dr. Dread, based on his training in medical school and his experiences as a physician, will testify as to the extent of Ms. K's injuries and as to her prognosis. Woody Nails, carpenter, will testify about the condition of the stairs. Let's pick up the trial with him.

Court:	Call your next witness.
Darrow:	Plaintiff calls Woody Nails.
Witness is sworn.	
Q: (by C. Darrow)	State your name and address for the record.
A:	Woody Nails. 5010 Randlett Drive.
Q:	What is your occupation?
A:	Carpenter. I have been a carpenter for thirty years.
Q:	Have you ever built staircases?
A:	More than I can count.
Q:	Do you ever have occasion to inspect staircases for safety?
A:	Quite often. Several insurance agents ask me to inspect buildings before they insure them. I pay particular attention to stairways because if they're not proper folks can get hurt real bad.
Q:	What happens if you find a staircase that is dangerous?

[*79*]

Q: (by Big Jim)   I object, Your Honor. This line of questioning isn't relevant to the issues of this case. What happens when this witness inspects other staircases is besides the point.

Q: (by C. Darrow)   Your Honor, this line of questioning is relevant to show this man's expertise. That insurance agents rely on him is evidence that he knows what he is talking about.

Court: Objection overruled.

Q: Again, what happens when you find a staircase that you think is unsafe?

A: I'll tell the owner or the agent. They have me repair it.

Q: Do they ever go ahead and insure the building without insisting on having the stairs repaired?

A: Not that I know of. It would be real dumb.

Q: Did you have occasion to inspect the back staircase at the Owl Apartments?

A: Yes. I went over there about two days after Ms. K fell.

Q: What was the result of your inspection?

A: The top stair was unsafe. It was loose and gave when you stepped on it. The problem

[*80*]

was that it had a big crack in it, about 6 inches long and a quarter of an inch wide.

Q: Could you determine how long the crack had been there?

Q: (by Big Jim)   Objection, Your Honor. There is nothing about this witness that would make him an expert in this matter. I let his testimony about "unsafe" pass but not this. Without some showing that this witness has some expertise in knowing how long conditions have existed, I object to the testimony.

Court: I'm going to allow the question. I think carpenters can make these decisions. You can cross-examine Mr. Nails about how he came to his conclusion. How much weight to give his testimony will be up to the jury but I will let it in.

Q: (by C. Darrow)   How long would you say the stair had been in that condition?

A: Well from the dirt and grime embedded in the crack, I'd say a fairly long time.

Q: Could you be more specific?

A: At least a couple of months.

Q: Thank you, no further questions. You may cross-examine.

Note the two step process. The judge decides whether or not to *admit* the evidence; once it is admitted, the jury decides whether or not to *believe* it. Admission of evidence is a question of law and you will see it at issue in several of the cases you read. The exclusionary rule, for example, makes certain evidence inadmissible: The jury will never hear it. On the other hand, just because evidence is admitted does not mean the jury must believe it. Even if a criminal defendant's confession is admitted in his trial, he can still testify to his innocence and attempt to convince the jury that his confession was not true because the police tricked him, beat him or whatever.

To illustrate something of cross, let's take the testimony of Joe Ham who, on direct, stated that two weeks before the accident he had told Larry Landlord of the bad condition of the stair and that Larry had said "That sounds dangerous. I will get it fixed immediately." Larry has told his lawyer, Big Jim, that the conversation never happened. As this is not something Joe could merely be mistaken about (like an eyewitness identification), it must be that Joe is lying (or Larry is). The purpose of cross examination in such cases is to suggest possible motives for perjury. Note, however, that Big Jim realizes that even hostile witnesses can be used to make needed points. Note too that the questions on cross are leading.

CROSS EXAMINATION OF JOE HAM

Q: (by Big Jim)   It's true that you used those stairs on several occasions both before and after Ms. K's fall.

A: Yes.

Q: And you never noticed the defective condition before the time you reported it to Larry Landlord.

A: That's right.

Q: So as far as you know, the condition was of fairly recent origin, isn't that right.

A: Well I didn't notice it before.

Q: So as far as you know, the stairway was not cracked before the time you reported it?

A: Yes.

Q: And that was two weeks before Ms. K's fall, and not a couple of months.

A: Yes.

Q: Thank you. Now you never fell on those stairs did you?

A: No.

Q: And you never heard of anyone else tripping on those stairs, isn't that right.

Q: (by C. Darrow)   Objection, Your Honor. The question is not relevant.

Q: (by Big Jim)   Your Honor, the lack of other accidents is relevant to the is-

	sue of whether the stairs were safe.
Court:	Objection overruled. You may answer the question.
A:	No, I never heard of anyone else falling.
Q:	Thank you. Now you are a very good friend of Ms. K's isn't that right.
A:	Yes.
Q:	And you want her to win this lawsuit, don't you?
A:	I think she should.
Q:	Please answer the question. Do you want her to win this lawsuit or don't you?
A:	I guess I do.
Q:	Do you guess or do you?
A:	I do.
Q:	And isn't it a fact that you don't like Larry Landlord?
A:	Well, maybe not.
Q:	Maybe not? Isn't it a fact that he evicted you two months ago?
A:	Yes.
Q:	And didn't you tell him at the time you would get even?
A:	No, I didn't say that.
Q:	Weren't you upset at being evicted?
A:	Of course.
Q:	And angry at Larry.

[*84*]

A: Yes.

Q: Nothing further.

During trial lawyers make points to use in closing argument. Big Jim's closing argument, as it
relates to Joe, will run something like this:

Ladies and Gentlemen, there is one glaring contra-
diction in this case. You remember Joe, the tenant
who had been evicted by Larry. He testified that he
told Larry of the faulty condition of the stairs a
good two weeks before the accident. Not only did
he tell him, but he told you Larry said "That sounds
dangerous. I'll get it fixed immediately." Now
that's quite convenient Larry said that. Note how
well it fits into the plaintiff's theory. It shows not
only Larry knew of the condition but also knew it
was quite dangerous. What better evidence could
you ask for?

Larry testified he never had that conversation with
Joe. You must decide who to believe. Someone is
lying to you. How can you decide who is telling the
truth? His Honor will instruct you that you can
consider the "character and quality of the testimony" and the existence of any bias or interest.

Does Joe's testimony make sense? To believe that
that conversation actually took place you must believe that Larry knew that there was a very dangerous condition on the stairway but simply failed to do
anything about it. Joe would have you believe that
Larry was content to wait until someone tripped and
fell, to wait until someone sued. Joe's story doesn't
make sense. Further, he continued to use the stairs.
Does it make sense to go on using a staircase after
you have reported its dangerous condition to the
landlord?

Joe's story just doesn't hold together. Had he told Larry of the condition, it is reasonable to assume Larry would have acted, not only to prevent someone's injury but also to avoid a lawsuit. Does Joe have a motive to make up his testimony? A motive to lie to you? You bet. He is a good friend of the plaintiff. He admitted that he wants her to win this case and obviously he knows his testimony is essential for her victory. And he dislikes Larry. Larry evicted him. Joe even admitted his anger.

No, Joe is not to be believed. He was simply lying about his conversation with Larry. Larry told you it never happened because it never did.

6. Closing Argument: Weaving Law and Fact

Effective closing argument relies on the primary lawyering skill, the ability to bring law and fact together. Here it is done in public. The witnesses who have testified and the documents and exhibits which have been introduced have put before the jury bits of information: that Joe was evicted by Larry, that the carpenter believes that the stairs had been in a state of bad repairs for a long time, that Ms. K fell. At closing the lawyer *marshals these bits of information into factual conclusions that have legal relevance.* To illustrate this let's pick up part of Darrow's closing argument.

Closing Argument: C. Darrow:

From the fact that Joe told Larry of the condition of the stairs and from the fact that they had been in disrepair for a long time, we can conclude that Larry

[*86*]

knew or should of known that the stair was dangerous.

Next Darrow shows the jury what these factual
conclusions mean in terms of law.

That Larry Landlord knew of the dangerous condition and yet did nothing about it means that he was
not acting as would an ordinarily careful person under the circumstances. An ordinarily careful person
would have done something to prevent the accident.
As the judge will instruct, if you find that Larry did
not do as would an ordinarily careful person, you are
to find him negligent.

This mode of analysis will become quite familiar.
It is the very same process law students use to
analyze exam questions. The bits of information
in the question are turned into factual conclusions which are then turned in legal conclusions.
More of this in Chapter 8.

Closing arguments are, however, more, much
more, than logic. They are emotion and power.
In the hands of a good criminal defense lawyer,
"reasonable doubt" becomes the finest and most
delicate flower of Western Civilization, a flower
about to be ground under the shiny black boot of
the State. Listening to a good personal injury
lawyer you experience the victim's anguish as he
lies sleepless in a hospital bed thinking of what
might have been. And you will experience few
moments as intense and as immediate as when
you make a closing argument yourself. At first
there will be the distractions, your nervousness,
your awareness of the spectators and the judge.

Soon, however, you soar. Forgotten are your notes and gone is the judge; for awhile it is just you, your argument, and the jurors.

7. Questions of Law and Questions of Fact

If the question is of law, you stand before the judge and coolly argue "Exoneration clauses should not be enforced." If the question is of fact, you rant and rave before the jury "Larry was negligent, thoughtless, heartless and surely no friend of Ms. K!" Whether a question is one of law or fact is important; it tells you where to stand. You will learn, however, that the line between questions of law and fact is often fuzzy. You will even find, to your consternation, that occasionally questions of fact become questions of law. I will leave all of that to your courses. Here I want to raise the fascinating issue of jurisprudence. Why are some questions of law and others of fact? Why shouldn't it be left to the jury to decide whether exoneration clauses in leases should be enforced? And why shouldn't the jury disregard a law if it thinks it unjust? Remember the jury instruction: "It is your *duty* to apply the law as I state it to you." Why not "It is your duty to apply the law *but only* if you think it is just." Do we fear that juries will run amuck? Do we believe that those of us with special training (and, of course, a higher average intelligence) have a better sense of justice than a cross section of our peers? Would jurors run amuck? Is justice a product of intelligence and

[*88*]

training? These are difficult questions; they go
to the root of our profession and system of justice. I urge you to consider them.

8. Cases as the Opportunity to *Do* Law

Reading cases affords the opportunity to *do
law*, and hence the opportunity to learn the central lawyering skill, the skill of analyzing the interplay of law and fact. This has been the theme
of the previous two chapters. We have covered
much material and a quick review is proper.

Questions of Law: The Art of Arguing and Distinguishing Cases

1. Our system is committed to the notion of follow-
    ing precedent. Does this make our system more
    predictable because precedent controls judicial
    whim? Do more just decisions come from con-
    sidering what other judges have done in similar
    situations? From realizing that one's own deci-
    sion will become precedent to decide future
    cases?

    Given the goal of treating like cases as alike,
    when are two cases alike? Before you can apply
    a *rule* of a case to a new situation, you must
    consider the *facts* of the case as well as the *ra-
    tionale* of the case. It is error to insist on too
    close a factual identity but it is also error to ap-
    ply rules without reference to the factual con-
    text in which they were announced.

2. Legal ping pong and how it can be played:
    Learn legal argument by restaging the argu-
    ment. Legal arguments have a certain ring to
    them. Although rules of law grow out of deep

emotions and philosophic notions of justice, legal argument is not directly about emotions and philosophy; it is always grounded in principles of law.

3. Often cases indirectly raise issues of role and ethics of lawyers. Consider them, discuss them with your classmates. They will be on your career and on your conscience.

Questions of Fact: The Trial Process

1. Trials are planned around jury instructions and jury instructions are nothing more than applied statutes and appellate decisions. When reading appellate decisions ask what will a jury be instructed, and consider what you would argue to the jury and what evidence you would introduce at trial.

2. Throughout the litigation process, there are various procedural devices to test the *legal sufficiency of fact.* Pretrial, they are motions to dismiss, demurrers, motions for summary judgment. During trial, the most common are objections to evidence. There are others you will consider in your Procedure course: Motions for Directed Verdict, Motions for Judgments Not Withstanding the Verdict.

3. The opinion rule in evidence keeps lawyers on specifics and teaches suspicion of factual conclusions and opinions.

4. One important allocation between judge and jury is that the judge decides whether evidence is *admissible* while the jury decides whether it is *believeable.*

5. There are ethical restrictions on lawyers during trial. While it is permissible to question witnesses to show their possible motives for perjury, it

is not permissible to ask questions in bad faith: When did you stop beating your wife?

Read cases to do law, not just to learn doctrine. You will find it difficult at first but eventually it will be fun. An added payoff is that you will learn the doctrine so much better. You will be *using it* rather than underlining it.

PART TWO

LAW SCHOOL SKILLS

CHAPTER 5

STUDYING LAW: LOOKING BUSY IS NOT ENOUGH

Stay involved with the materials; more bluntly, stay awake. It will not be easy. Much of what you will study is difficult; some, boring. The temptation to sleep, to close up shop, will be great. Your mind will cry:

Stop it! Let me rest! Just underline stuff for a while. If that doesn't do it, use a yellow highlighter. I don't care. Use pens with different colored ink. Buy an outline. Copy it. Just don't ask me to think! I can't take it anymore!

So sorry.

To determine the best way to study, begin with an idea of your goal. It is to learn the "law," not at the level of memorization, but rather at the level of application. Your legal education is not about committing long series of "legal rules" to memory by closing your eyes tight and concentrating hard. Your legal education is about developing the ability to see the legal problems in the situations your clients find themselves in and to solve those problems as a lawyer would—by applying principles of law in a lawyerlike way. This ability is developed by immersing yourself in law. You can't fade out when the going gets rough.

1. Learning by Writing

Study with pen in hand. Reading we "think" we understand; writing we realize we don't. My hunch is that we err because of speed. We read and think fast—speed allows us to skim over difficult links of reasoning and troubling points. Put pen to paper and the mind slows. New problems and new relationships emerge. Always write, always jot down questions and insights. Write not to store but to develop. Writing slows, writing focuses, writing deepens analysis.

Underlining and decorating your book with various color markers requires little thought and involvement even though you do "seem" busy. I'll grant you that. Far better to write in the margins. If you are not to be weaned of your yellow highlighter, summarize out loud what you have so neatly highlighted. Speaking slows the mind. You will discover your understanding of the material not as good as you "thought"; you will likely have to go back to see just how the author got from A to C without mentioning B and failing to see the implications of D.

Writing does not mean copying. Create what you write, be it a case brief or a course outline. Be clear on this: Those who write canned briefs and commercial outlines will do a much better job than you. Their briefs will be more concise and

their outlines more accurate. So be it. Yours is
not to learn the law at the level of memorization
where brevity and accuracy are essential. Yours
is to learn law at the level of application. Make
the case your own by restating its essentials in
your own words and make a course your own by
putting the cases and your class notes into a coherent whole of your own design.

Expect to be wrong. Expect to misstate legal
rules and confuse legal doctrines. It is the process, the struggle with ideas that matters, not the
result.

In order to *write* you need room. Leave *sufficient margins* on your briefs, class notes, and
outlines. Most bookstores sell paper with wide
three-inch margins and I recommend it.

2. Reading and Briefing Cases

There is a very famous Abbott and Costello
routine that pretty much sums up the first weeks
of law school. It's about a rather strange baseball team and begins when one friend asks another who plays first base.

"Who's on first?"

"No, Whos on second."

"What?"

"Whats on third!"

"Well, who's on first?"

"I told you, Whos on second."

[*94*]

Just figuring out what's going on in a case can
be very difficult. ("No, whats not going on in a
case, whats at third!") After what seem like
hours it finally hits you that the plaintiff and the
respondent are the *same* guy! ("Why didn't they
just say so?") Another flash: "That must mean
the defendant and the appellant are the same
too." Secure in your new knowledge, perhaps
even a tad pompous, you proceed to the next
case. Everything shatters—the plaintiff is now
the appellant and there isn't even a respondent,
only an appellee!

Expect to reread a case several times to understand the basics—*who sues whom, on what theory, who wins and why.* You will face a new vocabulary (get a legal dictionary), difficult
concepts and often impossible prose. Neither
panic nor lament: Everyone must struggle, and
it becomes much easier once you get the hang of
it. Once you understand the case, it is time to
brief it. Not to be confused with long written arguments lawyers submit to courts nor with men's
underwear, "briefs" are written summaries of
cases.

Briefing is a brilliant educational technique.
To brief a case means to reduce it to its essentials
and to restate those essentials in your own
words. What the court took four or five pages to
say, you reduce to perhaps half a page. As to all
the facts mentioned in the opinion, which are
key? Which make a difference in the court's decision? And, as to that lengthy discussion of le-

gal doctrine, what are the core thoughts? To brief a case means to understand it.

Briefs usually follow a certain format. The traditional, "fullblown" format is:
1. Case name and citation
2. Procedural posture of the case
3. Facts
4. Issue
5. Holding
6. Discussion

Some professors require a specific format; if they do, do what they say, it's their nickel.

Most briefs go awry in these critical areas:
1. Stating the precise issue before the court;
2. Stating the essential facts of the case; and
3. Discussing the legal doctrine applied by the court.

I will first discuss these aspects of a brief by presenting a checklist to use in reviewing your own briefs. After this discussion of the core concerns, I will discuss other aspects of briefing, such as the distinction between *dicta* and *holding*, and whether such things as the procedural history of the case, its date and even its name are important. These matters raise interesting questions of jurisprudence as well as telling you something of briefing.

To put the checklist in a specific context, we will use the short brief of *Globe* used in Chapter 3.

Globe

Facts: Plaintiff sues a credit bureau for negligently omitting a mortgage from a report it made to plaintiff. Because of the omission, plaintiff suffered an economic loss. The contract between plaintiff and defendant provided that defendant should not be liable for negligence. The court enforced the clause.

Rule: Exculpatory clauses are valid.

Rationale: The Court stressed the importance of freedom of contract. The court wrote: "If parties who make ordinary contracts cannot agree to limit the extent of liability, it is difficult to see where such a ruling would lead us."

a. Checklist for Briefs

Take one of your briefs and run it against the following.

(1) IS YOUR STATEMENT OF FACTS TOO LONG?

As to *each* fact recited, ask why. "If this particular fact were otherwise, would the outcome of the case be different?" If the answer is clearly no, then the fact is irrelevant and should *not* be included. Don't clutter your brief and your thought with irrelevancies. In *most* contract cases, it matters not whether the deal is for widgets or wadgets, for many or few, for much or little. In *most* tort cases it matters not whether the plaintiff broke his toe or his finger. How can you determine which facts are key? Sometimes they will jump out at you and occasionally the court will tell you directly: "If this had not happened, then we would not apply the rule." The difficulty comes when there are what seem to be very important facts but the court doesn't expressly say it is relying on them to decide the case. In *Globe,* the exoneration clause was in a *commercial* contract and the case involved *financial loss.* Are these facts key to the decision? If they were different, would the court's decision be different? A good argument can be made that it would. Include in your brief facts which are arguably pivotal.

(2) IS YOUR STATEMENT OF FACTS TOO SHORT?

It is error to reduce cases to mere abstract propositions of law: "Exculpatory clauses are enforceable." All statements of law are made in a *specific factual context.* Not knowing something of that context you will not be able to know whether the rule would be applied in a new fact situation. On an exam, for example, the question may raise the issue of an exoneration clause in an apartment house lease in a case involving personal injuries. Woe to you if you know only the abstract statement of the rule.

If your statement of facts is too short, reread the case to see if you have omitted essential facts.

[*98*]

(3) IS IT CLEAR WHY THE FACTS STATED ARE LEGALLY RELEVANT?

Under the traditional briefing format, one first recounts the "facts" and then, in a separate section, the "law." The separation is artificial. Discussing the facts separately leads to the mindless retelling of what is likely, at best, a boring tale. Facts are only important in relationship to principles of law. Good legal writing always involves the interplay of law and fact. Long recitations of the "facts" followed by long discussions of law do not trigger the key questions: "Which facts are important and why?" "Which legal discussions are important and why?"

If there are several key facts which you think should be included in the brief, the way to avoid the problem of long, unfocused statements of fact is to start the brief with a statement of the legal issue and thereafter state the facts. This way, the legal relevance of the facts will be clear.

(4) DOES YOUR BRIEF STATE THE FOCAL QUESTION SEPARATELY?

There is always a focal question, the question the court *must* answer to determine who wins. What exactly must the court decide? Once you have found the focal question, and sometimes it won't be easy, *state it separately.* It is of central importance as it joins the facts and the law.

Under the traditional briefing format, the focal question is known as the *issue:*

Issue: Are exculpatory clauses enforceable?

The *holding* of the case is the answer to the question posed in the *issue.*

Holding: Exculpatory clauses are enforceable.

Note that the *holding* can be called the *rule of the case.*

Rule: Exculpatory clauses are enforceable.

Note that the same core inquiry can be stated as an *issue,* as an *holding* or as a *rule.*   Although I am sure many of my colleagues will disagree, I do not believe it important what label you give your statement of the focal question.   What is important is that you find the focal question and state it carefully.

(5) IS THE FOCAL QUESTION (ISSUE) (HOLDING) (RULE) STATED TOO BROADLY OR TOO NARROWLY?

There is art, and argument, in stating the question carefully.   There is the danger of being too broad: "The issue is whether the contract is enforceable."   That is almost *always* the issue, except in Torts.   Conversely there is danger in stating the issue too narrowly: "The issue is whether the contract between Jones and Smith, dealing with first quality widgets, and calling for payments to be made each Tuesday . . . ."

The proper statement of the question (issue) (holding) (rule) is important as it relates directly to the precedential value of the case. State the rule too broadly and it will seem to apply in cases where it surely should not. State the rule too narrowly and it will seem not to apply to cases where it surely should. To test your statement of the rule, ask whether, as written, it would apply to cases where it doesn't seem it should. If it would, then likely the rule is stated too broadly. Conversely if you can think of cases where the rule should apply but, as written, would not, then likely the rule is written too narrowly.

"Exculpatory clauses are enforceable." Can you think of cases where it would seem not right to impose this rule? Say an exculpatory clause in a lease provides that the "landlord shall not be liable for anything" and the landlord takes a lead pipe to the tenant. Surely a court would not allow the landlord to escape liability by enforcing the clause but the rule, as written in the brief, would require enforcement. The rule is written too broadly.

"Exculpatory clauses releasing a party from liability for negligently failing to report a mortgage in a credit report are enforceable." Are there cases where the rule should apply but where, as written, it would not? Surely the rule should apply where the failure consisted of the failure to report something other than mortgages and should apply where the promised act is something other than a credit report. As written, the rule would not seem to apply to these cases. It is written too narrowly.

"Exculpatory clauses in commercial contracts releasing a party from negligent liability are enforceable when the injury sued upon is financial." This seems a fairly good statement of the rule as it gives us a sense of what kinds of future cases it will apply to *and* a sense of what kinds of cases it may not.

The quest is not for the perfect statement of the rule because, indeed, there is none. Good lawyers and judges will read a case differently, some finding that it stands for a narrow proposition of law, others finding that it stands for something broader. Much of the lawyer's art, and argument, goes to the issue of whether a case should be read narrowly or broadly. Stating the issue, holding or rule, your goal is not perfection; it is simply getting into the ball park. Good lawyers and judges will agree that some readings of a case are simply too broad while others are simply too narrow.

(6) IS YOUR DISCUSSION OF THE COURT'S REASONING IN YOUR OWN WORDS?

Why did the court rule the way it did? Many beginners aren't sure so they simply copy, or closely paraphrase, the court. This does not unlock the case. Your brief should identify and restate the key reasons. If your discussion of law is too long it may indicate lack of focus.

Do not quote in briefs. Convert the thoughts of others into your own. The one exception is when a case turns on specific statutory language. Because statutes are drafted with precision, each word tells, and copying them will increase your attention.

(7) HAVE YOU INCLUDED MATERIAL SIMPLY BECAUSE "IT'S THERE"?

Don't clutter your brief with irrelevancies out of the fear that "you never can tell." What strikes you now as trivial will most likely forever remain trivial and will not, at some future date, suddenly blossom into centrality. Don't mortgage your intellectual future by thinking: "When I review the case, then I will figure out whether it is important that the dog was a Collie. Right now, I'll just put it in and move on."

Briefing is a brilliant educational technique. To brief a case means to reduce it to its essentials. Or you can simply write down "what's there."

The checklist flags the major concerns. What are the key facts? The focal question? The essential law? We will now turn to collateral matters. Is it important to include the date of a case and the name of the judge? Is the procedural history of the case important? And what of this distinction between *dicta* and *holding*?

[*103*]

b. Citation, Dates, Court: What Should Be Included?

A typical caption might be:

Brown v. Finney
Penn. Supreme Court 1866
Opinion by Judge Tompson

Is this information necessary? To answer the question, ask why you brief cases. First, ~~you brief because you will need summaries for review; there will be too many cases to reread preparing for finals.~~ Second, ~~you brief cases in order to understand them.~~

Will it help you review (or does it show understanding) to include that the decision was by the Pennsylvania Supreme Court in 1866? In some cases, this information *might* be important. You will learn that, like the pigs of *Animal Farm*, some courts are more equal than others. In the development of common law principles, some state courts are quite respected. For example the New York Court of Appeals (the highest state court in New York) with Justice Cardozo and the California Supreme Court under Justice Traynor led the way in the development of many common law principles. Opinions of those courts carry particular weight. (To continue the animal metaphor, I'm not letting the cat out of the bag by suggesting that the 1866 Pennsylvania Supreme Court was not such a court).

Similarly the name of the judge who wrote the opinion *may* be important. Judges too are like pigs. In Constitutional Law courses, it's interesting to see how a particular Justice's philosphy plays out in several areas. However, in most courses, who wrote the opinion is of little interest (unless he's your uncle).

Dates are important *if* you are studying the historical development of a particular legal doctrine. *Usually* you aren't. Most cases are included in casebooks not to show you what the law *was* but to show you what the law *is*. The "Rule" of *Brown v. Finney* is as good today as it was in 1866. Legal education has been criticized for its ahistorical approach. The sense the student gets from reading old cases as current law is that the problems facing the law have always been the same and that the law itself is above history, that it is the product of neutral rational principles rather than the clash of competing philosophical, economic and social positions. This view is error. Oliver Wendell Holmes in his great essay, "The Path of the Law" (10 Harv.L. Rev. 457, 1897) wrote:

> I cannot but believe that if the training of lawyers led them habitually to consider more definitely and explicitly the social advantage on which the rule they lay down must be justified, they sometimes would hesitate where now they are confident, and see that really they were taking sides upon debatable and often burning questions.

And what is probably the most famous statement about law:

> The life of the law has not been logic: it has been experience. The felt necessities of the time, the prevalent moral and political theories, intuitions of public policy, avowed or unconscious, even the prejudices which judges share with their fellow-men, have had a good deal more to do than the syllogism in determining the rules by which men should be governed.

Law has a history and lawyers help shape its future. However as law is taught, history is not a paramount concern. Note the date in your brief only if you think it important. And be explicit—why is it important? Do you feel the case would not be followed today because it reflects different "felt necessities"? Just to note the date of an opinion, without saying why, is simply looking busy.

c. *Procedural History of Case*

Routine statements of the procedural history are not necessary.

> Jury found for plaintiff. Defendant appeals on basis of improper jury instruction. Appellate court reversed and plaintiff appeals. Affirmed.

This tells you nothing about the law and simply takes up space. Your interest is in what was the error in the jury instruction. This is not to say, however, that procedural history is irrelevant. It contributes to your understanding of the legal process. An opinion will end with "Affirmed" or "Reversed" but what does that mean to the litigants? Will there be a new trial or is that the end of the matter? *What happens next?*

Procedural history deepens your understanding of the interplay of law and fact. Procedural law allows for a series of devices to test the legal sufficiency and relevancy of fact. Pretrial, there are motions to strike and motions for summary judgment; during trial there are objections to evidence and arguments over jury instructions; and, after trial, there are motions for directed verdicts and for new trials. Thinking through the procedural history of particular cases helps you understand the trial process. It may also teach you something of trial strategy. Assuming the lawyer could have tested the legal relevance of the fact earlier or later in the proceeding, why now? Why did the lawyer wait until trial and until the witness was on the stand to object to a certain line of testimony when he could have challenged the relevancy of that testimony in a pretrial motion to strike the allegation which makes that testimony relevant? Procedural history also contributes to your understanding of the critical difference between questions of law and questions of fact. Is the court being asked to review a question of fact or a legal standard? You will find the distinction quite important to the appellant as courts are much more willing to reverse cases due to legal error than they are to reverse findings of fact.

Reading cases, pay attention to matters of procedure to learn the legal process. *Briefing*

cases, do not include them unless they contribute
to your understanding of the substantive rules of
law, rules about contracts, torts, property and
dog bite.

d.   Aside on Holding and Dicta

Holdings are statements of law necessary for
the decision in the case; *dicta* are statements of
law which aren't necessary for that decision.
Take the case of *Brown v. Finney* which involved
two men meeting in a bar and, after a few drinks,
making a supposed contract for the sale of coal.
The evidence disclosed that the seller was joking.
The appellate court reversed the judgment for
the buyer on the basis that the jury should have
been instructed that if the seller was joking he
should not be held to the contract. Suppose, in
the course of that opinion, the court stated "Intoxicated persons lack contractual capacity."
That statement would have been *dicta;* it was
not necessary for the court's decision which reversed on the issue of seriousness, not on the issue of intoxication. Conversely, in a case which
reversed a judgment because the defendant was
drunk when he made the offer, the same statement would be *holding*.

Lawyers use the distinction between holdings
and dicta to badmouth cases (distinguish them).
Say that the only case in the world is *Brown* and
in that case the court said "Intoxicated folks
don't have capacity to contract." The next case

in the world involves an intoxicated offeror. His
defense is that he should not be held to his promise because he was drunk when he made it. Assuming he, or his lawyer, could get it together, he
would argue, perhaps slur,

> Your Honor, *Brown* is a controlling decision here.
> It says "Intoxicated folks don't have the capacity to
> contract." So there! I win!

Distinguished opponent would, with great sobrie-
ty, sneer:

> This court is not obligated to follow *Brown*. This
> court is free to decide whether intoxicated persons
> should be held to their promises which, of course, I
> will argue they should be. As to the statement in
> *Brown* that "Intoxicated persons do not have con-
> tractual capacity," it is merely dicta. It was not nec-
> essary for the decision in that case. Brown involved
> pranksters, not drunks. It held that pranksters
> should be able to get out of their contracts. Its com-
> ments about drunks are totally beside the point.
> Hence this court is not obligated to follow the state-
> ment in Brown under the doctrine of *stare decisis*.

To which offeror, staggering to his feet, indig-
nantly responds:

> *Stare* what??? Your Honor, I strenuously object!
> This is an *American* court!

The distinction between holdings and dicta
makes sense. If something is really at issue, if
the case turns on it, likely the court thinks long
and hard before deciding. Compare those matters which are of the nature of "Oh by the way,
did you know that drunks . . . " Dicta are
not worth the same respect because likely they

are not the product of serious consideration—
nothing, in the particular case, turned on whether
drunks could contract or not. (Indeed, perhaps
the whole thing was simply the Judge's wishful
thinking.)

For a law student the distinction between holding and dicta can be quite useful as an analytic
ploy. Which statements of law are absolutely
necessary for the result reached? However once
you determine something is dictum, don't sneer
at it. Much of the law you will learn comes from
judicial asides.

e. *Some Final Pointers on Briefing*

1. Leave wide margins so that you can add points
    from class discusson and make further notes
    when you review.

2. Don't expect to write your brief the first time
    you read the case.

3. Some advise *not* to brief a case until you have
    read all of the cases in the same section of the
    casebook. This helps you see how the particular
    case fits.

4. A comment section at the end might prove help-
    ful. Do you agree or disagree with the opinion?
    What don't you understand about it?

A good brief forces you to examine a specific
legal rule in great depth. But there is also the
need to place the specific rule in a larger legal
context. You must occasionally step back from
the tree to see where you are in the forest. Periodic reviews help.

3. Periodic Review

A casebook's table of contents can be quite helpful in putting the specific into a larger context. The following is from Mueller and Rosett, *Contract Law and Its Application*, 2nd Edition.

V. Promises Tainted by Lack of Voluntary Assent

. . .

To ground a case in its larger context, begin with it and expand outward along the course-book's outline.

a. Are there any other cases in the same subsection? If so, how do those cases differ from the instant case? What additional information do they tell you about the topic of the subsection? Why are the cases presented in the order they are?

To illustrate, take the case of *Kuzmiak v. Brookchester* which appears in the subsection "Illegal Promises" with two other cases. What does it add to your understanding of "Illegal Promises" that the *McConnell* and *Allen* cases did not? Was *Kuzmiak* added to the casebook to show the same rule of law in a different factual context? To show a variation on the rule of law? Or to simply show off or allow the authors to fulfill their contract to produce a book of X pages? (And why did I throw in that last question?)

b. How does the subsection relate to the other subsections of similar rank? How are the principles of law different? How are they the same?

Under the larger division of "Transactions Outside the Area of Contract Exchange," there are two subdivisions, "Relationships that do not call for contractual recognition" and "Illegal Promises." Why did the authors make this division? Could they have made further divisions?

c. Continue the process outward. How does Section III, "Transactions Outside", relate to the topic of the Chapter? How does it relate to Roman II, "Words or Context Indicating Lack of Commitment"? No need to always look backward. In grounding *Kuzmiak*, for example, look ahead to the other categories. What might be "Vague and Indefinite Promises"?

I call this process a *Grounding Review* (whether this stems from gestalt psychology or the Forest/Tree metaphor need not detain us). I recommend that you do one each time you complete a subsection of the casebook. It should take only a few minutes; here I don't suggest you write, just sit, look at the table of contents and ask yourself questions. At first it will be difficult to even begin to answer the questions I have suggested and indeed some may be without rational answer. (Some cases seem to be in casebooks simply "Because they're there.") Still the questions take you beyond the narrow focus of the particular case and slowly the overall context clears. The trick is knowing both the particular and the general, seeing both the tree and the forest.

Another way to expand your vision, to see overriding connections, is to use the casebook's index.

4. Class Attendance

Elsewhere I write on the sheer terror of it. ("How I Stopped Worrying and Came to Love Civil Procedure!") Here a few brief points.

Spend a few minutes just before class skimming your briefs. In class you will hit the floor running.

Take notes, but not verbatim. A key phrase often will suffice if you go over your notes soon after class. Try to get the facts of the hypoes discussed in class. They can be helpful in review. Immediately after class, spend ten minutes going over your notes—filling in the gaps, writing out questions where things are unclear and generally reviewing what went on.

5. Study Groups

Law practice is social as well as solitary. There are times when you work alone, doing research, drafting documents or preparing a cross-examination. One of the real joys of law practice, however, comes in discussing difficult cases and problems with your colleagues. After law school I practiced with a Legal Services Program. Every Friday afternoon, we sat around the table in our small law library and talked about our cases. "Have you considered doing . . . ?" "I just read a case which might apply." "Did you hear what Judge Thames did?" There was challenge, humor, common purpose, sharing and connection.

Study groups can play a similar role. Ranging in size from two to six and usually meeting once a week, these groups allow for review and clarification of the week's work. They should also allow for hot discussions and high humor.

A few things to consider:

1. Everyone should agree to ask "dumb questions" and to admit confusion. Learn, don't maintain image.

2. Structure the session. Will you go over more than one subject? Will you review by discussing the cases or by working on problems, possibly old exam questions? How much time will be spent?

3. Consider having discussion leaders. Rotate them. "Next week, you do Property, I'll do Contracts." One effective way to learn is to teach: Planning and conducting a review session can be quite educational. Rotation shares this learning experience. It also copes with the problem some members of the group might have—the failure to realize that another way to learn is to listen!

4. It is *not* a good idea to divide the first year curriculum among the group to prepare outlines. "Kingsfield, you take Contracts." The true value of outlines comes in putting them together. Each person should outline each course.

Study groups are not for everyone. Some people work better alone. So be it! If study groups are not for you, you can get many of the same benefits by "talking law" with other students before class or over coffee. The only thing you have to worry about is what you're going to do Friday afternoons.

6. Asking Professors

One year, right after class, a student knocked on my door, came into my office, sat down, opened his notebook, took out his pen and announced "I missed class!"

Usually professors will welcome you. They love to discuss law. But don't ask them to fill in the gaps in your notes—that's what other students are for. Most will be happy however to explain difficult areas or argue troubling points. As one time law students, they know something of the personal side of law study. Many will be open to this topic as well.

On the other hand, professors have additional responsibilities—research, committee work, other courses. Sometimes they will not be able to spend time with you. However, my own assessment is that most professors are willing to spend time with students. You must make the first move—overcome that fear that says "Don't knock—go back!"

7. Preparing for Finals: Outlines and Old Exams

There is nothing magical about outlining except doing it. Its value is not the product but the production. It is yet another way to be actively involved with the material. ("Where does this interesting tidbit fit?")

Outlines combine your case briefs, class notes, and any outside reading you have done. For the major categories, consider using the Table of Contents of the casebook. And consider the questions raised in the discussion of *Periodic Re-*

view. Outlining, leave wide margins so that you can be writing while reviewing it.

Some students find it very helpful, toward the end of the semester, to review old finals. Many schools maintain files of them. There are also books giving typical exam questions. My own experience as a student was that I would look at an old exam and simply freeze—there was simply no way I could answer it. In the real test situation, of course, I had to overcome this panic and go ahead and answer the question. Like other study devices, going over old test questions is helpful to many, but not all, students.

A very good book, giving sample exam questions and model answers is Kinyon, *Law Study and Law Examinations in a Nutshell.*

8. Study Aids, Canned Briefs, and Commercial Outlines

Most professors advise not to rely on canned briefs or commercial outlines. I will join this chorus—knowing full well that you will believe the second year student sitting across the table in the Library who winks that someone in his class used nothing but canned briefs ("Didn't even buy the book!") and made Law Review. Believe second year students at your own risk.

One danger with study aids is that they do the work while you snooze. To succeed, you must stay awake and remain actively engaged with the materials. You must *do* law rather than memorize study aids.

Another difficulty with "outside" resources is that they may teach you more than you need to know. Here the analogy is to one of Poe's short stories. A man commits murder in the victim's living room. "I must wipe my fingerprints off the glass I was drinking from!" Fair enough, he does. "What about the table? Did I touch it?" A few extra minutes, no problem. "Maybe I went into the kitchen! Can't be too sure; it will take just a few minutes!" The story ends the next morning. The murderer is found in the attic wiping off old trunks.

There is always more to any legal topic than is covered in your casebook. The goal of first year courses is not to teach you "everything" about Torts, Civil Procedure or whatever. Treatises and hornbooks on these subjects, however, attempt to do just that. By using them, the danger is that you will concern yourself with areas not covered in your casebook, that you will get further and further afield, and end up, if not collapsed in an attic, at least slumped over volume 359 of the Pacific Reporter!

A similar danger of reading outside material is being prematurely swept up in the great theoretical debates that rage over the justifications and effects of law. In the field of Contracts, for example, some argue that the field is explained by basic moral injunction to keep promises. Not so,

claim others, the only way to understand Contracts is to understand economics. Still others
are actually rude enough to suggest the "Death
of Contract." While these are fascinating debates, do not engage in them until you have a
firm knowledge of the basics: is a promise to
make a gift enforceable? What if the donee relies on it?

If you don't use outside materials to do your
work and are aware of their dangers, they can be
quite valuable. If you are having a particularly
difficult time with an area, a treatise might help.
Go to one, however, only after you have strug-
gled. Treatises can also help you review. After
you have worked through a topic, it is helpful to
read a Nutshell or commercial treatise *as a
method of coming at the material from a different perspective.* Once you have done your own
work, you will learn more by seeing how others
have organized the material, reading how others
describe the rules, and thinking about examples
others have used to illustrate the doctrines.
Treatises can also help overcome the discreteness
of the case method by showing where a particular
topic is in the forest.

Outside sources can also broaden and deepen
your legal education. Spend some time nosing
around the law library. See what the current law
reviews are covering. Go beyond the "Reporters" to those things that look like real books,
books of different shapes, different colors and all

without numbers. You will be astounded at the diversity and complexity of books on the "law."

9. How Much Time?

Law study is demanding. A recent study of over one thousand students at seven law schools indicated that *on average* first year students spent about 36 hours a week in study, compared to 27 by second year students and 24 by third year students. These figures do *not* include time spent in class. For each group, study time was slightly over two and one-half hours for each hour spent in class (upper-year students spent less time in class). Again these figures represent averages and hence should be used simply as rough guidelines.

Structure your time. Some find that they study well in the early morning hours and that, come 9 p.m., they are blurry eyed. Set specific study times; study at times you are most productive and *don't* study at other times. It is quite possible to "study" 80 hours a week but this is neither necessary nor productive. Without limits, expect to wake up one morning in the attic, dust rag in hand.

10. Take Good Care of Yourself

Finally, be good to yourself. Put your first year in the context of the rest of your life. Keep a journal to step back from the day to day concerns. Get daily exercise. In writing this book, I have talked to many students and they have all stressed the importance of physical exercise. Go to movies, plays and concerts. Your uniqueness should not be squashed by casebooks. Even law students are children of the universe.

CHAPTER 6

LEGAL WRITING

Legal writing, it has been said, suffers from but two defects, style and content.

There is little we can do about content except lament the fact we weren't born musical, athletic or less squeamish. So be it. There is much we can do about style.

Make no mistake, matters of "style" are no mere backwater. George Orwell, in his brilliant essay, "Politics and the English Language" argues that we *think and act* badly partly because we *write* badly. Murder becomes "pacification" and "pacification" in turn allows for more murder.

> Modern English becomes ugly and inaccurate because our thoughts are foolish, but the slovenliness of our language makes it easier for us to have foolish thoughts. The point is that the process is reversible. Modern English is full of bad habits which spread by imitation and which can be avoided if one is willing to take the necessary trouble. If one gets rid of these habits one can think more clearly, and to think more clearly is a necessary first step towards political regeneration: so that the fight against bad English is not frivolous . . . .

One of the bad habits Orwell identifies is the use of ready-made phrases, "tacked together like sections of prefabricated hen-house". Using *In my opinion it is not an unjustifiable assump-*

tion that instead of *I think* gives a certain flow to your writing as ready-made phrases are arranged more or less euphonically; however you save mental effort only at "the cost of leaving your meaning vague, not only to your reader but for yourself."

Abstraction also prevents clear thought. The "concrete melts into the abstract" and a "mass of Latin words falls upon the facts like soft snow, blurring the outlines and covering up all details." To illustrate, Orwell rewrites a well-known verse from Ecclesiastes. The original reads:

> I returned and saw under the sun that the race is not to the swift, nor the battle to the strong, neither yet bread to the wise, nor yet riches to men of understanding, nor yet favor to men of skill; but time and chance happeneth to them all . . . .

The rewrite:

> Objective consideration of contemporary phenomena compels the conclusion that success or failure in competitive activities exhibits no tendency to be commensurate with innate capacity, but that a considerable element of the unpredictable must be taken into account . . . .

Orwell advises the writer to ask: What am I trying to say? What words will express it? What image will make it clearer? Is the image fresh enough to have an effect? Can I put it more concisely? If you simplify your English, Orwell concludes, when you make a stupid remark its stupidity will be obvious, even to you.

The fight against bad English is not frivolous. This chapter will supply ammunition. It will begin with three mindsets which hamper effective writing.

If it's law, it's gotta be complicated.

If I wrote it, it's gotta be important.

If I wrote it, it's gotta be good.

Next the hallmarks of good legal writing will be explored followed by some general tips on editing. An editing checklist is included. The chapter closes with some suggestions on how to get started, on how to get by those dreaded minutes when it is simply you and a blank piece of paper.

Writing is a very difficult business. Although this chapter focuses primarily on matters of style, your major struggle will be with matters of substance. Good writing is not about the conscious use of the maxims of good writing; good writing is about expressing your thoughts so that they can be understood by others. The question "How do I write that idea?" quickly becomes "What is it I think?" As Orwell suggests, clear writing forces clear thought. And that ain't easy.

Expect to work hard on your writing. Expect anger, frustration and moments of rage. I for one know what it is to rip paper from the typewriter, crumple it and throw it hard only to have it land soft with the other victims of aborted creativity. I know what it is to curse, to give up, to have sentences stop in the middle and refuse to

[*124*]

budge and to have paragraphs refuse to stop and meander off into gibberish. I know what it is to sit and stare, trying to capture a thought that flickers, and dances and always recedes.

I know too the thrill of a well-put phrase and the joy of suddenly seeing ideas come together. Out of chaos, occasionally comes order and that is deeply satisfying.

I know what it is to write. I pity you. I envy you.

1. Mind Sets Blocking Effective Writing

a. *"If It's Law It's Gotta Be Complicated"*

Almost all legal principles can be expressed simply. To a struggling first year student, adrift, that must strike you as an absurd proposition. Yet read someone really good, like Corbin. What will strike you is how easy it seems. "Why is that guy so famous? Everything he writes is self-evident."

Why is legal writing often complicated and difficult to understand? Partly it's because the writer quit the painful process of thought early, wrote the chaos rather than waiting for the order. Because of the expectation that legal prose is difficult to understand, writers tend to close up shop early.

Richard Wydick, in his fine book *Plain English for Lawyers*, suggests that lawyers write complicated prose because they believe they can be more precise. The word "said", for example, projects an aura of precision.

> The object of *said* conspiracy among *said* defendants was to fix *said* price of *said* products throughout *said* State of New York.

As Wydick points out, the aura of certainty disappears with analysis. If there were only one conspiracy, why not simply "the conspiracy"? If there were two conspiracies, the legalism "said" doesn't help clarity at all.

Legal writing must be precise. Be aware that complexity and the overuse of legalisms may simply create a false sense of precision, and often the effect is just the opposite, obfuscation.

Legal writing is a form of communication. It is not a peacock's dance. Rereading your legal prose several weeks after you wrote it, you should be struck with "Why was writing this so difficult? It reads clearly."

The Plain English Movement: A Caveat

Legal gobbledygook is under increasing attack.

Lawyer prose is described as "wordy, unclear, pompous and dull". Books and articles suggest that lawyers can and should write "Plain English". In government there are efforts to require that statutes and regulations be written in language which the average citizen can understand.

Not that I wish to come out in favor of legal gobbledygook. Indeed, this chapter is devoted to the premise that legal writing can be simplified. A few words of caution as concerning the rush to simplicity are in order, however, to use a most unplain term, *a caveat*.

The quest for law written in clear and simple language is not new. The great utilitarian, Jeremy Bentham, proposed in the early 1800's junking the complicated common law method and substituting a civil code:

> [I]f [a] general code were universally circulated . . . the laws would become truly known; every deviation from them would be [known], every citizen would be their guardian; there would be no mystery to conceal them—no monopoly in their explanation— no fraud or chicane to elude them.

This is a common longing. So too is Bentham's indictment of judges using the common law method:

> The judge, now conforming to the law, and now explaining it away, can always decide a case to suit his own designs. He is the charlatan who astonishes the spectators by making sweet and bitter run from the same cup. *(Principles of the Civil Code.)*

Yet the movements toward simplified legal codes have failed to produce laws "understandable by all". Indeed, it is quite common to hear lawyers say "I don't know what that statute means because it hasn't been interpreted." Why the failure? A very important question for you as a member of the profession.

[*127*]

No doubt the social and economic position of lawyers is enhanced by a system of complicated law. Have lawyers torpedoed the efforts to simplify, jealous of their "monopoly of explanation"? Or does the fault lie with the suspicion that simple words and sentences cannot capture all the nuances that make rules just?

Even if it were possible to capture our sense of justice in simple and precise language, there is a further danger. Precision can become a prison. In *The Ages of American Law*, Grant Gilmore makes this point in reference to New Deal legislation which was drafted with "superhuman precision". Since no one can predict future events, these old statutes often result in manifest injustice because there is no room for interpretation. He makes the rather startling suggestion that courts overrule "old statutes" just as they do "old cases" when circumstances have changed so that the old rule is now unwise.

Remember this when you are drafting contracts or other documents whose impact and influence will run into the future. There is something to be said for ambiguity; indeed, there is something to be said for leaving some room for the charlatan.

b.   *"If I Wrote It, It's Gotta Be Important"*

Revision is critical. Revision is cutting. Revision is painful.

Writers agree that wordiness is a major sin. "Omit Needless Words" counsel Strunk and White in the classic, *Elements of Style.* There are certain devices which can be used to cut excess verbiage, such as the use of the active voice, basic verbs and the elimination of "throat clearing" phrases. These devices will be explained later. Excess verbiage stems only in part from sloppy writing: it also stems from the mindset which assumes that everything in the draft must be important.

To avoid getting bogged down, in my first draft I include points I am not sure belong. I don't want to take the time to focus on them and, besides, I often can't tell if they belong until I have tried them out on paper. Well and good. Unfortunately, when it comes to revision, these try-them-out-to-see-if-they-work ideas suddenly take a life of their own and loudly insist that they are absolutely essential to the whole matter. I am often beguiled. Revision becomes simply a process of improving what I said rather than also questioning what I said; it becomes a process of omitting unnecessary words rather than also omitting unnecessary ideas. What I must remind myself is that those ideas, paragraphs and even pages wouldn't be there but for me. I wrote them, I can ax them. I am not, after all, revising the Declaration of Independence.

c.   *"If I Wrote It, It's Gotta Be Good"*

As professor, part of my job is to critique student papers. I do.

"This sentence is awkward."

"This paragraph makes no sense at all."

"Here I understand what you are saying but you are wrong."

As professor, another part of my job is to write. Without getting into the larger "publish or perish" controversy, let me offer one little justification for the requirement. It makes professors students.

I write a draft and give it to a colleague. She reads it and we discuss it.

"This sentence is awkward," she says. I force a smile.

"This paragraph makes no sense at all." My lips begin to quiver. I force myself to respond:

"Good, this is the kind of critique I need." My voice breaks.

"Here I understand what you are saying but you are wrong."

"Smile," I silently counsel myself. "Just smile. Forget the fact that she obviously can't read. Forget that she hasn't ever had an intelligent thought in her head. Just keep smiling. And please, oh please, don't cry."

Taking criticism is hard. But you must. Beyond the hurt I realize she is right. I rewrite to improve.

2. The Hallmarks of Good Legal Writing

a. Use Clear Conclusions and Transitions

Lawyers don't write to pass the time of day. They write to analyze problems, to advise clients, to convince judges. They write to do. Focus is sharp and style concise. Given the specific facts of the case and given the specific rules of law which govern, what result? Should a lawsuit be filed? Should the client be advised to plead? Should the court reverse? The result, the conclusion, is central. It links the world of analysis to the world of action. It tells us what to do next— our only real concern.

Your conclusion is star. Put it up front, before the analysis as to how it was reached. Knowing where you are going, the reader can test your analysis step-by-step. Surprise endings are out.

Knowing the ending does not spell boredom. We always know that the Lone Ranger will win; the interest is in how. A clear statement of your conclusion, plus a little of how you reached it, will involve the reader in what otherwise might be pretty dull prose. Knowing what you expect them to do (file a suit, advise a guilty plea, reverse a case) will enliven their interest: "Why should I do that?"

The Structure of Legal Writing: An Example of an Office Memorandum

You'll need a little law for this. A doctrine in contract law teaches that promises are not enforceable unless supported by consideration. Although there are a few exceptions, generally people will not be held to what they promise unless they got something for that promise. That something is called consideration. If I promise to give you $50, my promise is not enforceable because I got nothing in return. If I promise you $50 for your promise to fix my car, I'm bound. I got something for my promise: Your promise to fix my car. What if you save my life by jumping in front of the assassin's bullet? In gratitude, I promise to pay your medical expenses. If I pay them, well and good. That's a completed gift. But what if I refuse to honor my promise? Will the law enforce it? Many courts have held "no" because I received no consideration. I got nothing for the promise. As to my saved life, I had that already, before I made the promise.

So sorry.

A few courts have skirted the old common law doctrine and have enforced promises originating in "moral obligation". The Restatement of Contracts allows for enforcement of these kinds of promises in some circumstances. The memo which follows analyzes how a court following the Restatement would decide the famous case of *Mills v. Wyman*, 3 Pick. 207 (1825). The memo is addressed to a senior partner who must do something about the matter, either file a lawsuit or advise the disappointed party that such would be vain. Office memorandums impartially analyze the law; they are unlike court briefs which are argumentative analyses.

The memo follows one of many acceptable formats:

1. Caption
2. Facts
3. Issue
4. Conclusion
5. Statement of controlling law (when in statutory or Restatement form)
6. Analysis

The analysis section of the memo has been drastically edited so that the conclusion and transitions can stand out clearly.

OFFICE MEMORANDUM

To: Senior Partner

From: Humble Associate

Re: Contract Claim of Charles Mills

Facts: Levi Wyman, 25-year-old son of the potential defendant, fell sick upon his return from a sea voyage. Our client, Mr. Mills, cared for the young man for several weeks. Unfortunately the young man died.

Upon hearing of the kindness our client bestowed on his son, the potential defendant wrote Mills promising to pay the expenses he incurred in boarding and nursing his son. The father now refuses to pay on his promise and the question is whether his promise is enforceable.

Issue: Is Mr. Wyman's promise, made in recognition of services rendered Wyman's son, enforceable under section 89a of the Restatement of Contracts (Tent. Draft No. 2)?

Conclusion: I think the promise is enforceable under the Restatement.

Statement of Law:

Restatement Section 89a provides

(1) A promise made in recognition of a benefit previously received by the promisor is binding . . . .

(2) A promise is not binding under Subsection (1)

   (a) if the promisee conferred the benefit as a gift . . .; or

   (b) to the extent that its value is disproportionate to the benefit.

Analysis:

The first requirement under that Re-statement is that a promise must have been made. Was a promise made? A promise is defined as . . . . and applying it to the facts of this case, it seems a promise has been made.

Next, was the promise ''made in recognition of a benefit previously received''? That depends upon how the court would interpret ''benefit''. (The analysis continues).

But did the promisee confer that benefit as a gift?

Mills was acting voluntarily but that may not make his act a gift. How should the court interpret ''gift''? (Analysis continues).

The next question is whether the value of the promise ''disproportionate to the benefit''? . . .

First there are a few nice things about the memo. It is good to copy out, verbatim, statutes and Restatement Sections when you are analyzing them. This puts the reader in immediate contact with the source material and hence he need not rely upon your first level interpretation. Compare:

The Restatement would enforce a promise if it was made after the person making it receives some benefit and provided that the other person wasn't making a gift.

While that may or may not be an accurate reading of the Restatement, the reader will be forced
to take your word for it. Far better to quote the
Restatement itself. In quoting Restatements and
statutes often you will find parts that do not apply. You can edit out the material but be sure to
show that you have done so with ". . . ." Be
careful not to edit out things simply because they
are difficult to understand or because they go
against your position.

The draft memo also makes good use of quotes
within the analysis:

> Was the promise "made in recognition of a benefit
> previously received?"

Again the reader is brought face to face with the
legal requirements and need not rely on a paraphrase.

But what of our main concerns, conclusions
and transitions? The conclusion in the example
(page 134), really doesn't alert the reader as to
what will follow. It communicates next to nothing. Compare:

> *Conclusion:* The Restatement enforces promises
> made "in recognition of a benefit" previously re-
> ceived. If the benefit must be a direct material one,
> then the father's promise is not enforceable as the
> services were rendered to the son. However, if the
> court interprets "benefit" to include the benefit of
> knowing one's child died in peace, then the promise
> is enforceable as the other requirements of the Re-
> statement seem satisfied.

This statement of the conclusion flags the key issues to be discussed. The legal analysis will be easier to follow.

A good statement of your conclusion should contain more than simply your ultimate answer. It should *suggest* some of your reasoning as this will help your reader follow your detailed analysis. A delicate balance must be maintained. You want to suggest some of your reasoning but not get into your actual analysis. If you do, the section will fail to serve as an introduction.

What of the transitions? They can be improved. Transitions can, and generally should, do more than introduce the new topic. They can tie that topic to the previous material and can explicitly state the legal significance of that topic. The transitions used in the draft are compared with transitions that accomplish more:

The first requirement is that there be a promise . . . .

Compare: Next, was the promise made in "recognition of a benefit previously received?"

With: Even if there is a promise, it will not be enforced unless it was made in "recognition of a benefit previously received." Was there a benefit here?

Compare: But did the promisee confer the benefit as a gift?

With: If the court interprets "benefit" to include the kind of benefit the father received, the next issue is whether the benefit was conferred by the Good

[*137*]

Samaritan as a gift. If it was then the father's promise is not enforceable.

Compare: The next question is whether the value of the promise is "disproportionate to the benefit."

With: Assuming the court finds the requisite benefit and that it was not conferred by the Good Samaritan as a gift, the father's promise appears enforceable as the value of the promise (to pay expenses) does not seem "disproportionate to the benefit."

Transitions can accomplish three goals: they can *relate* the new topic to material discussed previously, they can *introduce* the topic, and they can show its *legal significance*, what legal difference to the topic makes. A mnemonic device might help you check your own transitions: RILS transitions:

*R*elate

*I*ntroduce

*L*egal *S*ignificance

There will be times when it will be very clear to the reader how the new topic relates to previous discussions and some occasions when the legal relevance of the discussion is so clear that it need not be stated. Nonetheless, check your transitions; if they are not RILS transitions, be sure that one is not needed.

A good transition introduces your topic. The discussion that follows it should revolve around that topic. Stick to the point and do not meander off into other issues. Mixing legal categories is worse than mixing beer and wine.

b. Don't Mix Legal Categories

It does seem that Wyman made a promise. But Mills, in caring for the son, acted without expectation of profit and perhaps this would mean his act would be found to be gift. While it is true that Wyman didn't receive a material benefit from Mills, the first thing people ask upon the death of a relative is whether they died in peace. Hence knowing that his son was cared for in his last days was a benefit of sorts.

This paragraph is confusing because it mixes two issues, the first being whether the father benefitted, the second being whether the Good Samaritan made a "gift". Meandering confuses you and your reader. Stay with an issue until you know what fits and what doesn't fit. Don't check out early and write the chaos.

c. Make Explicit Statements of Law and Fact

Compare the following:

1. The Good Samaritan cared for the son voluntarily.

2. The Good Samaritan cared for the son voluntarily and thus it may be said that his action was a gift.

3. The Good Samaritan cared for the son voluntarily and thus it may be said that his action was a gift. If so, then under the Restatement of Con-

tracts, the father's promise to pay for the services would not be enforceable.

The first statement simply identifies a fact. It fails to tell the reader why that fact is legally important. Does the writer know? The second statement is more explicit. It tells the reader that from the identified fact it may be concluded that the action was a gift. The third statement is more explicit. It tells the reader the legal significance of that conclusion, that the promise would not be enforceable.

Not only is explicitness essential in helping your reader understand, it is essential in helping you analyze the law. Simply stating that the Good Samaritan acted voluntarily and then going onto other matters, you will not consider the key legal issue. Are all voluntary acts "gifts"? By forcing yourself to tie your factual conclusions to principles of law, you immediately run into the essential legal questions. How should the word "gift" be interpreted?

To check to see if you are being explicit, ask yourself as to each point you make *So what?"* If you know, be sure you have told the reader. If you don't, stay with it until order emerges.

d. *Use Concrete Examples*

Abstractions "fall upon the facts like soft snow, blurring the outlines and covering up all details." Law is conceptually quite difficult, and without concrete and specific markers, it is easy to become lost. *Use examples.* Don't just write about the "intangible benefit the father received"; identify the benefit. "He now knows his son died in peace." Think in terms of specific events. Abstractly one might define a gift as "something done voluntarily without expectation of return." That sounds pretty good. But visualize Mills standing beside the bed of young Wyman, wiping his brow and administering to his needs. If someone asked you to describe the scene, would you describe it as someone making a gift? Most likely not. Checking the abstraction against a specific event suggests the abstraction wrong. "Gift" may mean something else.

There are other kinds of abstractions which are apt to confuse your written work:

> The promisee will argue that he did not confer the benefit as a gift.

Don't compel your reader to ask, "Who is the promisee here, Mills or Wyman." Instead, tell him.

> The promisee, Mr. Mills, will argue . . . .

Still your reader must ask, is Mills the father or the guy who helped the son?

> The promisee, Mr. Mills, the man who aided the son, will argue that he did not confer the benefit as a gift.

Good. But what is the benefit we are talking about?

The promisee, Mr. Mills, the man who aided the son, will argue that he did not confer the benefit, here caring for the son, as a gift.

Write in concrete terms so that the reader will know immediately and without thought whom and what you are talking about.

The plaintiff, the woman injured, ...

The respondent, the doctor who filed the false return . . . .

Avoid constructions like

As to the former argument, the plaintiff would argue . . . .

As to the latter . . . .

Under subsection 2a of the Restatement, the promise would not be enforceable.

These constructions always *stop* the reader. "Which was the *former* argument?" "What did subsection 2a provide?" These interruptions are irksome and can be easily avoided. You need not repeat the entire *former* argument, you can usually identify it in two or three words. The same is true in identifying particular subsections.

Under subsection 2a of the Restatement, dealing with benefits conferred as gifts, the promise would not be enforceable.

e. *Begin With Basic Propositions*

Law is complicated. Often your analysis will turn on a very technical point. Don't immediately go to that point or your reader will not understand. Start with the basic, elemental proposition of law and then take the reader by the hand until you reach troubled water. If you are dealing with a technical search and seizure issue, begin with a statement of the Fourth Amendment. Another illustration is proper:

Your firm represents Darth Vader. Darth has previously agreed with Princess Leia that she shall have the exclusive right to market his endorsement of various products. His favor helps a sale. In return for his promise, all that Leia promised was to turn over monies she received from the endorsements less her commission.

Their highly successful first effort showed the controlroom of a space ship. Darth and several sinister generals are watching a large TV screen which shows the beautiful blue marble. In the background, the voice counts 5-4-3-2-1. At "1" earth explodes. Darth and his generals smile and pat each other on the back. Up Music. "Now comes Miller Time."

Despite the success of this commercial, Darth wants out. He has been offered a large amount to do a "This Bud's for You" and, quite frankly, he doesn't want to count Leia in. Darth comes to your firm to discover whether he must honor his commitment. The Senior partner, after getting the fee up front (you never can be too careful), turns the matter over to you. You research the law. You submit the following memorandum.

To: Senior Partner

From: Abject Associate

Re: Darth Vader

<u>Facts</u>:   (You recite them)

<u>Issue</u>:   Did Darth get consideration for his promise? If not his promise is not enforceable.

<u>Conclusion</u>: Darth's promise is enforceable because Leia's return promise is sufficient consideration.

<u>Analysis</u>:   Darth's promise is enforceable because the return promise will be interpreted as requiring a good faith effort to market the endorsement. ''A promise may be lacking, and yet the whole writing may be 'instinct with an obligation,' imperfectly expressed.'' <u>Woods v. Lucy, Lady Duff-Gordon</u>, 222 N.Y. 88, 118 N.E. 214 (1917).

This memo shows that you know what you are talking about. It is doubtful, however, that the reader will know. The problem is that you have worked so much on the case, that *you assume* everyone knows the basic law as well as you. Most likely they do not. Unless you review the basics, they will be lost.

Before giving a better version, let me go through a method you can use to analyze legal problems. Play legal ping pong. Make the best argument you can for one side and then ask your-

self how you would respond as the opponent.
Let's try it:

Darth:　　　　Forget our deal, Leia. I'm making
a Bud commercial and you're not going to get anything out of the deal.
From now on, I'll market my own
stuff, what with the economy being
the way it is.

Princess Leia:　Oh no you're not. You promised me
that I would have the exclusive
right to market your endorsement.
"Exclusive" means you can't do it
anymore than anyone else can. If
you do you still owe me my percentage. I'll sue!

Darth:　　　　Granted my plan involves breaking
my promise to you. However that
promise is not enforceable. The
Empire enforces only promises supported by a consideration. As you
didn't give me anything for my
promise, I am not bound by it.

Princess Leia:　Gave you nothing, Sir? I gave my
promise to turn over the fees if I
got endorsements. And my word is
good, what with me being a princess.

Darth:　　　　My dear girl, that promise is illusory. You never promised to seek endorsements. You could do absolutely nothing and not break your
promise. Unless you sought endorsements, which you didn't promise to do, you would not have to
turn over the money. Your sup-

posed promise is like a promise "I promise to perform unless I change my mind." The courts of the Empire have repeatedly held that these promises are not sufficient consideration. It offends our fine tuned sense of justice to have one party bound while the other isn't, to have me bound by my promise to you while you are free to perform or not, totally in your discretion.

No, my dear girl, you promised nothing and therefore mine is unenforceable.

Princess Leia: If I had promised to use my best efforts to market your endorsement, then if I did nothing I would break my promise. That wouldn't be like a promise "I promise to perform unless I change my mind."

Darth: My dear girl, you should have been a lawyer. Had that been your promise, then I would have gotten something for mine and hence it would be enforceable. Unfortunately, you sweet young thing, you didn't promise that.

Princess Leia: Maybe I didn't but the courts will *imply* that I made such a promise and hence save the day.

Darth: Ee Gads! Do you have authority for that?

[*146*]

Princess Leia: Yes, Justice Cardozo in *Woods v. Lucy, Lady Duff-Gordon!*

Darth: Curses. Foiled again!

Curtain

Begin your legal analysis with the basics; begin with the first serve.

Darth made a promise to Princess Leia but now claims it is unenforceable as it is not supported by a sufficient consideration. It is well established that a promise made without consideration is unenforceable. It is also well established that consideration can consist of a return promise, provided that that promise is not illusory. A promise to perform "unless I change my mind" is an illusory promise as it really binds the person making it to nothing.

In this case, in return for Darth's promise of the exclusive, Princess Leia promised to turn over any money she made on it, less her fees. She did not however promise to actually seek endorsements. Thus it seems that her promise is illusory; she can change her mind, do nothing and not violate her undertaking. However, in cases like this, the court will imply in her agreement a duty to take action to generate fees. "A promise may be lacking, and yet the whole writing may be 'instinct with an obligation,' imperfectly expressed." *Woods v. Lucy, Lady Duff-Gordon* (plaintiff, suing for breach of contract, had exclusive right to market defendant's endorsement; he promised only to turn over the fees but Justice Cardozo held a promise to attempt to market the endorsement will be implied).

Here we begin with the basics. We do not assume the reader knows all that we do. Hopefully anyone can understand it, perhaps even a Senior partner.

f. *Write Down the Middle Yet Nod to Both Sides*

Ping pong is a great way to analyze legal problems. It is a lousy way to write. Don't write as if you were sportscaster.

Plaintiff asserts . . . .
Defendant responds . . . .
As to that, plaintiff argues . . . .
Defendant meets that argument by claiming
. . . .

Avoid broadcasting. It gets too sing/song. More critically, the form makes it difficult to tell the reader which side you find more compelling. To do so you must step outside the dialogue and pronounce your judgment. Writing down the middle allows for smoother analysis and makes it much easier for you to indicate the persuasiveness of the arguments while you are giving them.

Although it could be argued that . . . the response is . . . . However, that response overlooks . . . . On the other hand that last point loses validity when one considers . . . .

Courts write down the middle—they combine the competing arguments into a coherent whole. The point is so fundamental to good legal writing it deserves further illustration.

A typical judicial opinion reads like this:

Plaintiff is suing his mother's estate to recover the reasonable value of services he rendered to the mother before she died. Plaintiff alleges that his mother requested his services and that for several years he cared for her and her property. Plaintiff did not allege, however, that the mother ever expressly promised to pay him for the services.

Express promises are not always necessary to support contract actions. In some cases they can be implied. In ordering a hamburger at a restaurant, you impliedly promise to pay for it. However, cases in this jurisdiction hold that no implied promise arises from the performance of personal services by a son for the benefit of his mother (citations omitted) and we are of the opinion that this rule applies regardless of whether they are living together in the same household. The relationship of son and mother is so close that the implication is that services are rendered without the expectation of compensation.

Therefore we hold that the plaintiff has not stated a cause of action.

This is writing down the middle. A very good way to analyze a case is to pull it apart and restage the ping pong game. As to each point in an opinion, which side raised it and why?

Defendant: Even if the son rendered services to his mother, she never expressly promised to pay for them. That should be the end of the matter.

Plaintiff: Not so. In many circumstances a promise to pay for services rendered will be implied. If I go into a restaurant and order a hamburger, I cannot refuse to pay on the basis that I never expressly promised to pay. No, in cases like that the courts find that my promise can be implied from the fact that I asked for the hamburger. Here the mother asked for her son's services and she accepted them. From these facts a promise to pay should be implied.

Defendant: This case does not involve a commercial enterprise like a restaurant. A customer knows that such enterprises expect to be paid for the services they render. When he requests the services, it makes good sense to find that he has impliedly promised to pay for them. Not so in the case of a mother asking her son for help. She doesn't expect that the son will expect compensation. In fact we have cases in this jurisdiction that hold no implied promise arises from services rendered between family members.

Plaintiff: Those cases, your Honor, all involved family members living in the same household. In this case mother and son lived apart. The rule cited by defendant therefore does not apply.

Defendant: The fact that the parties lived apart is not significant. What is significant is the relationship. The relationship of parent and child is so close that the implication arises that whatever service one renders to the other the same is performed without expectation of compensation.

Plaintiff: Ee gads! Curses! Foiled again!

Analyzing legal problems, ping pong. Make your best arguments on both sides. Writing the results of your analysis, write down the middle.

[*150*]

g. Marry Law and Fact

Legal rules announced by courts have meaning only in context of the facts of the cases in which they were announced. To illustrate, take the case of the speeding delivery man.

> Defendant ordered a pizza. Upon learning that the delivery man broke the speed limit in delivering the pizza, the defendant refused to pay. Defendant has a good defense as it has been held that "no one will be allowed to profit from his own crime." *Riggs v. Palmer*, 115 N.Y. 506, 22 N.E. 188 (1889). Breaking the speeding law is a crime.

This sounds good. But are we sure that the rule of *Riggs v. Palmer* should apply? Compare the following:

> Defendant has a good defense as it has been held that "no one will be allowed to profit from his own crime." *Riggs v. Palmer* (preventing a murderer from inheriting from his victim.)

Stating the *facts* of *Riggs* greatly reduces the precedential value of the rule of *Riggs*. Speeding isn't murder.

In citing key cases in your written work, indicate briefly their facts. Otherwise the reader will not know whether the rule should apply. Abstract statements of law are *always suspect*.

3. General Tips on Editing

There are several generally accepted maxims of good writing. This part will review many. I also refer you to the many fine books and articles on legal writing, including Squires and Rombauer, *Legal Writing in a Nutshell,* Wydick, *Plain English for Lawyers* and Mellinkoff, *Legal Writing—Sense and Nonsense.*

Maxims are not, however, for memorization. Nor are they to be reviewed before you sit to write. Your first and foremost struggle is to force ideas from your head onto the paper. This struggle is always nip and tuck. Don't try to tame your ideas with the maxims of good writing at the same time you are formulating them. Get them down even if they are expressed clumsily. Once they are on paper, then is the time to focus on matters of style.

Reading this part, do not attempt to memorize maxims. To be valuable they must be learned at the level of application rather than abstraction. One way to apply the maxims is to make up your own examples to illustrate them as we go along. Another way is to apply them in editing your own work. The next section reduces the maxims to an editing checklist.

a.   Edit Needless Words and Awkward Constructions

The less cluttered your work, the more forceful and understandable it will be. Omitting needless words does not mean, caution Strunk and White, omitting detail and treating subjects only in outline form. It means that *each word must tell.*

There are several ways to reduce clutter, and small savings add up quickly. If you are able to cut at a rate of two words per ten word sentence, at the end of twenty pages you have saved your reader wading through four pages of excess verbiage. Most likely you can do a whole lot better than that.

Editing, pay particular attention to verbs. Sloppy use of verbs bogs down your prose. Best to use short verbs, the present tense and the active voice.

Present tense. Although much of what lawyers write about has already happened, with a little thought it is often possible to recount the events in the present tense.

Plaintiff's car then crashed into the tree. A fire broke out and the plaintiff was severely burned.

Plaintiff's car now crashes into a tree. A fire erupts and the plaintiff is severely burned.

Reading about something that is happening is simply more engrossing than reading about things that have happened. Prefer the active voice. (Actually, Groucho says it best: "We're past tense. We live in bungalows now.")

Active voice. An easy way to delete words is to find sentences written in the passive voice and rewrite them in the active.

"The case was reversed by the Supreme Court." Passive voice, eight words.

"The Supreme Court reversed the case." Active voice, six words.

In addition to being wordier, the passive voice can create ambiguity as it is possible to leave the subject out. Who did it?

"The case was reversed."

Often you don't care who did it and often you won't know who did it. In these cases, the passive voice is proper.

"I was mugged" illustrates, perhaps, both.

Use the passive voice in order to put key phrases where you think they might do the most good:

"Wordiness is often caused by use of the passive voice."

However, unless you have a good reason for using the passive voice, use the active.

Verb Derivatives. Undoubtedly language began with grunts—short, powerful and very much to the point. Over time these grunts became the basic vocabulary: "act", "decide", and "steal" being basic verbs. With civilization came decadence and with decadence came a fuzzing of the basic language. Basic verbs were replaced by verb derivatives which seemed perhaps more civil. Stick with the power and use basic verbs, not their derivatives: people you write of should *act*, not *take action;* they should *decide*, not *make decisions;* they should *steal*, not *obtain money feloniously.* Verb derivatives are weak and wordy. Write in grunts.

Excess verbs. Any sentence with more than one verb is a target for possible editing. Clauses

[*154*]

(a group of words with a verb) can often become phrases (a group of words without a verb).

"When the lawyer *was conducting* her cross-examination, the witness suddenly *got up and left.*"   15 words.

"During cross-examination, the witness suddenly got up and left."   10 words.

"The lawyer *had asked* the witness what he had for lunch, a question which *had been designed* to embarrass him."   20 words.

"The lawyer *asked* the witness what he had for lunch, a question *designed* to embarrass him."   16 words.

Sloppy use of verbs, the use of past tense and passive voice, the use of verb derivatives and the use of clauses rather than phrases, are not the only source of wordiness.   Take, for example, *inflated style.*

At the present time	now
In the event of	if
In the majority of instances	usually
With the exception that	except
For the reason that	because
In favor of	for
In order to	to
With a view to	to
In all likelihood	probably
In my considered opinion it is not an unjustifiable assumption that	I think

With these and countless other ready-made phrases we build our hen-houses.   The temptation is great.   As Orwell points out, they sound good and have a certain flow. They seem intelligent. We hope to shore up our simple ideas in respectability; instead we bury them in pomposity.

Don't flower your prose with inflated style. Far better to grunt. Another common problem stems from the false hope that our words, rather than our thoughts, will convice the reader. I call this *shouting*.

Thoughts, not volume, convince.
> It is important to note here
> It is critical to recall at this point
> It is interesting to realize
> Obviously
> Clearly

These and similar phrases are generally a waste of time. If what you have to say is interesting, profound, obvious or clear, it will be without your telling the reader so. On the other hand, few will be convinced with: It is *simply fascinating* to read about writing!!!

The overuse of *intensifiers, adjectives* and *adverbs* is another form of shouting and may even involve a little sleight-of-hand.

> The lecture was *very* boring. A few of the questions were *extremely* clever and one was *brilliant.* Outside the day was *scorching.*

The author is asking us to take his word for all these assertions. If he really wants to convince us that the lecture was boring, he should offer us some *facts.* "During the lecture I went to sleep."

Verbs and nouns tell. Adverbs and adjectives are simply the writer's opinion. H. L. Menchen makes a similar point in relation to an effective newspaper headline—it deals in facts, not abstractions and opinions:

It must be "McGinnis Steals $1,257,867.25," not "McGinnis Lacks Ethical Sense."

Repetitions cause your prose to be verbose. Do you use the same word twice in a sentence or have you used two words with the same meaning? 20 words.

Do you use the same word twice in a sentence or two words with the same meaning? 17 words.

Repetitions in various parts of your draft may signal organizational problems. An outline helps spot them.

Negative constructions are often wordy and ambiguous. *Rhetorical questions* are merely ambiguous. Both should be avoided.

Negative sentences lack the force of positive ones.

Positive sentences are more forceful than negative ones.

Positive statements are clearer and often save words:

Writing well is not easy. 5 words.

Writing well is difficult. 4 words.

b. Edit Sentence Length and Ambiguity

Richard Wydick advises that most sentences should contain only one main thought and, on the

average, should be less than twenty-five words
(about the length of this sentence. Nice touch!).
Longer sentences are difficult to understand as
the reader must hold more and more bits of information in mind before closure. Vary the length
of your sentence. Short ones spell relief. But
don't have too many short ones. It gets choppy.

Lawyers love to write long sentences, filled
with exceptions, and qualifications. In my first
year of law school I thought one had to summarize an entire Moot Court argument in *one* sentence. My sentence was half a page. Statutes
are the archetype of saving ink by omitting periods.

The following was passed by the California Legislature:

> (a) Any tax imposed pursuant to this part shall
> not apply with respect to any deed, instrument, or
> other writing which purports to transfer, divide, or
> allocate community, quasi-community, or quasi-mari-
> tal property assets between spouses for the purpose
> of effecting a division of community, quasi-communi-
> ty, or quasi-marital property which is required by a
> judgment decreeing a dissolution of the marriage or
> legal separation, by a judgment of nullity, or by any
> other judgment or order rendered pursuant to Part 5
> (commencing with Section 4000 of Division 4 of the
> Civil Code) or by a written agreement between the
> spouses, executed in contemplation of any such judg-
> ment or order, whether or not the written agreement
> is incorporated as part of any of those judgments or
> orders.

(b) In order to qualify for the exemption provided in subdivision (a), the deed, instrument, or other writing shall include a written recital, signed by either spouse, stating that the deed, instrument, or other writing is entitled to the exemption.

Professor Robert W. Benson's legislation class at the Loyola Law School in Los Angeles gave it the "Greatest Gobbledygook of the Year Award."

Okay, Professor, can your class do any better? Apparently:

There is no tax under this Act when husband and wife divide property between themselves because they are ending their marriage, or nullifying it, or legally separating.

On the document which would otherwise be taxed, husband or wife shall sign a statement saying that this exemption applies.

Squires and Rombauer, in *Legal Writing*, as well as recommending you start a sentence with its subject, not with a citation or some other interesting tidbit, state that if you keep the following simple rules in mind, your sentences will be clearer.

- Place the verb close to the subject

  "Square and Rombauer state . . . ."

- Place the object close to the verb

  "state that your sentences will be clearer"

- Place modifers next to what they modify

  Students who disobey these rules often get away with it. (If you do it *often*, do you always get away with it, or if you do it, do you *often* get away with it?)

Verbs and subjects cannot always be next to one another, nor can verbs and objects. However, the more words that are interposed, the more difficult the sentence. Squires and Rombauer recommend no more than a ten word separation and their reasoning is quite brilliant. We read and remember in segments. Indeed, we understand in segments. A written thought remains a string of words until there is closure, the mind's opportunity to assemble those words into a thought. The mind can hold only so many bits, seven to nine, before it must close. Otherwise the first bits will be forgotten. Hence, the more words which separate subject and verb, verb and object, the greater likelihood for confusion.

c.　*Edit for Forcefulness*

Legal writing should be forceful. Forcefulness is not overlooking competing arguments, personally attacking opponents, or shouting about the justice of your cause. Forcefulness is mostly a matter of the power of your logic. But it can also be a matter of order and a matter of word choice.

Order. First and last are the most important positions in sentences, paragraphs and arguments. Put important points either first or last; points in the middle tend to be overlooked and forgotten.

Compare:

Legal writing, it has been said, has but two defects, style and content.

It has been said that the style and content of legal writing are its only two defects.

The first is more forceful because it puts the key words, "legal writing" and "style and content" in the most forceful positions, first and last. This is a powerful concept.

1. At trial, put on your star witnesses first and last. The others go in between.

2. In oral advocacy,

- State your argument first
- State the opposition's argument
- Respond to the opposition's argument
- Restate your argument

   If you have three arguments, put the best two in the important positions, first and last.

3. In revising your work, does your paragraph order reflect this maxim? Do the sentences?

- Try not to begin a sentence with citation:

   In *Elements of Style*, 'Omit unnecessary words' wrote Strunk and White. 'Omit unnecessary words' wrote Strunk and White in *Elements of Style*.

- Try not to start sentences with long qualifiers or parts of the hen-house:

   It is very important to note that the order of thoughts in a sentence is important.

Word choice. Some words are strong, others weak. Prefer the strong.

Strong	Weak
copy	duplicate
burn	incinerate
make	produce
lie	fabrication
trap	enmesh
hoax	deception
give	contribute
need	necessity
write	compose
fight	altercation

At this point, recall Orwell's rewrite of Ecclesiastes. "Objective consideration of contemporary phenomena compels the conclusion . . . ."

First year students make word choice errors of a different sort. Courts don't "allege" "argue" "respond" or "refute"; courts are above the fray. Courts "hold" "decide" and "find". Parties and their lawyers allege, respond, argue and refute.

Another first year word choice problem is that of using legal words improperly. Some common words, such as "equitable" and "consideration," have legal connotations. Use these words *only* in their legal sense; otherwise you confuse the reader. And be sure, if you are using a legal word, to use it properly. Don't get into the mire of tossing legal terms around; best to avoid them unless you're sure.

d. Edit to Make the Copy Visually Inviting

Alice, of Wonderland, once remarked "What's the good of a book without pictures." Unfortunately, forget about using pictures to break up the type.

"Quotes can help."

"Yeah, but no one ever talks in legal writing."

"Oh."

At least make frequent use of paragraphs, varying their length. I am not suggesting arbitrary paragraphing, just frequent paragraphing. There is nothing worse than a page full of print and nothing better than an occasional paragraph of one or two sentences.

If we can't have pictures.

4. Editing Checklist: "If I Wrote It, I Can Dump It!"

Editing requires distance from your draft. Just after writing it will be difficult to spot trouble. You know what you meant; you just wrote it. Two devices help you read your writing as would a stranger. *Read it aloud.* You can hear problems you cannot see and, by focusing on each word, you can determine if those words actually say what you think they do. (If, in reading aloud, your face turns blue, check the length of your sentences.) *Put the draft aside for a few days and then read it.* Unfortunately you may find yourself in the good company of Robert Browning. When asked about the meaning of one of his poems, he ventured:

> God and I both knew what it meant once. Now God alone knows.

I suggest a three step editing process. First read the draft looking at its structure and legal analysis. Next return to any problem paragraphs and sentences you have identified. Finally, closely reread the draft, and omit any unnecessary words. The following checklist assumes you have read this chapter.

Step One: THE DRAFT AS A WHOLE

1. **Check the structure**

    a. *Is it clear?* Is there an introduction which overviews the paper? Do you state your *legal conclusions* before extended analysis? Do the statements of these conclusions alert the reader as to the major issues to be considered?

    Do you have clear *transitions* between issues? Are they RILS transitions, relating the topic to previous material, introducing the topic, and making explicit its legal significance?

    Could the structure be made more clear by the use of *headnotes* and *subtitles?*

    b. Is it logical? Do the paragraphs flow logically into each other? Do you find material being repeated, a sign that the draft needs reorganization.

    c. Is it the best? Do you lead and end with your most telling points?

 d. Problems with structure can be identified and remedied by making an *outline* of the draft.

2. Check the legal analysis

 a. *Do you tie together law and fact?* Is it always clear how the law you are discussing relates to the facts? How the facts you are discussing relate to a principle of law? Long discussions of facts by themselves and long discussions of law without references to specific facts *are always suspect.*

 b. *Are you explicit?* Do you explicitly state your factual and legal conclusions or are you hoping the reader will do the work for you? Ask to each point you make "So what?"

 c. *Do you mix legal categories?* Within each section, do you stay on point, with all your factual and legal analysis going to the issue of that section? Or do you mosey about some?

Step Two: WORKING ON PROBLEM PARAGRAPHS AND SENTENCES

 Often paragraphs and sentences are confusing simply because they are verbose, the vice attacked in the last editing stage. Here structural problems are addressed. In reading your draft, mark the trouble spots and come back to consider the following.

1. Problem paragraphs

 a. *Is it too long?* Paragraphs longer than half a page should be examined with care. Readers need an occasional break, called "closure," to put it all together. They cannot hold too much information without losing it. *Short* paragraphs should be used for contrast and visual effect; too many paragraphs become irritating however.

[*165*]

b. *Does it attempt to cover too much?* Usually a paragraph will develop one theme, a theme introduced by the first sentence. You can vary this, but if you find a paragraph confusing it may be because it is covering too many ideas.

c. *Does it mix legal categories?*

d. *Is it explicit?*

e. *Does the first sentence introduce the theme and the last summarize it?* Sometimes you can start a paragraph in the middle and get away with it. However, most often you can't. Again, if you don't use introductory and summary sentences, still say something important in these key positions.

2. **Problem sentences**

a. Does it contain more than one idea?

b. Is it too long?

Usually sentences shouldn't exceed 25 words. Longer sentences can be shortened by

1. Dividing them or

2. Making a tabulation

Sentences with "and" "but" "or" are easy to break into two sentences by dropping the conjunction and adding a period.

c. Do too many words come between subject and verb, verb and object?

d. Are the modifiers next to what is modified?

e. Is the sentence cluttered with a citation in the beginning or a long citation in the middle?

f. Is it stated negatively?

g. Is it ambiguous because it is a rhetorical question?

Step Three: EDIT BY OMITTING NEEDLESS WORDS

Carefully reread your draft looking for needless words. Make a game of it, the more you destroy, the better (a kind of intellectual Atari). Before starting, review the likely targets.

1. Eliminate stowaways

As to each point, ask, did I intend it? Is it essential? Remember many will have sneaked in during the draft. Throw them out despite their cries "Not me, take the next sentence! I'm the key to the whole thing!"

2. Check passive verbs: can they be made active?

- The draft was edited.

- I edited the draft.

3. Eliminate most verb derivations

- You are not *doing a revision,* you are *revising.*

4. Check clauses: can they be turned to phrases?

- When you have completed the revision, you'll be happy.

- Completing the revision, you'll be happy.

5. Eliminate inflated style

- It is my considered opinion and judgment that in a majority of instances you will find some.

- You'll usually find some.

6. Don't shout!

- Clearly it is obvious that it is of utmost importance to call one's attention to the fact that it is the points one makes, rather than the volume with which they are made, which ultimately convince the reader.

- Don't shout.

7. Check for repetitions

If you use the same or related word more than once in a sentence or even in a paragraph, you may be able to cut or substitute.

8. *Play again* if you have been unable to eliminate at least two words out of every ten!

5.   How to Start Writing

You can't revise what you haven't written. So how do you get started?

One effective way to *organize* your thoughts is to use 3x5 cards. Write each point on a separate card, put alike cards in separate piles, and place the piles in logical order. Off you go. While writing, jot additional thoughts on new cards. Throw out cards when you incorporate their points in your draft. There, there goes one right now.

The more complicated the subject, the more helpful a *rough* outline, one indicating the major sections of the draft and listing some of the points in each. I don't think a more detailed outline (one listing all your points in the order you will write them) is possible. Much of your analysis will come to you while writing. (Someone was asked what they thought of a current political issue. "I don't know, I haven't written anything on it.") *After* you have a draft, an outline may help sort out organizational problems.

Once you have a rough idea of what you are going to say, get started. Don't dwell on your introduction until it is perfect. Good writers often write the introduction last, *after* they see what they have said. Striving for early perfection will just block your efforts, keep you running around the room, cursing, kicking over chairs, and tearing up paper. Just start writing, and keep writing, knowing that you will make it all brilliant during the revision.

Finally, when you finish writing, conclude on a positive note:

> Writing is easy. You just sit looking at a blank piece of paper until blood forms on your forehead.
>
> Gene Fowler

CHAPTER 7

MOOT COURT

Just when you begin to get comfortable, they spring Moot Court. The purpose is to give you practice briefing and arguing an appellate case. Welcome the opportunity; it is rich in potential.

You will be assigned to one side of an appellate argument. If you are *petitioner* (appellant), yours is to convince the court to reverse the decision of a lower tribunal. If *respondent* (appellee) befalls your lot, yours is to defend the insight and courage of the lower tribunal, perhaps with a few bars of "Nothing could be finer." In many schools you will work with a partner, in some you will work alone. Each side writes and exchanges written briefs. Petitioner files a brief urging reversal. Respondent responds to that brief by pinpointing its errors and arguing why the lower tribunal's decision should not be reversed. Quite frequently petitioner has the opportunity to file a *reply brief*. Hence each side gets a shot at each other's written work.

The finale of moot court is oral argument. The court is usually composed of a second or third year student, a practicing lawyer or judge, and, if that is not bad enough, a professor. Each side has an equal number of minutes to argue and usually the side going first "reserves" part of its time for rebuttal. Petitioner goes first because it

[*170*]

is the side that would disturb the universe. The members of the court *will* interrupt with questions. After each side has concluded, the court will take the matter under advisement. Then comes critique of the oral presentations:

"You were quite good. *However* . . . ."

Moot court can be a profound learning experience. From this "hands on" experience, you will gain stronger grasp on what constitutes effective legal argument and will understand more deeply the dynamics of the appellate process. Thereafter you will read "cases" somewhat differently, knowing how they came to be and knowing how lawyers use them as tools in future cases. In addition to learning something of the law, you will discover something of lawyering and perhaps of yourself.

For the first time you will use advocacy skills in a formal setting. Begin to explore the question of what kind of lawyer you would like to become. Some lawyers, trial lawyers in particular, are almost constantly pitted in adversity; others seldom are. Do you enjoy the gladiatorial fray? Do you find great satisfaction in fielding a judge's difficult question? Experience a rush in turning your opponent's best argument around? Or do you find the whole process "yuck"? Surely career decisions should not be based on moot court but it can be an illuminating initiation.

Moot court exposes the emotional side of lawyering. Do you think you will become more or less convinced of your position as you develop your argument? Do you think you will gain more or less respect for your opponent? Do you believe you will become more or less concerned with the justice of the controversy? Keep track of your emotional reactions and make use of your Journal.

In *real* appellate court arguments, the goal is to convince specific human beings to do a specific thing—affirm or reverse a lower tribunal's decision. In *real* appellate court arguments, judges ask questions because they want to know; they want to decide the case properly and look upon the lawyers as experts in the facts and law of the case.

Moot court is an educational enterprise. This causes some skewing of the process. Judges may ask questions not because they want to know, but to see if you do. In real cases, the judges' knowledge that a decision must be made maintains focus on the critical issues; in moot court, as judges do not actually decide the controversy, focus often gives way to collage. Unfortunately, moot court often becomes a place, not where you try to convince, but where you try to survive.

This chapter will ignore the skewing effects and will assume that your goal is to convince the court. We will spend little time on brief writing, more on oral argument. Before that, "How to convince a Judge?"

1. A Theory of Appellate Advocacy: How Judges Decide

The best way to learn how people decide is to decide. Then back up and analyze the process. "Why did I decide as I did?" As a lawyer you will often attempt to influence the decision of juries and judges. Serve on an actual jury; if you can't, watch a real trial as a spectator, or volunteer to play juror in a trial advocacy course. Reach a verdict. Then ask which of the lawyer ploys worked? What kind of evidence was most convincing? Did the closing argument influence your decision or had you already decided?

It will be more difficult to duplicate the role of judge. Try this. Read the briefs on a moot court problem, sit through oral argument, decide the case and write an opinion. This will take several hours but may provide profound insight into how judges decide and hence into how to convince them. After you have written your opinion, ask:

1. When did you decide the case? After reading the facts? After reading the briefs? After listening to oral arguments? Or only when you were writing the opinion? (Are some decisions simply not writable?)

2. What most influenced your decision—law, fact or presentation?

3. How could the briefs have been improved? How could the oral argument?

Deciding cases judges will likely be concerned with three things, (1) doing justice between the parties, (2) correctly applying existing law and (3) creating good precedent. Both in written and oral argument you can address these concerns.

a. *Justice Between the Parties: The Statement of Facts*

It is too cynical to suggest that judges, given the flexibility of the law, can decide whatever they want; it is too simplistic to suggest that judging is a matter of gut rather than of mind. And yet . . . .

Judges want to do the "right thing" between the parties—no one can fault them for that. As an advocate your task is to convince the court that the "right thing" is finding for your client. Most often this is done by making a compelling statement of the facts of the case. John W. Davis, appellate lawyer extraordinaire, asserts that the statement of facts is critical. It is "not merely part of the argument, it is more often than not the argument itself. A case well stated is far more than half argued." "The Argument of an Appeal," 26 *A.B.A.J.* 896 (1940).

Before working on your statement of facts it is essential that you are clear on just *why your client should win*. Most likely this will come down to a very simple statement of key facts. What is compelling about your client's situation? How would he tell it to justify his position? Try this.

[*174*]

Without indicating what side you are on, tell a
non-lawyer friend the facts of the case from the
perspective of your client. Don't argue the case,
just state the facts. Ask who should win. If
your friend is unsure, then most likely *you* are
not sure why your client should prevail. Keep at
it until you have convinced yourself, as a simple
matter of fact, why justice favors you.

Work hard on the statement of facts both in
your brief and in your oral argument. A mere
recounting of what happened is opportunity lost.
Personalize your client. You represent a particular human being, not merely a "Plaintiff" or "Respondent." Tales can be told in radically different ways and each rendition can be perfectly
honest. Tell your tale in a way that the listener
will want to find for your client, in a way that it
makes only "common sense" and "basic fairness"
to do so. Try out your statement of the case on
non-lawyers. Can they understand what happened? Who do they think should win?

In telling the story, be absolutely honest. If
you misstate facts (or overlook inconvenient
facts) you undermine your credibility with the
court. Good story telling is not sentimental goo
nor is it a fairy tale where things are all black
and white. Good story telling is truth presented
powerfully from a certain point of view.

To illustrate the power of factual statement,
consider two renditions of the "facts" involved in
the Supreme Court case of *Paul v. Davis*, 424

U.S. 693 (1976). The first version comes from a law review note on the case (43 Brooklyn L.Rev. 147) while the second is the Court's statement of the facts:

In June of 1971, plaintiff Edward Charles Davis, a photographer for the Louisville Courier-Journal and Times, was arrested in Louisville, Kentucky on a charge of shoplifting. He pleaded not guilty. In September, the charge was "filed away with leave [to reinstate]," but he was never called upon to face that charge in court. With the onset of the Christmas season in 1972, defendants McDaniel and Paul, the chiefs of police for Jefferson County and Louisville, jointly prepared a five-page flyer containing the names and mug-shots of "Active Shoplifters." Copies of this bulletin were distributed to local merchants in the Louisville area, warning them of possible shoplifters. In fact, the flyer was composed not only of persons actually convicted of shoplifting, but included persons who had merely been arrested for shoplifting either in 1971 or 1972. Plaintiff's name and mug-shot were included in the flyer, even though the charge against him was dropped six days after the flyer was distributed. After discovering the affront, Davis commenced a civil rights action in the District Court for the Western District of Kentucky . . . .

Based on these "facts" who do you think should win? Now consider the Court's statement of the facts. Note that focus has shifted from the plaintiff Davis to the defendant police chiefs, Paul and McDaniel:

> Petitioner Paul is the Chief of Police of the Louisville, Ky., Division of Police, while petitioner McDaniel occupies the same position in the Jefferson County, Ky., Division of Police. In late 1972 they agreed to combine their efforts for the purpose of alerting local area merchants to possible shoplifters who might be operating during the Christmas season. In early December petitioners distributed to approximately 800 merchants in the Louisville metropolitan area a "flyer," . . . [of active shoplifters].

> The flyer consisted of five pages of "mug shot" photos, arranged alphabetically . . . . In approximately the center of page 2 there appeared photos and the name of the respondent, Edward Charles Davis III.

Guess who won?

Again consider the key question: As a simple matter of fact, why should your client win?

Much has been said of "projecting belief" in your cause. The problem is not so much "projecting belief" as it is "having belief." Once you are clear why your client should prevail, an emotional commitment flows naturally. It will actually matter to you whether or not he is victorious. Once you have this emotional commitment to your case, project it. Some students fail to do this because they dislike being assertive and are uncomfortable with taking strong positions. Realize this: It is not your cause, it is your client's cause. State it vigorously and powerfully even if, if the cause were yours, you would take a more timid and cautious approach.

Effective advocacy is more than presenting compelling factual statements. A compelling factual statement motivates the court to rule in your favor; now you must establish a rationale that permits it to do so. Even if the court wants to decide for you, it will not unless it is convinced prior law allows for it to do so (or, if it does not, is willing to overrule that law). The court must also believe that its decision will be a good precedent (or, if not, so narrow and garbled as to be no precedent at all).

b. *Consistency With Existing Law*

Under the doctrine of *stare decisis* courts must follow the rules of law announced in prior controlling decisions unless (1) those decisions are distinguishable or (2) the court is willing to overrule those prior decisions, a thing most courts are generally loath to do. (As a technical matter, lower courts do not have the *power* to overrule decisions of higher tribunals. Federal District Courts, for example, cannot overrule decisions of the United States Supreme Court although, admittedly, some have tried. In moot court it is generally assumed that the court you are ad-

[*178*]

dressing has the power to overrule any prior decision of any court.)

In Chapter 3 I have presented the method of arguing and distinguishing cases. Review it before embarking on your moot court adventure. Note that *even if* you are able to convince the court that a case is distinguishable, all you have done is to convince the court that it *need not* apply the rule of the case. It still can apply the rule as a matter of its own choice. "We see your point counselor. We don't *have to* apply that rule of law. However, it seems like a good rule to us."

Given the operation of *stare decisis*, a "morning line" on appellate arguments is possible.

1. *If precedent is with you, you're favored.* Convince the court the prior cases are indistinguishable, you win. Unless, of course, the court is willing to overrule those cases. Against the overruling of precedent you have several powerful stock arguments:

   a. Overruling in this instance is a bad idea because people relied on the rule announced in prior decisions.

   b. Overruling in *any* instance is a bad idea because it rejects the wisdom of the past and creates uncertainty in the legal order. The more decisions that are reversed, the less any can be relied upon.

2. *If precedent is against you, try harder.* Even if you convince the court that the prior cases are distinguishable, you still are not a winner. All that you have done is show the court it *need not*

[*179*]

apply the rule to your case. Still, not only must you show that the precedent is distinguishable you must also convince the court that the rule embodied in that precedent is a bad one. And *even if* you convince the court that the old rule is a bad one, you must also convince the court that the rule you are proposing in its stead is a good one. Will the new rule be a good precedent?

c. Creating Good Precedent

It is quite proper for the court to consider the further implications of its decision—the decision will become precedent and will thereafter be followed by other courts in similar cases. As advocate, be prepared to answer the court's concerns:

1. If it rules in your favor, will it be opening the "flood gates" (allowing for a great increase in the amount of litigation)? Given the general cautious nature of the judicial mind, best to convince the court that no flood gates will be opened. If you can't argue this, admit to the flood and argue that it is a good, rather than bad, thing.

2. Will the "rule" you ask for always produce justice or will it lead to ridiculous results?

3. Is the "rule" operational in the sense that juries can understand it, lawyers work with it, other legal functionaries administer it?

4. In short, counselor, what impact would this rule have in the real world?

Prepare for these questions. They are legitimate concerns of a court which not only decides the controversy between the parties before it but also fashions a rule which will govern controversies and parties in the future.

To recap the theory of appellate advocacy: There are three main concerns, convincing the court that a decision in your favor (1) will produce justice between the parties, (2) will be consistent with prior authority and (3) will establish "good" precedent. You have two cracks at it, the written brief and oral argument.

2. The Written Brief

Briefs should be well written. Consult the chapter on legal writing. Realize too that your brief *is not the end of the matter*. You will have to justify your arguments before the court on oral argument. Therefore:

1. Before committing an argument to paper, think about how your opponent will respond to it and visualize yourself defending it to the court. Beginners often get carried away in their own rhetoric as if there is no tomorrow. There is. "Well, Your Honors, it sounded good when I wrote it," is not an eloquent response.

2. In responding to your opponent's written or oral argument, don't engage in personal attacks: "If my opponent had bothered to read the cases" and "My opponent's argument is totally confusing but I think she is saying . . . ." Insults simply anger; they convince no one. And, as petitioner, don't ridicule the tribunal whose decision you want reversed. It's like attacking family.

Briefs must follow a certain format which will be given you by those in charge. A good guide to brief form, citation form and related matters is the *Handbook of Appellate Advocacy* (West).

3. Oral Argument

Clutching the podium as you look into those somber, unsympathetic faces, your main task is staying conscious. This should not be, however, your *only* task. Try to make an argument that the judges can *understand.* The primary difficulty will be that the judges *hear* the argument. It is simply more difficult to follow an oral argument than it is a written one. You must take special steps to assure clarity. Your final task will be to make a *convincing* argument. Partly this will be a matter of maintaining credibility with the judges and partly a matter of discovering what they are thinking. You need to answer their concerns, not yours.

Maintaining consciousness is most pressing. Make a garbled, ridiculous argument, you remain safely within the pack; pass out, you become the stuff of legends. Despite this obvious priority I will discuss the psychological dimension last, here simply noting that all judges, even the famous ones, are simply law students in robes.

a. Helping the Court Understand Your Argument

Many moot court arguments seem garbled because the student attempts to cover too much. There is no need to cover every point raised in your brief nor to respond to every point your opponent makes. You do not concede points you do not orally argue. *At most* argue three or four points and that is probably too many. John W. Davis, who routinely argued in the land's highest courts, advises to *go for the jugular* and asserts that in most cases there will be one, perhaps two or three, cardinal points. The best appellate lawyer Davis knew often argued but *one*. The more issues you argue the more likely the judges will become confused and bewildered. The chaff buries the wheat. Decisions do not turn on minor nitpicks; they turn on the very few hub issues involved in the case.

Moot court arguments can also be confusing if they have no clear structure. Points are merely made, not introduced or fitted into an overall analysis. The student may know why these floating tidbits are important, but quite likely the judges will not.

Typical Structure of a Moot Court Argument

1. *Introduce yourself and who you represent.*
    "May it please the court, my name is C. Darrow

[*183*]

and I represent D. Vader, the defendant in the action below and the petitioner here."

2. ~~State the nature of the case~~ (contract, tort, criminal) ~~and briefly describe its procedural history~~. "This is a breach of contract action filed against Darth Vader by the plaintiff Princess Leia. After a jury trial, judgment was for the plaintiff. We appeal on the judge's failure to direct a verdict in favor of the defendant on the basis that the alleged contract is unenforceable because it lacks consideration and further that it is unenforceable under the Statute of Frauds."

3. ~~State the facts of the case.~~ Remember they are extremely important. "The facts of this case are that . . . ." Often the court will cut you off with "We are familiar with the facts, proceed with argument." Dashed, the hope of killing the first several minutes on safe turf!

4. ~~State the legal issues and overview the points you intend to argue.~~ A clear introduction to your legal argument is critical. Otherwise the judges will not follow it.

"It is our contention that Darth Vader's promise is unenforceable because it is not supported by any consideration at all. He got nothing for his promise and such promises have always been unenforceable. As a separate and independent defense to this suit, it is our position that the promise is unenforceable under the Statute of Frauds. I intend to address the consideration issue first unless the court prefers another order."

Now the court knows where the argument is going. It can be quite effective to ask the court if it prefers another order. It may pay surprising dividends in discovering what the court is thinking.

"Yes, counselor, I would prefer if you discussed the Statute of Frauds issue first as that seems most troubling to me."

5. *Argue the case.* As with your written work, your oral argument will be improved by the effective use of transitions.

Not: "The next issue is the Statute of Frauds."

But: "That concludes my discussion of the issue of consideration. Unless there are any questions, I would like to now address the matter of the Statute of Frauds for *even if* this court decides there was consideration for the promise, the promise is still unenforceable under the Statute of Frauds."

As more fully described in the chapter on legal writing, RILS transitions are best:

They *R*elate the new issue to previous issues;

They *I*ntroduce the new issue; and

They show the *L*egal *S*ignificance of that issue.

The more *explicit* your argument, the more you *tie law and fact* together, and the more *concrete examples* you use, the clearer your argument will be. Consult the chapter of legal writing for further explanation of these hallmarks of clarity.

6. *Rejoice if the court asks you questions.* Why you should rejoice rather than faint is a matter to be discussed later.

7. *Conclude and sit down.* In moot court, as in most appellate courts, you are allotted a certain

[*185*]

amount of time. There is no requirement, however, that you use it all. If you are done, sit down. To avoid mindless meanderings, have a concise and powerful conclusion in mind. Tell the court exactly what you want it to do and state your best reason for why it should.

Moot court arguments require clear introductions, clear transitions and clear summaries. These will mean some repetition but in oral argument this is proper and necessary. Listening, we can't go back to see how the arguments fit together and often our minds wander. Repetition is needed. Related to the problem of lack of structure is the problem which may be caused because you will be so familiar with the arguments and law of the case that you will assume that everyone must be. Not so. Even if the judges have studied your written brief, they will not know your case as well as you. Don't jump to the heart of your argument which may turn on a rather fine point of law. Put that argument in context. As with legal writing, *begin with the basics*.

b. *Making a Convincing Argument*

What is the proper goal for the appellate lawyer? Surprisingly one of the best, again John W. Davis, says that it is the "single and sincere desire to be helpful to the Court." Judges face the anguish of decision and they need the help of the lawyers who are expert in the law and facts of the case they must decide. What judges don't need is theatrics or bombast. I do not take Davis to mean that one becomes a friend of the court rather than an advocate; what I take him to mean is that you realize the difficult task the judges face and that you address their concerns, rather than yours, and that you do so in an open and honest way. To do so you must first discover those concerns and then you must deal with them in a credible fashion.

Finding out what the court is thinking. Legal argument is not a group of friends sitting around a table drinking coffee. It is highly stylized. You stand and make an argument; they, the judges, sit and look down. How do you know that you are addressing the issues that concern them? Two devices can help. First, maintain eye contact and second encourage questions. And once you know what concerns the judges, be flexible enough to address those concerns rather than those arguments which you find more elegant.

By maintaining eye contact you will sense which of your arguments are making headway, which are beside the point, which are not understood, which are hopeless. This means *no reading*. Have with you only a general topic outline or perhaps note cards with key phrases. It is a good idea to write out your argument before giving it. This slows the mind and allows you to see weak spots as well as additional strengths. However, once you have done this, outline the basic argument. You will *not* forget—if you do, the buzz words on your pad will get you going. ~~In preparing for your oral argument practice~~ *speaking* ~~it out;~~ don't just *think* about it. Hear your voice making the argument before you actually make it.

Encourage questions. Don't freeze up and die at the first one—humane judges most likely won't ask another; you will never know what they are thinking. Another way to discourage questions is to answer, "I'm coming to that." Don't do it. Yours is to encourage questions by responding to them. Ask the judges if they have any questions. Project the feeling that you want to answer questions. You do this by *wanting* to answer questions. Answering questions will help you relax; there is nothing worse than a wooden argument given to wooden judges. Watch someone give a formal speech. Most often the prepared remarks are lifeless and the presentation strained. Come the question and answer period and the speaker becomes vital. Even his jokes are better. The reason is that there is spontaneity and creative moment in the exchange.

Preparing for oral argument, anticipate the questions. If you are working with a partner, have him ask you questions. With some thought it is possible to determine most of what may be asked. For example, a typical question is, "Your opponent in her brief argues . . . . How do you answer that argument?"

Keep flexible. The goal is not to make your argument, it is to convince the court. By listening and watching you may discover

- the court is already convinced of a particular point and there is no need for your most brilliant argument
- the court will decide an issue in your favor but on a far cruder and less elegant ground than you propose
- there is no way the court is going to buy a particular argument even though it is clearly correct

Be prepared to jettison your masterpiece. It will be painful but it may mean survival.

The court is looking for your help and it is absolutely essential that it trust you. *How to maintain your credibility?* First, do not make arguments you do not believe in. What is of interest is that this is so infrequently a problem. Once you research and write your argument what at first looked like a loser becomes a sure thing. What I most often observe is the converse problem, the problem of over-contentiousness, the brazen denial of the opposition's "good arguments." That attitude destroys credibility; your desire is not to help the court but rather to fool the court. Enough of you!

Admit to your opponent's good points and deal with them.

Your Honors, my opponent points to a very real concern when she argues that if you strike a term in a lease which exempts the landlord from liability, other litigants may come before you asking that other

terms be struck. However, I believe, for reasons
that I will detail momentarily, that exculpatory
clauses are so unique that to strike them will not
lead you to the slippery slope of rewriting other contract terms. But even if I'm wrong about that, an
exculpatory clause is so repugnant to public policy
that voiding it is justified even if it leads to difficult
decisions in the future.

Over-contentiousness breeds adversity; questions from the bench are looked upon with suspicion.

"Counselor, if we hold that this exculpatory clause is
invalid, would we have to hold invalid a clause requiring the tenant, in event of late payment, to sacrifice his first born?"

"Absolutely not, Your Honor. Those cases are
clearly distinguishable."

Don't assume all questions are hostile. Some are
merely for clarification, others are designed to
help you out by suggesting new arguments.

"Yes, Your Honor. As your question suggests, the
courts will void certain terms as against public policy even though, in theory, it opens the door to attacks on all terms."

c. *A Few Points on Delivery*

1. It is atrocious to read long quotes to the court.
   If you must quote specific language from a statute or opinion, it is well to refer to the page in
   your brief where you quote the language so that
   the judges can follow along as you read it.

2. If you are citing a case it is usually best to describe briefly the facts of that case. Rules of

law are always announced in specific factual contexts and abstract statements of law are always suspect.

3. Judges, like the rest of us, get bored. Involving them in your argument by encouraging questions is one antidote. So too statements like, "This is a question of first impression," "This appears to be a novel question of law," and even "My opponent makes a very telling point." Falling silent during your argument will also tend to raise the interest of the bench.

4. Stop clutching the podium. You will not drift off into the audience. Natural gestures not only enliven your presentation, they help you relax.

5. Avoid monotone. Vary your volume, speed and pitch. Not everything you have to say is of equal status. Pauses can highlight. It might be helpful to record your argument before you give it and then you can check on how you sound.

6. Keep your voice up and avoid the tendency to let it drop at the end of sentences. Avoid the space fillers of "em" "er" "um" "ya know." There is *no* need for you to be making noise *all* the time. When asked a question, *don't* immediately reply. Think about your answer. What may seem like a long intolerable silence to you will seem a very short period to your listeners. Occasionally even consider: "That's a very good question which I hadn't considered. Let me think a few moments."

7. Be aware of the tendency to talk too fast when you are nervous. Keep in mind the distinction between periods and commas. Force yourself to take an occasional deep breath.

8. Keep your hands away from your face and avoid those numerous habits of smoothing hair and playing with glasses.

9. Look at the judges, not at your notes or even the flag.

10. Keep the ball high to their backhands! (You gotta have 10.)

For an excellent selection of readings and text on Argument, consult Bellow and Moulton, *The Lawyering Process*, Chapter 7.

d. On Not Passing Out

Coping with nervousness. Sitting there, stop thinking "Oh no, I'm next!" One way to cope with nervousness is to get your mind off yourself. Concentrate on your opponent's argument while he argues. Listen to what the judges ask him and watch the judges when he responds. You may want to change your argument in light of what you hear and see. While you argue, concentrate on the argument, not on how you are doing.

Remember to breathe. Nervousness often leads to shallow breathing which leads to oxygen deficiency which leads to more nervousness. Take deep breaths; relax your jaw and the back of your neck.

The only reason you are nervous, of course, is because you are afraid you'll make a fool of yourself. To avoid this, pretend that you aren't you

[*192*]

at all, that you're really Darrow up there. If he
makes a mistake, well that's his problem.

Remember too that you appear much less nervous than you are. That is the overwhelming
comment students make viewing themselves on
video-tape. This truism should help you get
through your own argument; it will also give you
some understanding of your smug opponent who
"looks" so cool, so self-possessed.

Defining and stating your intention. Ultimately the problem of nervousness stems from
confusion as to what you are about. In making
an oral argument to a court, your goal is not really "don't be the fool" nor is it even to "appear
brilliant." Your goal, your intention, should be
to convince specific people, the judges, of specific
factual or legal conclusions. If you are clear
about what you are about, your general demean-
or, gestures and arguments will reinforce that intention without conscious effort on your part.
This is an insight of the great Russian drama director, Stanislavski. See generally, McGraw,
Acting is Believing.

We often get confused about goals. As students, our goal in studying is not "to get to ten
o'clock, cover 20 pages and write many notes."
As lawyers our goal in interviewing clients is not
to "appear knowledgeable." Ask "What should
my intention be?" And then state it.

On that fateful day, just before you walk to the podium, silently repeat your precise intention:

My intention is to convince Judges Binder, Boland and Bergman that Vader, despite his faults, got a raw deal in the trial court.

CHAPTER 8

WRITING LAW SCHOOL EXAMS: THE ONLY SKILL WORTH HAVING!

The first thing you'll notice about law school exams is that they are quite often written in Greek, occasionally in Chinese. Whatever the language, when you first look at the exam, you are confronted with an indistinguishable mass of words, all blurred, all running together, all running on and on. Let me give you an example:

allkdfj pqwiur nbvmznx kdk ieur pire jdjo ghjhgfiyr oiyu re otjhg lkpqyr pqlxh plvhgfd qwert yuiop asdf fgh zxcvb mjuik opk kiuy juyhgr dqwsxcgy plmbht fdghj qmpzwno hyde nhyu cdew mkoiy asdfqwer.

Discuss.

Your hands tremble, sweat runs into your eyes. The little voice in your head goes berserk. "There, there, I told you! It's worse, far worse than you thought. You're a goner for sure! Oh, no, you wouldn't listen to me, you had to go ahead and apply. Look around, ninny. People are already starting to write!!!"

Relax. Slowly take a few deep breaths. You are a child of the universe. Loosen your jaw.

"Why yes! Those are English words, at least the short ones are. Yes indeed! It seems to be some kind of story. Interesting! People are arguing, treating each other lousy. Yes, this must be a law school exam!"

At least you are in the right building—it isn't Modern Languages after all. You begin to relax. Suddenly the suffocating panic returns: "I'm in the wrong room! This must be an Antitrust test, or one on Wills, perhaps it's even the Bar Itself! There is nothing about Torts at all. Torts? What are Torts? Look! Everyone is writing now!"

The Fundamental Rule: All law school exam questions relate to, are somehow about, the material you covered in the course. Discounting extreme sadism or early senility of the professor, you *can* answer each question. Again, relax. And don't worry that you didn't get "enough" sleep the night before—while advisable, sometimes sleep just doesn't come. Remember this: In my experience no one has ever, not ever, gone to sleep during a law school exam.

"Fine," you say, clenching your teeth. "I'll relax. Now hurry up and tell me how to pass!" Check the tension in your neck and shoulders. Is your jaw tight or loose? You see, you can't even read about law school examinations without being tense. Listen, you can't rush this whole thing, you can't pounce, chew it all up and somehow have it. You must relax and take it as it comes.

What to do when you freeze up? Remember that you *can* answer the question and that you

[*196*]

will answer the question. Relax, think about other things for a few moments. Right now a trucker in some small roadside cafe is ordering a cup of coffee. Elsewhere waves break along a deserted beach. Picture a scene far away and far removed. If you are still stuck, skip to the next question.

And remember this. Those students who write while you sweat are probably jumping too quickly into the exam, rushing ahead without taking ample time to organize their thoughts and to develop a concise response to the question. Forget what others are doing. Focus on the test.

Stay loose, not only in writing exams but in reading about how to write them. What you read here is not to be chewed up, ingested and thereafter "possessed." Be with the materials. At times you will find them puzzling and confusing. Well and good. When the going gets rough, don't depart the materials to engage in self-pity or self-flagellation: "I knew it, I'll never make it!" Stay with the materials and out of puzzlement and confusion will come understanding. Do not fear puzzlement and confusion as evidence of your own incompetence. Welcome them as opportunities to learn.

The rest of this chapter is organized as follows:
1. I will set out a short examination question. You should write an answer. I will first give some principles of law so that you have a basis for constructing an answer.

2. Two typical answers to the question will then be presented. Compare them with your own in order to begin to verbalize the standards of good legal writing.

3. I will then discuss the overall goal of law school examinations: to see if you are "thinking like a lawyer." I will attempt to describe what this means.

4. Then I will analyze the two model answers in order to determine what it means to "write like a lawyer." These standards will apply to all your legal writing for they are basically the standards of good legal analysis.

5. Finally, I will offer some thoughts on the mechanics of writing the exam.

This chapter is designed to give you practice writing a law school exam. It is also designed to involve you in developing the criteria of good legal analysis and writing. Ideally you should plan to *spend two to three hours* working it through.

1.   Practice Law Exam Question

a.   Some Rules of Law to Apply

I envision that you actually write an answer to the question. Get a pen and paper, preferably a blue book. Have a watch to time yourself. Before you attempt to answer the practice question, however, you must know some "law." Here are some principles of law that may or may not be

[*198*]

relevant to the practice question. Study them a few minutes before writing.

1. In order for there to be an enforceable contract, there must a valid offer and acceptance. What if one of the parties makes an offer she is not serious about? What if she is joking or is simply "off-the-cuff?" Take the King who says "My Kingdom for a horse!"? Can a mere peasant ascend to the throne with a mere "I accept! Here, take mine!" ? The law protects the *reasonable* expectations of the person accepting an offer. If the peasant reasonably believes the King is making a serious offer, then the acceptance is valid, even if the King can later convince us that he was really only joking. On the other hand, if the peasant knows or should know the King is joking, then his acceptance does not a contract make. And how does the law judge what a reasonable peasant would believe? By looking at the circumstances surrounding the offer—was it made at the height of battle, for example, or during a drunken party?

2. There is something in the universe which is called the Statute of Frauds, which requires that some, not all, agreements be in writing. It generally goes something like this:

   The following contracts are invalid, unless the same, or note or memorandum thereof, is in writing and signed by the party to be charged:

   1. An agreement for the sale of real property.

   2. . . .

Cases interpreting the Statute of Frauds have indicated that it fulfills two purposes. The first purpose is to protect against false claims. A writing is good evidence that the parties actually agreed and that no one is making things up. The second purpose of the Statute is cautionary. People shouldn't enter into important legal transactions, such as the sale of realty, orally. Written contracts ensure greater reflection on the part of the contracting parties.

3. Contracts for an illegal purpose are void and unenforceable. For example, a "contract" as in "there is a contract out on the Godfather" is unenforceable. Even if the assassin does his part, he can't sue to recover his promised fee. Such contracts are illegal on their "face," that is, the illegality appears in the agreement itself: "I'll waste Jones for $5,000."

4. Gift promises, as in "I promise to give you a Big Wheel for your birthday," are not enforceable. The kid cannot sue you if you renege. (I'm sorry I had to tell you that.) To be enforceable a promise must be supported by an adequate "consideration." The person making the promise must "get something" for it. "I promise to give you my Big Wheel for $20." This promise is enforceable. The promisor got something for it, in this case $20. The promise is supported by an adequate consideration.

Spend some time reflecting on these rules of law before attempting to answer the question.

b. *The Question*

COLLEGE OF LAW

CONTRACTS (Final Exam)   Page 1 of 10
Professor Quibble Weaver
Spring Semester,   PLEASE CHECK TO
                             SEE IF EXAM IS
                             COMPLETE

Friday, April 1,
8:00 a.m. (4 hours)
Room 24

Instructions

1. You have four hours to complete your answers.
2. This is a closed book examination.
3. Use ink or typewriter and write only on one side of each page.
4. If in any question you find it necessary to make any assumptions of fact or law, state them explicitly.
5. The grading weight is indicated at the beginning of each question by the amount of time suggested for the question. Use your time accordingly.
6. Use only your student examination number to identify your answers.

Question 1: 40 minutes

Sleazy Sam and Billy Bigmouth ran into each other at the Lazy J Bar.

After several drinks, Billy says, ''You know, I think I'll blow this town and get into pictures.''

[201]

''Oh yeah? How are you going to support yourself in Hollywood until they discover your major talent?'' asked Sam.

''Why I'll sell my house. You can have it for $40,000. Last week it was appraised at $80,000.''

''You must be joking, that deal is too good to be true,'' replied Sam, having another drink.

''Man, it's just that you don't have the money.''

''Look, I can have $40,000 cash at the end of the week.''

''Bring it by.''

''Are you serious?''

''Sure. You'll be seeing me in the movies,'' laughed Bigmouth.

''Well, I can use a place for my bookmaking activities.''

''What you do with the place is your business,'' said Bigmouth, ''Let's shake.'' The men shook and left the bar.

Three days later Sam received the following letter from Bigmouth:

Dear Sam,

Of course I was joking when I promised to sell you my house for $40,000 cash at the end of the week. In any event I don't want to do it. So there.

Yours truly,

Billy Bigmouth

Billy Bigmouth

MUST BILL MAKE GOOD ON HIS PROMISE TO
SAM? DISCUSS HIS LEGAL POSITION.

Take 40 minutes to answer the question.
Write your answer. If you just "think" about an
answer, you won't learn as much from this exercise. Two quick points before beginning. Funny
names like "Sleazy Sam" and "Billy Bigmouth"
are a law school tradition. If you find absolutely
nothing humorous in your exams, you are taking
them too seriously. Loosen up.

Note too that law profs do not have a good ear
for dialogue.

You may begin!

After you have completed your answer, put it
aside and read the two below. Read them relatively quickly and then spend a few minutes, pen
in hand, jotting down your answers to the following questions:
1. Which answer was easier to follow? Why?
2. Which answer displayed a better understanding
   of the law? Why?
3. Did you have difficulties following specific parts
   of either answer? Why?

Once you have completed this general analysis,
return to the two answers and compare them
more closely. Each discusses the same main issues. Compare these discussions and ask which
is better and why.

Only after you have completed your analysis of the answers, should you consider mine. I think it vital that you do your own analysis first. The criteria of good writing comes from simply asking questions about writing. "Why is that paragraph confusing? Why does this paragraph flow so well?" It is hard work to answer these questions but if you do the work you will come to understand good writing at a more profound level. My analysis then becomes a conversation rather than a lecture.

c. *Two Answers*

Answer Number 1

This case is about Sam and Bill who met in a bar and began to talk about the selling of Bill's house to Sam for $40,000. The issue is whether the alleged contract is enforceable or not.

First, Bill was clearly drunk.

Second, Bill was joking. He said as much in his letter to Sam. Who on earth would sell an $80,000 house for $40,000 in order to go get into pictures? Sam was going to use the house for bookmaking activities and that's illegal. And remember that Sam didn't think Bill was serious because he asked him ''Are you serious?'' Sam knew Bill was joking.

Because this deals with the sale of real property, the Statute of Frauds applies. The first English Statute of Frauds was enacted nearly 300 years ago to prevent fraud. In California the Statute is Civil Code § 1624. Many commentators in law reviews have argued that the statute, which has been adopted with modifications in many states, causes more fraud than it prevents. That is, it allows people who have made promises to get out of them simply because they are not in writing. Courts often try to get around the Statute of Frauds. One way around the statute is part performance. Had Sam built a garage or some other structure on Bill's property, then he could claim part performance and raise an estoppel. Realtors always require things to be in writing and there must be a legal description of the property. What if Bill had two houses?

Finally the law holds that promises are only enforceable if they are supported by a sufficient consideration. Had Bill promised to give the house to Sam, his promise would not be enforceable because he got no consideration. However, if Sam had relied on the promise then maybe he could have it enforced. However, because Bill was asking $40,000, there is consideration.

Bill will clearly win.

Answer Number 2

There are several issues to be considered in this question:

1. Did Bill make a serious offer to sell his house to Sam?

2. Assuming that the Statute of Frauds applies, does the letter of Bill to Sam satisfy it?

3. Is the contract void because Sam intended to use the house for an illegal activity?

The first issue is whether or not there was a valid offer. Even though Bill may have been joking in making the offer, the question is whether he appeared to be serious. The law is designed to protect the reasonable expectations of people accepting offers: was it reasonable for Sam to think Bill really wanted to sell him the house? Bill will claim he was joking and that Sam either knew it or should have known it. He will point out that both men accidentally met in a bar. There is no indication that they met to discuss the sale of the house. He will also point out that both men were drinking. (If Bill had been drunk, and Sam knew he was drunk, that would be another defense.) He will argue that no reasonable person would believe he wanted to sell a $80,000 house for $40,000 in order to go into pictures. Note that there was nothing put in writing—it is reasonable to assume that if Bill were seriously thinking about selling a house for $40,000 it would be in writing.

On the other hand, Sam will argue that Bill appeared to seriously want to sell his home. First, Bill initiated the discussion. Second, he mentioned that the house had been recently appraised— one does that when one is planning to sell. Third, Bill told Sam he was serious and both men shook hands, a traditional way to conclude a deal. If Bill had been joking, he would have told Sam so rather than shake hands. Finally, Bill himself thought the deal serious because he wrote the letter to Sam—had the joke been clear, he wouldn't have thought to write claiming it was a joke.

On balance, it seems that Sam will have the better argument here.

Even if it was found that Bill was serious, however, the agreement might be unenforceable because of the Statute of Frauds. The Statute applies because the deal concerns the sale of real property. Was there a note or memorandum signed by the party to be charged? The original agreement was oral. However, Bill wrote Sam saying he wanted out of the deal. He signed that letter. The question becomes, then, can a letter denying the seriousness of a promise be used to satisfy the Statute of Frauds? On the one hand, it seems as if it might. One of the purposes of the Statute is to prevent fraud—by signing the letter, Bill admits he made the promise to sell the house. Sam didn't make up the agreement. On the other hand, another purpose of the Statute is cautionary—to insure that people reflect before committing themselves to important deals. Obviously a letter trying to get out of a deal cannot be said to fulfill any cautionary function: it comes too late.

Even if the letter could be used to satisfy the Statute, I don't know how specific the letter would have to be. Must it describe the property? Must it say when delivery is to be made? I really don't know the answer.

Even if Bill was serious in making the offer and even if his letter satisfies the Statute of Frauds, there is another possible defense, that of illegality. The law states that contracts illegal on their face are unenforceable. However, this contract isn't illegal on its face—it is not for bookmaking, it is

[*207*]

for the sale of a house. Assuming a
seller knows that the buyer is to use
what is purchased for an illegal activity, can he, must he, refuse to go ahead
with the deal? I assume that contracts
for illegal acts are not enforced in order to deter illegal activity. That
policy would apply here and make the
contract unenforceable.

To summarize, I think a court would
find that Bill made a serious offer but
that the agreement would not be enforced
because of illegality. The court could
go either way on the Statute of Frauds
issue.

Which of the two answers is best? Why? Go
back and reread them. The more you attempt to
verbalize the standards of good writing, the more
you will learn. And how to "verbalize the standards of good writing"? From your sense of
what is good and bad, begin to ask yourself
"Why?"

———

Legal writing is essentially, and not particularly profoundly, a means of communication. In
your comparison of the two answers, you might
have come up with the standards of clarity and
brevity.

A brief aside. After a long day of harangues,
headaches and other lawyer activity, the successful practitioner comes home, seeking relaxation
and harmony.

"You know, Dad," his teenage daughter greets him, "You really can't write at all."

Touching! A denial. More accusations. Further denials. A test, finally negotiated. The daughter would submit one of her father's briefs for analysis by her Creative Writing teacher.

The verdict: "He agrees—you can't write at all!" Daughter is pleased. (Live by contentiousness, die by contentiousness.) "Your sentences are too short; your paragraphs are too short and besides anyone can understand it!"

Good exam writing must communicate. It should communicate your knowledge of the law and that you "think like a lawyer." What is it to think like a lawyer?

2. Thinking Like a Lawyer

As you have undoubtedly been told, in law school you will learn to "think like a lawyer." Expect to wake up one morning "thinking like a lawyer". What this does to your breakfast plans is unclear. Nonetheless it will surely be a major event in your life. You will be different, improved, better.

In the sixth grade I was told by the big kids what it was going to be like in the seventh, the first year of Junior High. No more sitting in the same room with the same teacher all day. Kid stuff! Instead, different rooms with different teachers! And exotic classes, like Journalism and Boys' Cooking. Moreover, and to me much more

[*209*]

impressive and threatening, each student had to take a pencil to every class! "Boy," I thought, "the seventh grade must be really IT." No more the childish, immature kid, I was to be somebody substantial, someone important.

In short, I was going to learn to "think like a seventh grader."

Well, I took my pencil every day, changed classes every time the bell rang. But, alas, it was the same old "me" doing it. But just you wait until High School . . . .

Whether or not law school proves to be really IT for you, whether or not you will really begin to "think differently," it is clear that you *will* be doing new and different things, both as a law student and as a lawyer. The *main thing* lawyers do (but not nearly the only thing) is to *apply law to fact.* Law school exams test the ability to do this. (To the extent that lawyers do many other things as well, law exams do not test for lawyering success.)

Good exam answers, like any good legal analysis, be it a written brief or an oral argument to a court, involve the *interplay of law and fact— one should never discuss one without the other.* Clients will come to you, professors will come to you, with fact patterns—be they past fact patterns (the tragic crash, the grisly crime), or future fact patterns (the hoped for successful partnership, the well-planned estate). Your job is not simply to construct clever, even compelling, factual arguments—after all, even a seventh grader, with or without pencil, can argue convincingly that "It's just not fair to make Bill sell his house for $40,000." Nor is your job simply to discuss the law in the abstract—no professor or client is even going to ask, "Please tell me everything you know about Contracts, or Torts, or the Rule Against Perpetuities." The questions will always be *"Given these facts, what are my legal rights and obligations?"*

Given the question, how does a lawyer go about answering it?

a. Spotting the Issues

The first task is to recognize and identify the legal problems and potentials lurking within the facts presented. Few seventh graders, for example, would have spotted the Statute of Frauds problem. (Much can be said for that innocent state.) Recognizing the legal problems, spotting the issues, is of utmost importance in both law practice and exam taking. The practice exam was not much of a test of this ability as the issues were pretty well given you. Suggestions on how to "spot issues" will come later but for now grasp the *crucial point*: in law exams you are not telling what you know but *applying* what you know. Spotting issues you are applying what you know by perceiving elements in the facts that non-lawyers would not see.

Spotting issues is not enough. No client, or professor, will be satisfied with "From what you tell me, you have a Statute of Frauds problem." The next step is to apply the law to given facts. There are two basic patterns, one in which the law is clear and the facts muddied, the other in which the facts are clear and the law muddied.

b. *Applying a Legal Rule to Facts*

~~Often the legal rule will be relatively clear. Your task is to predict or analyze how that rule would be applied to the facts at hand.~~ For example, take the rule of law that for offers to be operative it must appear to a reasonable person that the person making the offer is serious and not joking. There is no question that the rule governs the offer Bill made to sell his house. But what will be the result of the rule in the case? Would a reasonable person conclude that Bill was serious or that he was joking? Here the lawyer's, and law student's, skill is to analyze, interpret and marshal the facts. "On the one hand, these facts point toward one conclusion, on the other hand, these facts point toward the opposite conclusion."

c. *Deciding Which Legal Rule Applies*

Often the problem facing the lawyer is not *how* a given rule will be applied in a given factual context but rather *whether* a given rule should be applied. ~~Should a specific rule of law be applied~~

~~to what is admittedly a new and quite different factual context?~~ A rule of law states that contracts which are, on their face, illegal, will not be enforced. Should that rule be extended to contracts which are legal on their face but where one of the parties plans to use the product of the contract for an illegal purpose? There is nothing illegal on the face of a contract concerning the purchase and sale of a house. But what if the seller knows the buyer plans to conduct illegal activities in the house? Should the "illegal contract" rule provide the seller with a legal excuse to break his promise?

Again, there is a statute that requires some kinds of contracts to be in writing. If someone writes a letter saying he didn't mean to contract, should that satisfy the requirement of the statute? Here the skill is to *argue policy and purposes*: Do the reasons behind the rule on illegal contracts apply equally to the new situation? What are the implications of applying the rule in the new situation? Does a signed written letter denying the intent to contract satisfy whatever policies or interests the statute requiring a written agreement was designed to protect?

"To think like a lawyer" means being able to see legal problems and opportunities that others might miss. It also means being able to analyze how the law would impact on those problems and opportunities by either (a) analyzing the facts to determine how the legal rule would apply or (b) in cases where the legal rule itself is up for grabs, analyzing which legal standard a court would likely apply.

Which of the two answers best reflects "thinking like a lawyer?" A quick reread of the two answers with this question in mind might help cement some of the previous discussion.

Law exams test the ability to think like a lawyer. In order to show this ability it is also necessary to write like a lawyer.

3. Writing Like a Lawyer

Good exam writing is but an instance of good legal analysis and expression. Many of the points that follow apply to all forms of legal expression, both written and oral. There will be some overlap with the chapters on Legal Writing and Moot Court. So be it. The points deserve repeating. Here the illustrations will be drawn from the previous exam question. If you have skipped ahead, go back.

a. Don't Force Your Reader to Guess

A major failure in legal writing is the tendency to put things down without bothering to tell the reader exactly why those things are being put down, exactly why they are important. This I call "implicit" writing. It forces the reader to guess. Explicit writing is where the reader is told exactly how everything fits together in clear, unambiguous terms. Examples help.

[214]

In answering the exam question, a student might write "Remember, the men met *accidentally* and they were drinking!" This is implicit—the reader might well ask "So what?" but, of course, the student is now on semester break. Reading an exam question, certain facts will jump out. Don't just note them in your answer. Ask yourself why these facts seem important. Once you know, tell the reader.

Your thought process might run something like this:

> It strikes me that it is important that the men met accidentally. Why? Well maybe it shows that they weren't of a serious frame of mind. Are there any other facts in the problem that support that conclusion? Well, yes. The men had been drinking.

> But even if the men weren't in a serious frame of mind, so what? If they weren't, then that might be a defense to the contract. I remember a rule of law which states that if the offeree knows the offeror isn't serious making an offer, no contract will result.

Note the process. Your legal training has made you sensitive to certain fact patterns. Reading an exam question, a fact "jumps out." Asking why it did focuses your concentration and leads to a possible factual conclusion, that the men weren't serious. From that tentative conclusion come further insights into the question. "Are there other facts which support that factual conclusion? Facts that go against it?" Finally, mulling over the facts triggers the recollection of the rule of law. "Why is it I'm so concerned with whether the men were serious?"

The question "Why?" leads to insights. Once you have them, share them with your reader.

> The fact that the men met accidentally indicates that they didn't come planning to talk business. Thus it is more likely the conversation was "off-the-cuff." This undercuts the notion that the men were in a serious state of mind. Reinforcing the idea that the men were in a less than serious frame of mind is the fact that both had been drinking.

This analysis makes explicit the *factual conclusion* drawn from the bits of information given in the problem. You should be explicit as to the *legal conclusion* as well:

> If a reasonable person would have concluded that Bill was not seriously proposing the sale of his house, then Bill would have a valid defense. The law holds that only the reasonable expectations of people accepting offers will be protected.

To recap the process. From the given facts the lawyer must draw factual and legal conclusions.

A. Bits of information (the raw facts, such as the men met accidentally)

B. Factual conclusion (from the bits of information one can conclude Bill did not appear serious)

C. Legal conclusion (if that is the factual conclusion the legal rule would apply in the following fashion: it would prevent enforcement)

To steal a wonderful phrase, the events of the world are "bloomin' confusion." The job of the lawyer, and law student, is to impose some order, first by recognizing factual patterns and then drawing legal conclusions.

b. Legal Analysis Involves the Interplay of Law and Fact, Don't Leave Home Without Both of Them!

This is another way of saying "Be explicit!" "Why are you discussing these facts anyway?" "And what does the Statute of Frauds have to do with the facts of this case?"

If you persist too long discussing the facts or too long discussing the law, you are wandering off into insanity. Come back.

c. Don't Mix Categories

Legal thought is categorical thought, logical thought, Vulcan thought. Recently a legal services attorney quit, remarking that she was tired of attempting to fit "filthy" prison conditions into "cruel and unusual punishment." But that is the way the law works. The Constitution does not prohibit "filthy conditions." It prohibits "cruel and unusual punishment." Unless filthy conditions can be fitted into the cruel and unusual category, the courts are powerless to act.

Many students are unclear about the category they are discussing. This stems from the failure to be explicit. Other students tend to mix up the categories. In a paragraph discussing whether the parties were serious, don't suddenly throw in something about the illegality issue. *These are*

[*217*]

separate legal categories and must be discussed separately.

Note, however, that the same fact may be used in more than one category. You could argue, for example, that because the deal involved an illegal activity, it is more likely that the men were joking. If you are doing this, however, be clear. Again, how does this "fact" fit into the category?

d. Use Transitions and Words of Contrast

These tell the reader just how your arguments fit together. Is the issue you are discussing an independent defense or is it a sub-issue of another defense? Does the fact you are discussing tend to put the case within the rule or does it take it outside the rule? Again, transitions tell the reader "So what." And by forcing yourself to use transitions, you force yourself to understand "what's so."

In the exam there are three issues—seriousness, Statute of Frauds, illegality. A new paragraph will indicate to the reader a new category is being considered but does not tell the reader how the categories relate to the ultimate disposition of the case. Compare the opening sentences of the paragraph immediately after the discussion of "seriousness":

A. "The next issue involves the Statute of Frauds."

B. "Even if Bill was found to be serious, another defense would be that enforcement of the contract is prohibited by the Statute of Frauds."

"B" is preferable because it shows how the issue of the Statute of Frauds relates to that of seriousness. It is clear that the defense is in addition to that of lack of seriousness: "Even if Bill was found to be serious, another defense . . . ." Much of legal analysis is the analysis of relationships between rules of law and between facts. Good legal writing is full of words indicating relationships:

although

nonetheless

instead

on the other hand

even though

despite the fact

Get used to using such words.

e. Don't Take Sides and Consider What Both Sides Would Argue

As part of a "What Do Parents Do?" program, I went to my son's fourth grade class. Not wishing to embarrass him, I did not discuss what I actually do. Rather I staged a trial. I took two students, Tom and Joe, out in the hall. I told them to fake an argument and then stage a brief shoving match. I called three or four other students out in the hall on some pretext. They were to be the witnesses. When they arrived, the incident was staged. The trial was to fix blame for the assault. Students played judge, lawyers and

jurors. After the evidence was presented, I whispered instructions to the judge.

"Tell the jury to decide the case only on the evidence they heard. They shouldn't decide simply
because they like Tom or Joe better."

"I got ya," the judge whispered back. He
turned to the jury.

"Ladies and Gentlemen of the Jury," he began,
"decide this case fairly. Forget the fact that Joe
is better than Tom."

Taking exams, you forget it too. *Never take
sides*, unless the instructions tell you to, which
they generally won't. After the exam question
you may be told:

"Advise Bill as to his legal rights and obligations."

"Discuss Bill's defenses."

"Advise Sam."

All of these come to the same thing! You are
not to assume that you are Bill's lawyer, or
Sam's, and then argue only things in favor of
your client. Your position is "brooding omnipresence"—you are to evaluate the case impartially,
making the strongest arguments possible for
each side. And, of course, even if you are instructed to "take sides," you must consider what
the other side may argue in order to represent
your client effectively.

In making factual or legal arguments *always*
consider possible responses. In discussing the
seriousness issue, don't just look at the evidence

which supports the view that the men weren't serious. What would you, if you were on the other side, respond?

> There is evidence that the men were serious. Both men shook hands, a traditional method of showing serious intent. Additionally Sam asked Bill if he was serious and Bill said he was. Further . . . .

Developing both sides of an argument is part of not taking sides. Some students consider both sides but make a devastating error nonetheless. They first state one side's position on *all* the issues and then state the other side's positions on all the issues.

> As to seriousness, the plaintiff will say . . . .
>
> As to illegality, the plaintiff will say . . . .
>
> As to the Statute of Frauds, the plaintiff will say . . . .
>
> As to seriousness, the defendant will say . . . .
>
> As to illegality, the defendant will say . . . .
>
> As to the Statute of Frauds, the defendant will say . . . .

This format is wordy and confusing.

Far clearer is the format that analyzes both positions on a given issue together.

> As to the issue of seriousness, there is evidence that the men were not in a serious frame of mind. That evidence is . . . . Contrariwise, there is evidence supporting the conclusion that the men were serious . . . .
>
> As to the issue of illegality . . . .

Note that when you bring competing contentions together in one place your analysis deepens.

Thrust: There is a doctrine that illegal contracts will not be enforced. That doctrine should apply here because Sam planned to use the house for an illegal activity, bookmaking.

Parry: The doctrine is that contracts *on their face* are not enforceable. The contract at issue here is simply one to sell a house. There is nothing illegal about that.

Thrust: Although the doctrine generally applies to contracts illegal on their face, the notion behind it is that courts should not enforce contracts if that would encourage illegality. Once a party knows that the other party plans to do something illegal with the fruits of an otherwise legal contract, that party should have the legal right to refuse to carry out the contract. Otherwise, he will be forced to perform the contract and hence illegal activity will be encouraged.

Parry: Does that mean that a car dealer can refuse to sell a car because the purchaser might speed? That doctrine would disrupt too many contracts. It is best to hold the illegality doctrine to contracts which themselves involve illegality.

Thrust: We are not talking about speeding. We are talking about a serious crime. The doctrine could be restricted to cases where the threatened illegality is of serious nature.

Parry: The law needs to be predictable. Who can predict what is a "serious" illegality? The proposed rule would leave things too much in the air and should be rejected on that basis.

Thrust: The law usually needs to be predictable. People should be allowed to plan. But should the courts worry about people planning illegal acts?

And so it goes.

f. Read the Question Carefully

Often more than two people and more than one event will be involved in an exam question. If the instructions read "Discuss Mary's claim against Tom," it will do you absolutely no good to develop a brilliant theory holding David liable for slandering Bruce's dog.

g. Don't Kill Time or Show Off

The person who wrote the question *knows* the facts. Don't merely repeat them. Discuss the facts only in relation to the law. As to long discussions of the law, remember that you aren't Corbin nor, presumably, were you meant to be. A law school exam is not the place to show off how much general law you know. (What else are resentful friends for?) Long discussions of general law should not be included. Discuss only the law which applies.

[*223*]

Related to this is the problem of *non-issues*. For example, in a criminal law exam the student might write:

> Had the victim died, then the defendant might be guilty of murder. There are, under the Model Penal Code, several degrees of murder.

And the answer continues, telling us more and more about murder. The student then concludes:

> But, as the victim only stubbed his toe, the defendant probably will not be guilty of murder—under any of the definitions discussed above.

We all have an investment in what we learned. It took a long time to memorize all those degrees of murder and, by gosh, we want some recognition. Again, however, better to bore your friends than your prof. There is a tricky problem here, however. How do you distinguish the true issue from the false? The more developed your legal sense, the easier it will be. However, in case of doubt, *include* the issue. If the prof thinks it a true issue, by omitting it you have forfeited points allotted to it. If the prof thinks it a false issue, probably the only cost will be a sneer and the loss of time it took it write it out.

One nice solution to the true/false issue quandary is to treat what you take to be collateral issues quite summarily. How to do this will be shown later.

h. Don't Chicken Out!

You may see an issue but duck it because you don't know how to resolve it. For example, you might think "This contract isn't illegal on its face—buying and selling a house isn't. But here the seller knows the buyer will use it for an illegal purpose. Does that make the contract void? Gee, I don't know. I better just skip it."

Chickening out you may miss a key issue. Even if you don't know how to resolve the issue, at least mention it.

> Contracts illegal on their face are void. This contract isn't but the seller knows the buyer will use the house for an illegal purpose. Quite frankly I don't know if this would make the contract void but it would be worth looking into.

By doing this, you will get some points for seeing the issue and maybe even one or two for candor. To improve the answer, however, try to reason through how a court might resolve the issue. What factors might a court consider relevant?

> Where the seller knows the buyer is to act illegally, the contract should be void in order to discourage illegal activity. But such a rule might be too difficult to enforce and might make too many contracts unenforceable—can a car salesman get out of a contract because he learns the buyer repeatedly parks illegally?

i. *Don't Assume Your Professor Can't Make Up Good Tests*

"There is no question but the confession will be suppressed."

"The defendant will undoubtedly be held to be negligent."

"There was obviously no consideration."

If the issue seems too easy, it is likely either a non-issue, one your professor does not expect you to discuss, *or* it only seems an easy issue because you haven't thought it through.

j. *Use Examples, Simple Ones*

This stuff is hard enough, even for your prof. Purely abstract discussions will confuse you both. *Ground abstractions in examples.* It will help you think out problems and help your prof follow your discussion. Take the argument whether the illegality defense should be extended to contracts, not illegal on their face, but where one party knows the other plans to use the fruit of that contract illegally. An abstract discussion could go on and on and be essentially meaningless. Discussion becomes so much more focused with the use of examples:

What of the gun dealer who knows there is murder in the customer's heart?

What of the car dealer who knows there is an illegal left turn in the customer's heart?

[*226*]

One's intuitive sense is to treat these cases quite differently. The discussion quickly comes to the critical issue: If the defense were extended is it possible to draw a meaningful line between the two examples? To protect the gun dealer, must the law also give the defense to the car dealer? Or, to protect the car purchaser, must it also allow the disappointed murderer's suit?

All legal discourse is improved with examples.

k. Don't Misspell Words—It Makes You Look Dumb

If you are, like me, a bad speller, spend some time learning the words you are likely to use in the exam. Some examples:

affidavit	hearsay
amendment	judgment
appellant	principal, principle
argument	receive
attorney	separate
counsel	solely
defendant	subpoena
defense	suppress

Speaking of words, don't throw around legal jargon unless you are very sure you are using it correctly. When I read an exam answer nothing undermines belief quicker than the misuse of legal words. I get the sense that the student is merely throwing words at the problem, hoping to get lucky. Don't do it. It won't work.

And speaking of looking dumb, try to do something about your handwriting if it is bad. Write on every other line in your bluebook. I have found that using an ink pen, as opposed to a ballpoint pen, improves my handwriting because it slows me down. With ballpoint my scrawl flies across the page.

And, of course, there is always typing.

Reread the two model answers in light of the maxims of writing like a lawyer:

1. Don't force your reader to guess

2. Intertwine law and fact

3. Don't mix legal categories

4. Use transitions and words of contrast

5. Don't take sides and consider both sides

6. Read the question carefully

7. Don't kill time or show off

8. Don't chicken out

9. Don't assume your prof can't make up good exams

10. Use examples, preferably easy ones

11. Don't misspell words

Searching for examples in the model answers will help you understand the material. After you have made your analysis, read mine.

[*228*]

4. The Model Answers Analyzed

a. Answer 1

Answer One begins:

> This case is about Sam and Bill who met in a bar and began to talk about the selling of Bill's house to Sam for $40,000. The issue is whether the alleged contract is enforceable or not.

This is a weak opening because it tells the reader nothing that is not already known and does not focus the issues at all. The issue "is the contract enforceable" is so broad as to be meaningless.

Now examine the opening paragraph in the second answer:

> There are several issues to be considered in this question:
>
> 1. Did Bill make a serious offer to sell his house to Sam?
>
> 2. Assuming that the Statute of Frauds applies, does the letter from Bill to Sam satisfy it?
>
> 3. Is the contract void because Sam intended to use the house for an illegal activity?

Two points. Leave some room after #3 because you may think of a number 4 as you write. Note as well that the student does not say "There are *three* issues to be considered."

An introduction listing the issues to be discussed serves two purposes. It focuses your thinking and it shows the prof that you at least saw the issues if you run out of time and fail to discuss them all.

Answer One continues:

First, Bill was clearly drunk.

There are two problems with this. First the student has manufactured facts—the question did not say Bill was drunk, simply that he was drinking. Be *very* careful to get the facts straight. An important lawyer skill is careful reading and an acute awareness of the critical distinction between *observed data* and *inference*. Exams often test for this awareness. The second problem is that the statement is implicit: So what if Bill was drunk? If Bill was drunk, it would make a legal difference—*but* it is the student's job to tell us what that difference would be.

Observe that the second answer avoids both of these problems: "Had Bill been drunk, and Sam knew it, that would be another defense." Bill's intoxication is probably a non-issue in this case, but it would be something a careful lawyer might examine. Note that the second answer deals with the problem of the non-issue by simply noting the issue. There is no lengthy discussion, yet there is a recognition that it is a possible issue.

Second, Bill was joking. He said as much in his letter to Sam. Who would sell an $80,000 house for $40,000 in order to go get into pictures? Sam was going to use the house for bookmaking activities and that's illegal. And remember that Sam didn't think Bill was serious because he asked him "Are you serious?" Sam knew Bill was joking.

There are multiple problems here. First, it appears that the writer is taking sides, looking only at Bill's position. Had the student asked, "What would the other side say when Bill's lawyer argued Bill was joking?" all the counter facts would have been brought forward. Second, the writer is making an implicit argument. *So what* if Bill were joking? The reader is forced to guess the legal relevance of that factual conclusion. Third, the writer mixes legal categories— the business of illegality is thrown into a discussion of seriousness. Not good. Finally there is no basis in the facts recounted to conclude "Sam knew Bill was joking." When one takes sides, when one becomes contentious, one is more likely to manufacture facts.

Because this deals with the sale of real property, the Statute of Frauds applies. The first English Statute of Frauds was enacted nearly 300 years ago to prevent fraud. In California the Statute is Civil Code § 1624. Many commentators in law reviews have argued that the statute, which has been adopted with modifications in many states, causes more fraud than it prevents. That is, it allows people who have made promises to get out of them simply because they are not in writing. Courts often try to get around the Statute of Frauds. One way around the statute is part performance. Had Sam built a garage or something like that on Bill's property, then he could claim part performance and raise an estoppel.

This paragraph starts out well enough but could be improved by the use of a transition

showing how the Statute of Frauds analysis fits
with that of seriousness. A good, effective transition might read: "Assuming that Bill made a
serious offer, the Statute of Frauds may prevent
enforcement."

Recounting on the history of the Statute of
Frauds is showing off. *Or* desperation! No one,
least of all Bill and Sam, are interested in a history lesson. The question is whether the statute
will prevent Sam from successfully suing Bill.
That some courts have been hostile to the Statute
of Frauds *may* be relevant to this but again there
is the need to be explicit: "Because the courts
have been hostile to the Statute, it is likely that
they will interpret it to allow for enforcement of
promises by holding that a letter denying the obligation satisfies the Statute."

Fortunately, there is usually little need, in law
exams, to cite specific code sections ("Civil Code
§ 1624") or, for that matter, specific cases. Case
names may be important in some courses, such as
Constitutional Law. In most first year courses,
however, case names are not significant. To be
sure, ask your professor.

Now the business about Sam building a garage
is unabashed—one gets the idea that the student
is simply trying to fill up space because the student does not know what else to do. This is a
dangerous idea for your prof to get about your
exam.

Realtors always require things to be in writing and there must be a legal description of the property. What if Bill had two houses?

Answers should reflect what you learned in the course, not interesting tidbits that you picked up elsewhere. It is also dangerous to let on that you once sold real estate. The paragraph does contain two choice kernels which, unfortunately, are not developed. What of this matter of the "legal description?" And what if Bill had two houses? If the student had asked *"So what?"* perhaps these interesting points would have led to deeper mines. For example, the student might think, "If Bill had two houses, then the failure to describe the house he meant to sell may mean that his offer is too ambiguous. How specific must offers be, anyway?" Great. And what if the student doesn't know how specific offers must be? Don't chicken out! Mention the issue and move on.

Finally the law is that promises are only enforceable if they are supported by a sufficient consideration. Had Bill promised to give the house to Sam, his promise would not be enforceable because he got no consideration. However, if Sam had relied on the promise then maybe he could have it enforced. However, because Bill was asking $40,000, there is consideration.

Another example of a false issue. Again, if you want to hedge your bets, or simply show that you considered everything, do something like this:

> To be enforceable, promises must be supported by an adequate consideration and there is no doubt that the promise to pay $40,000 is adequate.

Finally:

> Bill will clearly win.

If it were that clear, the question would not have been asked.

b. *Answer 2*

There are several issues to be considered in this question:

1. Did Bill make a serious offer to sell his house to Sam?

2. Assuming that the Statute of Frauds applies, does the letter from Bill to Sam satisfy it?

3. Is the contract void because Sam intended to use the house for an illegal activity?

The first issue is whether or not there was a valid offer. Even though Bill may have been joking in making the offer, the question is whether he appeared to be serious. The law is designed to protect the reasonable expectations of people accepting offers: was it reasonable for Sam to think Bill really wanted to sell him the house? Bill will claim he was joking and that Sam either knew it or should have known it. He will point out that both men accidentally met in a bar (there is no indication that they met to discuss the sale of the house). He will also point out that both men were drinking. (Had Bill been drunk, and Sam knew it, that would be another defense.) He will argue that no reasonable person would believe he wanted to sell a $80,000 house for $40,000 in order to go into pictures. Note that there was nothing put in writing—it is reasonable to assume that if Bill were seriously thinking about selling a house for $40,000 it would be in writing.

The introductory paragraph has already been commented on. The second paragraph is excellent. It starts off discussing the law. *Precise statements of law* are not required. You need *not* memorize the language of statutes or Restatements or the key language from opinions. In fact, as a matter of learning, it is best to put thoughts in your own words—it is possible to memorize without understanding.

The seriousness issue requires the student to apply a relatively clear legal standard to an ambigious fact pattern. The paragraph shows good factual analysis. For example, note the use of the fact that the deal was not put in writing. There is a *separate* issue concerning the Statute of Frauds but here the fact of no writing is skillfully used as evidence of lack of serious intent. Well done!

On the other hand, Sam will argue that Bill appeared to seriously want to sell his home. First, Bill initiated the discussion. Second, he mentioned that the house had been recently appraised—one does that when one is planning to sell. Third, Bill told Sam he was serious and both men shook hands, a traditional way to conclude a deal. If Bill had been joking, he would have told Sam rather than shake hands. Finally, Bill himself thought the deal serious because he wrote the letter to Sam—had the joke been clear, he wouldn't have thought to write claiming it was a joke. On balance, it seems that Sam will have the better argument here.

This paragraph answers the essential question "What will the other side say?" After you state each side, is it necessary for you to reach some conclusion as to who has "the better argument?" Generally, *yes*. A conclusion is appropriate as a way of indicating that you know some arguments are better than others. Once you become adept at arguing both sides, you will always be able to come up with some argument, even if it is unconvincing. If you simply state "Of course the defendant could argue that the plaintiff should not have come to California in the first place," the prof may think you actually find this convincing. Hence, weighing of the arguments is often essential.

This demands further elaboration because it is a matter of great confusion. In law school exams, *conclusions are analyses, not solutions*. Take the issue of whether Bill's letter satisfies the Statute of Frauds. The competing contentions would be:

Bill: My letter could not satisfy the Statute of Frauds because the goal of the Statute is to force people to reflect before they enter into important deals. My letter was written *after* I made my hasty promise. To allow it to satisfy the Statute would defeat its purpose.

Sam: Not so. The main purpose of the Statute of Frauds is to prevent false claims from being made. It requires that before one person can

sue another for the breach of certain kinds of
promises, that that person produce written
evidence that that promise was made. And
there is that evidence, Bill's letter.

Developing the competing contentions is the main
work. It shows that you know how to analyze
problems as would a lawyer. To further that
analysis it is often proper to reach a conclusion,
not because it is necessary to reach the "right"
conclusion, but rather to round off the analysis,
to show the reader that you have a legal sense
that some arguments are better than others.
Two important learnings come from this discussion:

1. Don't freeze up in fear you won't reach the prop-
    er conclusion.
2. Don't simply assert your conclusion; always jus-
    tify it.

If you have analyzed the problem properly,
don't fear that your prof may disagree with your
ultimate conclusion. Most exam questions are
close questions; you will not be dealing with two
plus two. That conclusions are not solutions but
are rather analyses will also teach you that un-
supported conclusions count for little or nothing.
Take the following conclusion:

I think that Sam will win the Statute of Frauds issue.

Well and good. Perhaps, in a real court, he
would. Yet, as written, the conclusion tells us
nothing about the only thing we are really interested in: the student's ability to analyze prob-

lems. Perhaps the student simply made a lucky guess—after all, the odds aren't all that bad. Compare:

> I think Sam will win the Statute of Frauds issue. Although Bill's letter was written after the promise, and hence could not fulfill any cautionary function, it seems that the main thrust of the Statute is to prevent false claims. Here we know Bill made the promise because we have his signed letter to prove it.

Here we know the student understands.

In sum, while analysis may stand without conclusion, conclusion can never stand without analysis.

> Even if it was found that Bill was serious, however, the agreement might be unenforceable because of the Statute of Frauds. The statute applies because the deal concerns the sale of real property. Was there a note or memorandum signed by the party to be charged? The original agreement was oral. However, Bill wrote Sam saying he wanted out of the deal. He signed that letter. The question becomes, then, can a letter denying the seriousness of a promise be used to satisfy the Statute of Frauds? On the one hand, it seems like it might. One of the purposes of the Statute is to prevent fraud—by signing the letter, Bill admits he made the promise to sell the house. Sam didn't invent this. On the other hand, another purpose of the Statute is cautionary— to insure that people reflect before committing themselves to important deals. Obviously a letter trying to get out of a deal cannot be said to fulfill any cautionary function: it comes too late.

Another job well done. Nice transition. Good statement of the law and of the issue. Here the facts are clear and hence the student faces a pure legal question: Should the letter satisfy the Statute? The model answer uses the proper mode of analysis. Because the Statute does not tell us what it means by "notes" and "memorandums," we must define those terms in light of the purposes and goals of the Statute. Would they be furthered or defeated by allowing the letter to count?

> Even if the letter could be used to satisfy the statute, I don't know how specific the letter would have to be. Must it describe the property? Must it say when delivery is to be made? I really don't know the answer.

This is a fine example of not chickening out. Perhaps the student could have developed some notion of sufficiency of the memorandum by returning to the purposes of the Statute of Frauds. This is what the courts must do when faced with such an issue. Here we have a piece of writing that neither mentions the delivery date nor describes the property. Does it satisfy the Statute? The Statute doesn't prescribe precisely what is necessary. One can only answer the question by examining the purposes of the Statute. (Or one can look up cases that indicate how specific the memorandum must be. The way those courts determined the issue, however, was by turning to the purposes of the Statute: This is what legal reasoning is all about.)

[*239*]

Even if Bill were serious in making the offer and
even if his letter satisfies the Statute of Frauds,
there is another possible defense, that of illegality.
The law is that contracts illegal on their face are unenforceable. However, this contract isn't illegal on
its face—it is not for bookmaking, it is for the sale
of a house. Assuming a seller knows that the buyer
is to use what is purchased for an illegal activity,
can he, must he, refuse to go ahead with the deal? I
assume that contracts for illegal acts are not enforced in order to deter illegal activity. That policy
would apply here and make the contract unenforceable.

This starts well. There is a good transition.
We know that even if Sam wins on the serious
issue and on the Statute of Frauds point, he still
may be a loser if he blows the illegality point.

Important: You are to discuss *all* issues that
are *fairly raised* in the problem *even though* you
may think one would be determinative. For example, even if you were convinced Bill would win
his case on the Statute of Frauds point, you must
still discuss seriousness and illegality because
they are fairly raised in the problem. The exam
tests your ability to recognize legal issues.

Returning to the answer, the discussion of illegality would be much improved had the student
asked "What will the other side argue?" There
are powerful arguments against Bill's position
here, so powerful, in fact, that courts will likely
reject the defense—although that is an issue I
will leave to your Contracts course.

To summarize, I think a court would find that Bill made a serious offer but that the agreement would not be enforced because of illegality. The court could go either way on the Statute of Frauds issue.

Concluding gracefully presents difficulties. Believing that they should summarize their answer at the end, some students get into the unfortunate morass of repeating and repeating their previous analysis. Grades are not improved for mere repetition and profs find reading the same points over and over irksome.

The ideal ending summary is not a rehash, it is *further analysis*. Rather than repeating previous points, it shows how the points *relate* to one another. Well written summaries, like the one above, can be effective.

Avoid summaries which merely repeat previous analysis. Use summaries that show how the various issues relate to one another. And that, dear friends, is my best effort at concluding this part gracefully. Now some thoughts on the mechanics of writing an exam.

5. The Mechanics of Writing the Exam

The Dreaded Day will someday arrive. After all that study, after all that struggle, one morning you will enter the room, just you and your bluebook. It all comes to this. You will be given a copy of the exam, face down, pending further instructions. It looks so terribly long. After the instructions, the words which you will never forget:

"You may begin."

Of course you will be nervous and of course you will have a hard time getting started. My expectation is that, after the panic, you will *enjoy* the exam. It is a fascinating intellectual puzzle. It will push you, confound you and delight you. *Exams are not awful.* The prospects of exams are awful. Grades are awful. Exams themselves are adrenalin, discovery and adventure. Enjoy them.

This part discusses three problems you will face during the intellectual roller coaster which is the law exam: spotting the issues, capturing the issues and finally organizing the issues.

a. Spotting the Issues

Probably the *most* important element in taking law school exams is discussing all the relevant legal issues posed. While it is nice to be brilliant on one issue, it is generally far better to do an adequate job on all or most of the issues posed. Most professors grade by allocating points to each issue presented. If an issue is not discussed, no points are awarded. This grading system tends to reward *broad coverage rather than deep analysis.* This preference is not without its support in the world of lawyering—as Sam's lawyer, no matter how brilliant your theory that Bill's letter satisfies the Statute of

Frauds, you will come up a loser if you overlook
and hence do not prepare for the illegality defense.

From this notion that you should discuss as
many issues as you can, two rules and one warning follow:

   a. *Budget your time!* Don't spend too much time
      on one issue. Zeroes hurt more than Tens help!

   b. *Discuss all the issues* even if you conclude that
      one would determine the matter conclusively.

   c. *Warning:* In the quest to discuss all the issues,
      don't create false issues.

How do you spot the issues? The more you
have prepared for the course and the better you
understand the material, the easier it is to spot
the issues. Indeed, they rush out at you as you
read the question.

"Look, Bill might be joking! But he says he isn't!
And what about the drinking? Isn't bookmaking illegal? And there was nothing in writing!"

The problem will often be channeling this flood of
ideas into a coherent whole. But what if the
flood doesn't begin, are there any tricks to help
spot issues?

First I will discuss the use of checklists to spot
issues. This is often recommended but I dissent.
Then I'll offer my own advice on spotting issues.

Checklists. Some recommend that you convert
the subject matter of the course into a huge
checklist, covering every possible issue. For ex-

[*243*]

ample, a checklist for Contracts might read like this:

1. Offer—was it specific enough?
2. Acceptance—was it the mirror image?

                    had the offer lapsed?

                    was the offer revoked?

Even if you make a checklist, it's not likely you'll be allowed to take it into the exam with you. (Some professors will allow you to bring notes and other materials to the exam.) To rely on the checklist, as checklist, you will have to memorize it, perhaps by using a mnemonic device, preferably one that spells something witty or crude. Once you are in the exam, you are to match the checklist to the question—is there a mirror image issue here?

I don't recommend the use of mental checklists because I don't think good exam writing happens that way. *If* you have prepared and *if* you understand the material, the issues *jump* out at you—there will be no need for a checklist. And checklists may tend to lead you toward false issues (because you are responding to your checklist instead of the problem) and may actually prevent you from perceiving issues that are not on your checklist. To my mind good exam writing comes from being totally absorbed in the problem, responding to it directly rather than through the filter of a checklist.

Preparing a checklist can be quite valuable, however. Anything that gets you actively involved with the material is worthwhile. Preparing a checklist will deepen your understanding and more issues will "jump out" during the exam. However I doubt that any mnemonic will save you—even if it spells "I'd rather be in Philadelphia."

If not checklists, what do I recommend to help you spot issues? First realize that everything in a question is there for a purpose. Second follow the dictates of good exam writing: they are designed to deepen your analysis as well as to communicate that analysis.

Exam Questions as Art. Read the question carefully at least twice. Do not assume that you saw all the issues the first time through. Read carefully. Pretend you are reading orally; it will force you to read words, not sentences. As to each fact, ask "Why is this here?" Exams are not thrown together like prefab chicken coops— each question is worked on, labored on, rewritten. While others write poems, design buildings, paint pictures, we profs make up exam questions! So be it. Every fact is there for a purpose. Is it to raise an issue? To help resolve an issue? Or is it, alas, just to confuse you? Ask these questions—nothing is there to kill time. "Why was it the defendant's *ugly* dog that did all those nasty things?"

Exam Answers as Art. The dictates of good legal writing will help you spot and develop issues: being explicit (asking *"So what?"*), asking

"What will the opponent say?", and using clear transitions to show how the various categories fit together. These devices not only help the reader understand your answer, but they also help you to think out your answer.

b. Capturing the Issues

The goal is to be actively involved with the question. You are neither a casual reader, looking for "interesting" points nor a disinterested critic looking to see if the issues you thought might be on the exam are there or not. You are to be engaged and excited by the question, perhaps even overwhelmed by it.

"Why is this fact in the problem?" "Is this a simple illegality issue or is there something trickier here?" "Why is it important that they were drinking?" "If one side argues that the Statute of Frauds would make the deal unenforceable, what will the other side say?" "Help!"

The problem is to control the flood.

Underlining and noting ideas in the margin. As you read the problems, ideas, issues, and questions will pop out. You must note these flashes and insights lest you forget them. But be not dazzled by them—initially, none demands refinement or thought. Until you have finished reading the question, you won't be able to sense the whole. *Premature focus on one issue will force others out of view.* The first issue you see may not be even germane to the problem as it unfolds. The dilemma: keeping track of your insights as they come while avoiding premature closure.

As a law student, I found the best solution was to underline what I thought important as I read the problem the first time. I would also make quick notes in the margin. I would then reread the question, writing additional reminders in the margins and underlining additional items which now appeared important because of events revealed later in the problem. An example:

Sleazy Sam and Billy Bigmouth <u>ran into each</u> other at the Lazy J. Bar. <u>After several drinks</u>, Billy says, "You know, I think I'll blow this town and get into pictures." "Oh Yeah? How are you going to support yourself in Hollywood until they discover your major talent?" asked Sam.

"Why I'll sell my house. You can have it for <u>$40,000</u>. Last week it was appraised at <u>$80,000</u>."

Serious Offer?

"You must be <u>joking</u>, that deal is too good to be true," replied Sam, having <u>another drink</u>.

"Man, it's just that you don't have the money."

"Look, I can have $40,000 cash at the end of the week."

"Bring it by."

"Are you serious?"

"Sure. You'll be seeing me in the movies," laughed Bigmouth.

"Well, I can use a place for <u>my bookmaking activities</u>."

"What you do with the place is your business." said Bigmouth. "<u>Let's shake!</u>" The men shook and left the bar.

Three days later Sam gets the following letter from Bigmouth:

Dear Sam,

Of course I was joking when I promised to sell you my house for $40,000 cash at the end of the week. In any event I don't want to do it. So there.

Yours truly,

Billy Bigmouth
Billy Bigmouth

Once you noted your insights in the margins, you must organize them before setting them out on paper.

c.   *Organizing the Issues*

Make a rough category outline. Use a piece of scratch paper to break the problem into the *major issues* it presents. Under each, simply note your ideas; perhaps a rough statement of the law, a list of important facts, arguments pro and con. A formal outline is not required—time will prevent it in any event. All you need is to jot down your ideas as you begin to focus on the issues.

A rough outline might look something like this:

```
Serious?
    Shook hands, asked if was serious
    But price real low
      men drinking
    Law: Would reasonable offeree think
      Bill making a serious offer?
Statute Frauds
    Nothing in writing before Bill's let-
    ter
    Involves sale of real property there-
    fore within statute
Should Bill's letter count?
    Doesn't show reflection
    Bill can't argue he never made promise
    Must letter mention which house, if
      more than one?
What about Sam's bookmaking?
    Illegal Contract?
    Not illegal on face. Extend rule?
    Car dealer & customer illegal left
      turn?
```

The process of thought is quite fluid. Thinking about one issue, a key point in another will pop into your head. As your rough outline shows the major issues, it allows you to jot down insights *where they belong*. For example, thinking about the illegality issue, it may strike you that the men met accidentally at the bar. "Where does that point fit? Under seriousness." You note it and return to considering illegality.

Once you have your rough outline, time to write. The outline format helps assure that you do not mix legal categories and helps with the matter of transitions.

Expect the fluid nature of thought to continue while writing the exam. New insights and perhaps new issues will come to you. Write so that you can easily accommodate this happening. Don't handcuff yourself with assertions like "There are two issues in this problem"—you may see more as you write. Also, write every other line in your bluebook, both to improve readability and to allow for last minute inspiration. (Unfortunately, the fluid nature of the process continues *after* you have completed the exam. You will be relaxing after the exam, watching a movie, perhaps talking with friends, when the cold chill hits you—"Oh no! I forgot the illegality issue!" Don't be overly concerned with this state of disquietude. First, very seldom does a student get all the issues and, second, the panic usually subsides after a few months.)

How long should you mull over the problem before you start to write? How long should you look for issues and organize your thoughts? Some recommend that you spend a third of your time thinking and organizing before writing. Rules of thumb, however, may prove dangerous. I can simply advise that it is of critical importance that you do spend *some* time and not begin writing immediately after you read the question. But be aware that tests are timed. It is far better to write something on all the questions than to write on only one, no matter how well organized that one answer might be. Remember that you have "miles to ride before you sleep."

6. Some Final Thoughts and Warranty

Be with the exam. Your engagement with the exam must be total. *Don't* have an agenda going in. Don't figure out beforehand what "is surely going to be covered" and expect to find it. Don't listen to second year students—never listen to second year students!—when they say "In Professor Quibble's class, all you need do is spot the issues" (or "All you need do is develop one or two issues in depth" or "Always come out on the side of the criminal defendant because Quibble is a communist!"). You will have so much to do in seeing, organizing, and writing about the issues that you won't have time to structure your answer to conform to what you "think" are the idiosyncrasies of the individual professor.

Similarly, don't spend too much time thinking about the *form* of your answer by asking "Are my transitions good? Am I being explicit? Am I considering both sides? Am I making up false issues?" These preoccupations will pull you away from the question. Your focus must remain on it.

Learn from the exam. After your first exam, spend some time with your Journal. Focus on the process of exam writing. What was going on with you? What did you do right? What mistakes did you make? How would you approach the exam differently? How would you study differently? Your insights, I am sure, will be more to the point than mine are.

Warranty. I cannot promise great success. I can promise, however, that if you work with this chapter, that if you do flunk, you will flunk with dignity!

PART THREE

BEYOND SKILLS

CHAPTER 9

FEAR AND LOATHING IN THE FIRST YEAR

A first year student at Harvard captures the feeling:

Why did I bother? Why did I care? Why was I afraid?

Imagine, is all that I can answer.

You have a stake. You have given up a job, a career, to do this. Or you have wanted to be a lawyer all your life.

All your life you've been good in school. All your life it's been something you could count on. You know that it's a privilege to be here. You've studied hours on a case that is a half page long. You couldn't understand most of what you read at first, but you have turned the passage inside out, drawn diagrams, written briefs. You could not be more prepared.

And when you get to class that demigod who knows all the answers, finds another student to say things you never could have. Clearer statements, more precise. And worse—far worse—notions, concepts, whole constellations of ideas that never turned inside your head.

Yes, there are achievements in the past. They're nice to bandage up your wounded self-esteem. But "I graduated college *magna cum laude*" is not the

Heglund Study & Practice—10 [*253*]

proper answer when the professor has just posed a question and awaits your response with the 140 other persons in the class.

The feeling aroused by all of that was something near to panic, a ferocious, grasping sense of uncertainty, and it held me, and I believe most of my classmates, often during that first week and for a long while after. On many occasions I discovered that I didn't even understand what I didn't know until I was halfway through a class. Nor could I ever see how anyone else seemed to arrive at the right answer. Maybe they were all geniuses. Maybe I was the dumbest guy around.

Scott Turow, *One L*

. . .

Much in this chapter will be negative. Law study is trying, disorienting, humiliating. It is also exhilarating, challenging, confidence building. Professor Kingsfield, dreaded Contracts Professor of *Paperchase*, bellows at his first year class:

Your minds are filled with mush. You will teach yourself the law. I will teach you how to think!

Pompous and overstated, yes. Yet there is something to it.

The first year is intellectual dynamite. Gone the lectures of undergraduate days, gone the endless, meandering discussions of Great Issues. Lectures fall to the "Socratic method"—students, not faculty, to bring forth knowledge. The great issues remain, yet in law there is a critical difference; they matter. Here a Hobbesian view of human nature means a certain criminal defendant

[*254*]

will go to prison rather than remain free; here, classical economic thought means the enforcement, rather than non-enforcement, of a specific contract. Here theories determine outcomes. Tested by reality, abstractions become more focused and urgent. When all is said and done, someone wins, someone loses.

Most law students, when they aren't complaining, discuss law. It is heady and fascinating stuff.

Another very positive aspect of the first year is the satisfaction that comes with mastering a new and difficult discipline. At first you will be doing it wrong; you will garble facts, misstate issues, and confuse holdings. After much hard work, you will do it right. That accomplishment is deeply satisfying.

On the other hand . . . .

There is a "ferocious, grasping sense of uncertainty." You've always been successful at school. You want to do well now. But how?

What is expected of me? How should I study? Is it worth the effort? Do I really want to be a lawyer? What is it I'm trying to learn? Will I flunk out?

Students going into other graduate programs, schools of education, philosophy, social work, have a fairly good idea what to expect because those graduate schools are not qualitatively different from their undergraduate programs. Law school is, in marked contrast, a whole new game.

[*255*]

Don't expect the sense of uncertainty to abate early. There is *very little feedback*. Traditionally there are no term papers or midterms. You will sit in a large class, classes over 100 are not uncommon, awaiting the *one and only* test, the final. Finals come and go and quite likely there is still no meaningful feedback; grades don't tell you what you are doing right or wrong.

Lack of feedback is one of the most bitter complaints of law students. Why the lack of feedback? Partly, perhaps mostly, economics. Legal education is graduate education on the cheap, one professor handling a class of 140! Recently there has been improvement. Many law schools now offer small classes in the first year. Students in these schools will take one of their courses in a class of 20 to 30. And, in the second and third years, there will be seminars and clinical courses that have a lower student/faculty ratio and hence more feedback. With these exceptions, the general law school model holds: large classes followed by a single final. Legal education simply does not look like other graduate education, a small group of students sitting around the table chatting with the professor.

This chapter will look at the psychological tensions of the first year. It will explore two common beliefs: "I'm the dumbest one here" and "Everyone here is viciously competitive, except me and my friends." It will then examine the fear of participation in class and the psychological impact of grades. The "ferocious, grasping sense of uncertainty" effects them all. The chapter will end with a discussion of two haunting first year questions: "Am I being turned into an intellectual zombie?"   "Is it okay to be a lawyer?"

1. Two Common First Year Beliefs

a. *I'm the Dumbest One Here!*

Take heart! *Every* first year student believes this. Only one is right! (The bad news is . . . .)

After the first few weeks in law school, I was convinced that all my classmates were geniuses. They said such profound, insightful things, things that would never, ever, occur to me. "It's curtains for me, I'll flunk out for sure!" I did find some solace in the fact that Boalt Hall, like most law schools today, flunked out very few students. (As admission standards rose, failure rates fell. Gone the classic First Day Greeting: "Look to the person to your right, look to the person at your left . . . .") Using the rumored "flunk out rate" as a basis, I concluded that I had to be smarter than only 3 or 4 of the 120 students in my section. Not bad odds. I would come to class, looking and listening to discover someone dumber than me. Weeks would pass. I grew desperate. Finally someone would say something that seemed wildly beside the point. Mark one down. At the end of the first semester the count

stood at three. It was going to be a cliffhanger.
(As it developed one of the three ended up in the
top 10% of the class. One of the really unnerving
things about the first year is that you can't even
tell who's dumb!)

As a law school teacher I think I know how to
account for the "everyone's smarter than me"
syndrome. It's that there are so many interesting and profound things to say. Student A and
student B will both have interesting, insightful
comments to make about a case, comments which
are, however, quite different. Student A recites;
student B is dumbstruck—"I would never have
thought of that; there are notions, concepts,
whole constellations of ideas that never turn inside my head!"

The insecurity, although understandable, leads
to viciousness. I, sitting, watching, counting, is
one example. Another is the pathetic posturing
that occurs.

    "I don't study more than an hour a day and under-
stand everything."

    "My LSAT is in the 99th percentile. What's
yours?"

    "Personally, I find Kingsfield a little weak on con-
sideration!"

How to cope with posturing? Take a tip from
a defensive linesman. Broadcasting a professional football game he told the following story. As
a player, often friends would ask him, "Doesn't
so-and-so play the same position as you do with

the Jets?" Indeed, so-and-so, did. "And what's-his-face, he plays the same position for the Rams?" Indeed he did. "Well those two guys always sack the quarterback. Why don't you?"

"Did you ever consider that they're better football players than I am?"

You can lose the posturing game ("I'll never make it with such talented people!") or you can attempt to win by inventing your own killer sword ("I didn't do that well on the LSAT but I do have a doctorate in philosophy!") Best, however, not to play: "Gee, did you ever consider you're smarter than I?"

b. *Law Students Are Viciously Competitive!*

Law students are aggressive, competitive, humorless and, worst of all, they study all the time. Now, of course, *I* wasn't that way as a law student, nor were my close friends. I am sure you and your friends aren't that way either. But we can agree that everyone else is.

One of my students wrote of her first day at law school. She met another woman and thought "She's smarter than I, more beautiful than I, and more emotionally stable." She took an instant dislike.

Who are you, the person seeing the other as "smarter, better looking" or the person being observed as "smarter, better looking?" You are, of course, *both*. As the observer, realize that your own insecurities and uncertainties may cause you

[*259*]

to improperly label and reject many of your classmates. They have much to offer you—don't reject them simply because they had the affront to
come to law school. If it hadn't been them, it
would have been someone else.

It is difficult to believe that you are also the
person being observed as smarter and better
looking. "What? Me scary?" Shocking, but
true. Think of it. All those super bright men
and women who are your classmates are terrified
of your intelligence, wit and emotional stability.
You, scary. It's true.

Competitiveness and aggressiveness are not
just psychological projections. They are also
quite real. Your classmates are competitive and
so are you. It is important to confront and contain your aggressiveness and competitiveness. It
will not do to simply deny these feelings, "Oh, I
don't care what grades I get or how I do; I just
want to get by!" Some students take denial to
the extreme of not trying; they do a minimum
amount of studying and miss class frequently.
(If you refuse to try, then failure will be less
painful. On the other hand, there is always the
possibility of the ultimate seventh grade fanta-
sy—an "A" in Math, an "F" for Effort.) You are
competitive or you wouldn't be in law school.
You have achieved recognition and pleasure in
competing successfully in the past. This is not
shameful. Accept this part of yourself; however, do not let it consume you.

Scott Turow, the author of *One L*, describes an incident from his first year. He and members of his study group were discussing whether they should share their class outlines with other students. Turow surprised himself by arguing that they should not:

> "I want the advantage," I said. "I want the competitive advantage. I don't give a damn about anybody else. I want to do better than they."
>
> My tone was ugly . . . .
>
> It took me a while to believe I had actually said that. I told myself I was kidding . . . . What had been suppressed all year was in the open now. All along there had been a tension between looking out for ourselves and helping each other; in the end, I did not expect anybody—not myself, either—to renounce a wish to prosper, to succeed. But I could not believe how *extreme* I had let things become, the kind of grasping creature I had been reduced to. I had not been talking about gentlemanly competition . . . . I had not been talking about any innocent striving to achieve. There had been murder in my voice . . . .
>
> That night I sat in my study and counseled myself . . . . It's a tough place, I told myself. Bad things are happening. Work hard. Do your best. Learn the law. But don't suffer, I thought. Don't fear. And for God's sake, don't give up your decency . . . .
>
> I had finally met my enemy, I figured, face to face.

One final thought on how competitive your classmates are. Much of what you will hear is simply false rumor or incorrect supposition.

Once after a few weeks of class a student came to me aghast. "Several people have already finished reading the book! What am I to do?" "How do you know they've finished reading the book?" "Because I saw their books. They're underlined all the way through!" Realize this: Some buy used books.

2.　Confusion and Terror in the Classroom

A typical first year scenario. You study one case half the night. The first several times through, nothing. You stick with it. You consult your law dictionary. You reread the case. Suddenly a glimmer; more slowly, order. Finally you are ready. Confidently you go to class. You are quickly shattered. "What does what we're talking about have to do with the case I read? I didn't understand it at all; maybe it's not even the same case!" The pain of trying hard and failing, the confusion and the panic that accompany it, often turn to bitterness. "These professors can't teach, even if they wanted to, which they don't; they just want to confuse!" It is as if they swore to some terrible misreading of the Prayer of St. Francis, "Where there is understanding, let me sow confusion."

Not so. A "case" is an invitation to *do* law. Your professor is trying to help you understand what it is to do law; she assumes you have a basic understanding of the case and quickly goes beyond it. "You will teach yourself the law; I will teach you how to think."

Expect your professors to understand the cases at different levels than you. They are lawyers; they know how to read cases; they know much law. What strikes them as important about a case likely will not be what you find important— it is a question of differing experiences and understandings. Do not lament.

A great cause of frustration is that students come to class expecting answers and get, instead, only more questions. Law school is confusing enough—naturally students long for rules to hold onto, such as "Public officials, to sue for libel, must allege malice." In class, the rules and the security they offer dissolve into a series of difficult questions. "What," queries the professor, "is malice?" "Is a basketball coach a public official?"

Law professors are part of the current intellectual milieu which downplays the ability to arrive at clear and certain answers. Psychology teaches the importance of the observer's point of view in what is observed; so too Physics. Anthropology teaches the relativism of beliefs and truth itself falls to the Sociology of Knowledge. Law has not been immune. Was a time that it was thought possible to have clear and certain laws; was a time when the following made sense:

> Certainty is the mother of repose; thus the law aims at certainty.

With a brilliant turn of phrase, Holmes captured the modern view:

Certainty is generally illusion and repose is not the destiny of man.

No wonder that law professors, committed to this view, are accused of "hiding the ball"; they don't believe there is one.

What of the terror of being called on? Partly it comes from our fear of "getting found out." Deep down we all know that we really aren't all that "hot." Sure, we've been able to fool the others but that "demigod" up front might prove too much. Relax. In all likelihood that demigod is not as tough as he looks. Likely he'll be unable to expose the real you, the incompetent you. (Indeed, he probably fears, deep down, that he's not that hot, that he doesn't measure up to Kingsfield!)

a. Being Called on in Class: Herein the Socratic Method

You'll be in class one day, just sitting there, minding your own business, actually rather enjoying the discussion, when, without warning, you hear someone calling your name. The Professor! All eyes turn to you. There is total silence. The Professor is good enough to repeat the question:

Quis outouc ptyo xovbiyeous oppeuawud ipptons?

Relax! Take a deep breath, loosen your jaw. Shift your attention from "Oh no, it's happening

to me!" Focus on the question. If necessary ask
that it be repeated. Answering the question remember that you are probably doing a whole lot
better than you think you are. Just because *you*
thought of something, just because *you* understood a point, doesn't mean that it is so obvious it
doesn't justify discussion. What you have to say
might be terrific. Realize that you appear less
nervous than you feel. When your classmates recite, they do not *appear* nervous even though
they surely are. Listening to someone recite you
do not hear the pounding of his heart nor feel the
quiver in his lips.

Confront, finally, the dreaded fear: You make
a total fool of yourself and your classmates actually laugh at your bumbling, inept response.
You will walk from the room shattered, unable to
look your classmates in the eye. Nonetheless
you will overhear smatterings of their conversa-
tions. Suddenly it will strike you:

"What? They're talking about other things, law,
baseball, the weather. No one is talking about my
shame, my disgrace."

Be the fool and learn that the world goes on
much as before. This is a valuable, although
somewhat disappointing, lesson. The willingness
to risk being the fool is absolutely essential to effective lawyering. Who was foolish enough to
first assert that separate means unequal? To argue that, despite tradition and practice, police
must warn defendants of their right to remain silent? To suggest that manufacturers of goods

could be held "strictly liable" for injuries their products cause? Law demands creativity; creativity demands we try new things; fear of playing the fool demands we don't.

Welcome the opportunity that law school affords, that of being the fool before 120 classmates. Let them laugh as you learn to risk and hence free your creativity. Of course, the worse you are, the more they will love you. As you stammer and fret, there will be a collective sign— "There's one more we can mark down." They'll see.

What happens if you *don't* fall on your face at the first question? What if you are actually able to answer it? Then expect another. Survive that, expect a third. Welcome to the *Socratic Method.* There is probably no more controversial aspect of law school than the method wherein the professor presses the student to justify his opinion, meeting answers with questions and arguments with counter-arguments. Some denounce the method as destructive of the student's self-esteem, as a device of verbal terror designed to expose the student's ignorance and to ridicule him before his fellows. Others see the ultimate irony. In law school, the argument runs, the method is not used to pursue Truth but rather to destroy Truth. The process of demanding justifications, of meeting argument with counter-argument, destroys the student's basic moral outlook. Extreme relativism reigns. Watergate becomes the expectation.

Plato himself saw the possible danger. In *The Republic* he warns against "plunging the young into philosophical discussion" as it destroys notions of honor and right learned in childhood.

> [S]uppose he's confronted by the question, "What does 'honorable' mean?" He gives the answer he has been taught by the lawmaker, but he is argued out of his position. He is refuted again and again from many different points of view and at last is reduced to thinking that what he called honorable might just as well be called disgraceful. He comes to the same conclusion about justice, goodness, and all the things most revered . . . .

> [W]e shall see him renounce all morality and become a lawless rebel.

The *goal* of the method is not to inculcate relativism; the *goal* is not to expose student ignorance; the *goal* is not to ridicule. The *result* of the method may be all these things. Hopefully if you understand the goal you will be able to deal with the hurt and correct for the negative results.

The goal of the method is *to force students to justify their positions, to consider other points of view and to realize that even the best of arguments, even the best of theories, suffer from "inconvenient facts."*

To illustrate take a case in which a tenant is suing the landlord for negligently maintaining a common stairway. The landlord sets up as defense a clause in the lease wherein the tenant

agreed not to sue the landlord for negligence.   Is
the clause valid?

> Student: I don't think the tenant should be held
> to her promise not to sue if that promise
> was buried in the small print in the
> lease.
>
> Professor: Why not?
>
> Student: It just isn't fair.
>
> Professor: Why not?

Here the student may feel that she is being attacked. Still worse, the student may feel that
she is being argued out of her sense of justice.
This is not the professor's goal; rather it is to
force the student to get to bedrock as to why she
feels the way she does, indeed, as to why her
sense of justice dictates it.

> Student: Well, it seems to me that one reason we
> enforce a person's promises is to pro-
> tect, to further, personal autonomy.
> The whole notion of contract is prem-
> ised on actual choice. Now if the tenant
> didn't know what she was signing, then
> the whole justification for enforcing
> promises collapses.

Behind our sense of justice often lie good sound
reasons. For the professor to insist upon their
verbalization is not to attack them.

> Professor: Good. But what if the evidence showed
> she read the contract? Would you still
> think the agreement unfair?
>
> Student: Yes. The facts show that she was poor
> and probably not that well educated.

> She really didn't know that she was giving up valuable rights.

Professor: Good. But isn't that a little paternalistic? If the law doesn't enforce her promise because she is poor and not well educated, aren't we saying that she is legally incompetent? That she doesn't have that most basic of rights, the right to mean what she says?

The professor is not attacking the student, not trying to trip her up and humiliate her. Nor is the professor trying to argue her out of her position and turn her into a mouthpiece for landlords. The professor is attempting to force her to consider other points of view, to adopt the "yes, but" form of reasoning. "Yes, my initial reaction is valid but there are counter considerations."

Max Weber, the great sociologist, wrote in "Science as a Vocation" that the "primary task of a useful teacher is to teach his students to recognize 'inconvenient' facts . . . . [F]or every opinion there are facts that are extremely inconvenient, for my own no less than for others."

The teacher should force the student to understand what his opinions and arguments entail. Weber continues:

> If you take such and such a stand, then . . . you have to use such and such means in order to carry out your conviction. Now, these means are perhaps such that you believe you must reject them . . . . Does the end "justify" the means? Or does it not? The teacher can confront you with the necessity of this choice . . . .

[*269*]

[The teacher] can force the individual, or at least we
can help him, to give himself an *account of the ultimate meaning of his own conduct*. This appears to
me as not so trifling a thing to do, even for one's
own personal life. Again, I am tempted to say of a
teacher who succeeds in this: he stands in the service of "moral" forces; he fulfills the duty of bringing about self-clarification and a sense of responsibility.

Without question few of us succeed at this
very often and, without question, our successes
as well as failures create tensions. Having made
a very compelling argument why the tenant
should be excused from her promise to pay, it is
discomforting to have the professor point out
that the argument entails paternalism and seems
to deny tenants the very basic right to "mean
what they say." Again, in Weber's analysis, the
professor is not suggesting that the promise
should be enforced; the professor is forcing the
student to realize the important values which
would be sacrificed if the promise were not enforced. "The teacher can confront you with the
necessity of choice."

Knowing the goals of the Socratic Method may
lessen hostility to it. Knowing what it is to conduct a Socratic class may lessen the hurt. Classes never go as well as written dialogue; my classes seldom go as I planned. "Hurly-burly" is the
best adjective; "roller coaster" is the best analogy.

Preparing for class I see the cases raising key issues, issues important for the class to discuss. I carefully note them on my pad. I even rehearse the class in my mind. (Let me assure you, it always goes brilliantly.) But mine is not to lecture about what I see in the cases; mine is to help the student bring out what is important. Glancing at my pad and then the seating chart, I ask a student to recite the case. Often the student will raise wildly tangential points. It is not so much that he is wrong, it is that he is not approaching the case as he must if he is to practice law. Take one example. A torts case, out of Iowa in the 1930's, involved a plaintiff who attended a circus, sat in the front row and was defecated on by a horse. The *legal* question is assumption of risk. There are many other interesting questions. Why would someone in the 1930's in Iowa be so upset about the incident so as to sue? This may be a better, more profound question; but it is not a *legal* question. As the professor your job is to help students recognize and deal with legal questions. Asking a student to recite you can expect almost anything. Seldom do you get the response you were planning on; you must instantaneously decide if the tangential remark is worth pursuing (often I find that I overlooked important legal issues in a case) and, if the point is not worth pursuing, how to gently bring the student back.

It ain't easy. Undoubtedly, I often too quickly reject what the student believes is a valid point;

undoubtedly, I am too abrupt with students
whom I feel meandering; and, undoubtedly, the
shock and dismay I occasionally experience
shows. These are but inadvertent and unfortunate slights and insults caused by the intellectually challenging and unplanned nature of Socratic
discourse. Forgive them.

b. *Volunteering in Class*

For a law school class to succeed students must
participate, must share their insights, questions
and experiences. You can't sit on your hands
and then complain that the class is boring. A
good class is as much the doing of the students
as it is the professor's. Both sides have a responsibility.

You have an obligation to participate, to take
the chance of being wrong by making a point you
think valid, of playing the fool by asking what
might be a "dumb question." (If you have a
dumb question probably everyone else in the
class does too—you will be a hero for asking it.)
It is irresponsible to just sit in every class, always taking and never risking.

Volunteering has payoffs as well. Even if it
isn't "counted" towards your grade, volunteering
gives you experience trying out your ideas and
thinking on your feet, important lawyering skills.

Don't volunteer all the time as there is a definite drawback. Volunteering requires blocking
out remarks of other students while you wait un-

til you are called on. It is difficult to listen and
retain what you want to say or ask. (Try jotting
down a few words and then turn attention to the
class). And, if you volunteer too much, other students will resent you. (As the person doing the
resenting, consider who is responsible for the
"Bigmouths." The professor needs participation
and is likely as sick of them as you. But if
they're the only ones raising their hands
. . . .)

The main point about volunteering is that it
should be a matter of choice, not fear. William
Blake has a marvelous phrase, "mind-forged
manacles." Don't forge: "I'm just not the kind
of student who raises her hand!" Volunteer at
least occasionally, first because you have an obligation to your classmates, second because you
have an obligation to yourself not to imprison
yourself in a closet.

3. Grades

Take a group of exceptional students, students
with distinguished academic accomplishments and
with varied and significant life experiences.
With a wave of the bluebook, turn most "average." Magic. The magic of grading also anoints
the select few. No matter in which group you
fall, you run grave dangers, dangers which will
be presently discussed. First a few words on the
incredible dimensions grades assume in the life of
the law student.

Grading is done anonymously. Professors don't know whose paper they are grading. To maintain anonymity, you use your "number" on your exam, not your name. Getting your exam number is a significant event in itself. While it may take several hours, you will be able to figure out just why your number is extremely lucky—do you realize that 32 is three 7's and one 11? Lucky number.

Grades are posted by exam number. Where I went to law school, we were graded, not by letter grades, but by number grades. The posted grades look something like this:

Corporations—Professor Jenkins

Student	Grade	
18	65	
20	77	
24	72	
25	80	
27	60	
32	88	(I told you that 32 was a lucky number)
35	74	
39	68	
43	72	
50	69	
56	81	
58	74	
62	61	

You would think that such a list would interest only students in the particular class. Surely first year students would have no interest—Corporations is a second year class. Wrong! First year

[*274*]

students swarm when the grades are posted. They are silent, in awe. In a hushed, respectful tone, one will offer:

"Look at 27. 60!"

"Yeah, look at 62!"

"Gosh, 32 got an 88. That's the top grade."

Law school grades have a wildly disproportionate effect. Never mind their previous accomplishments, never mind the kind of people they are, 27 is a 60, 32 an 88.

First I'll talk to 32.

If you do well gradewise you should feel extremely proud. It should be a time of celebration. It should also be a time of reflection. You are gifted—to excel in such a competitive environment is more than a product of hard work— almost everyone worked hard. You can't take total credit for your success. You have a special gift. What are you going to do with it? Sell it to the highest bidder or consider using it for the greatest good?

"Stars" can fall victim to pomposity. They peacock down the corridors on their way to the office of Law Review and suddenly take everything they say seriously. They hang out only with "good" students. If you want to become a disagreeable person, that's your affair. If you cut yourself off from "average students," however, you are cutting yourself off from a great deal of talent, insight and wisdom.

Don't be seduced. In the rush of success you may not end up where you originally wanted to be. Law school success will open many "prestige" jobs; there is nothing wrong with a "prestige" job unless you wanted to do something different all along. Professional seduction is one danger, the other is intellectual seduction. As a "winner" in the system it will be more difficult for you to critically test the underlying premises of that system. Like other institutions, law schools rest on certain assumptions. Are they correct? There is a serious and significant debate over legal education and the values it reflects. The danger is that it is difficult to fault the institution that has crowned you. Stars too quickly embrace the institution's world view and too quickly and too defensively label criticisms "sour grapes."

What if you end up in the middle of the class? Don't forget who you are. You are a talented person or you would not have been admitted. Some students stage dramatic "academic comebacks." Realize too that "average" law students make good lawyers and incredible contributions. Earl Warren had an undistinguished career as a law student.

The danger the "average" student faces is intellectually dropping out of law school, living off of commercial outlines and feeding on the false rumor "What you learn in law school hasn't anything to do with practice!" Unable to cope with being "average," some students reject the institution which bestowed the label. The institution survives, the student suffers. There is much to be learned in the second and third years of law school; by continuing to work, you may never get an "88" but you will know much more when you graduate and you will be a much better lawyer.

Finally, what if you do terribly? Some don't catch on at first, others are handicapped by personal problems. These students can "turn it around." The law isn't for everyone, however. If you don't do well at something, likely you won't enjoy doing it. While lawyering involves many skills that aren't "tested for" in law school, practice also involves the skill that is tested for. Why continue with something that looks like it will be a continued struggle for you? Obviously this is a question that can be considered *only after* you get your grades.

———————

Fear and Loathing. Note the relationship. Much of our loathing is a product of our fear. But not all. Surely not all. Some professors abuse their power; some, believing it important to toughen you up, forget restraint. I know because I too was a law student. Some law students *are* viciously competitive; some, for whatever reason, have hatred in their hearts. All of the negatives you might see in law school are not simply projections born of fear. Some are real. Your mission is simply to survive them and not become their victim. Solace may be found in writing your Journal.

I have only two further points before turning to the Haunting First Year Questions. The first is to recommend a book, *Becoming A Lawyer: A Humanistic Perspective on Legal Education and Professionalism* (Dvorkin *et al.*). Despite its cumbersome title, the book is rich in ideas and compassion. I have learned much from it. The format is to offer a short selection by the likes of Tolstoy or Carl Rogers followed by reaction pieces by lawyers, law professors and law students. It addresses many significant issues. I recommend it, preferably for semester break or after the first year—before then you have too much law to learn.

Finally, as to fear and loathing, know that too much can be made of it. One year at the first year orientation the topic was "Psychological Pressures on the First Year Student." Many spoke and office hours of the campus psychologists were posted. Five weeks into the semester a student came to me, aghast.

"I can't understand it. I still have friends. I'm still married. I go to occasional movies and read a few novels. What am I doing wrong?"

————————

Much ink (and beer) has been spilt on the issue of whether, and if whether, now and in what direction, legal education affects law students. Often these scholarly articles (and late night discussions) come to (degenerate into) the issue of whether any decent human being could actually become a lawyer. The remainder of this chapter highlights some of the arguments. They are the stuff of journal entries. How is legal education affecting *you*? How can *you* become a lawyer?

4. *Haunting First Year Question Number One:* Is Law School Turning Me Into an Intellectual Zombie?

There is little doubt that you will experience the world differently once you have completed your legal education. Mark Twain said it best. He describes, in *Life on the Mississippi*, how, as a river boat captain, he came to read nature, to recognize that a floating log means a rising river, that a slanting mark on the water means a deadly reef ready to sink a steamship, that a particular sun means a wind tomorrow.

Now when I had mastered the language of this water . . . I had made a valuable acquisition. But I had lost something too . . . . All the grace, the beauty, the poetry, had gone out of the majestic river . . . .

The romance and the beauty were all gone from the river. All the value any feature of it had for me now was the amount of usefulness it could furnish toward compassing the safe piloting of a steamboat. Since those days, I have pitied doctors from my heart. What does the lovely flush in a beauty's cheek mean to a doctor but a "break" that ripples above some deadly disease? Are not all her visible charms sown thick with what are to him the signs

[*279*]

and symbols of hidden decay?   Does he ever see her
beauty at all, or doesn't he simply view her profes-
sionally, and comment upon her unwholesome condition all to himself?   And doesn't he sometimes wonder whether he has gained most or lost most by
learning his trade?

Whether you gain most or lose most from learning your trade is a quite important question, one
with which you must grapple. Your journal
would be a good turf. Before I offer my own
opinions, consider the following questions. Return to them as a third year student.

	Answer as a 1st year student	Answer as a 3rd year student
Law school will increase my respect for law, lawyers and courts.		
Law school will sharpen my analytical ability.		
Law school will increase my sense of justice, fairness and morality.		
Law school will increase my self-confidence.		
Law school will increase my respect for and appreciation of other people, both within and without law school.		

[*280*]

	Answer as a 1st year student	Answer as a 3rd year student
Most of my classmates are ethical.		
Most of my classmates are motivated primarily by big bucks and social prestige.		
I would recommend law school to a good friend or close relative.		
I will find being a lawyer meaningful.		

The usual rap is that law school deadens your sense of justice. Perhaps. By forcing you to recognize facts inconvenient to your sense of justice, law school dampens your outrage. This I take to be a good rather than bad thing. Justice does not need outrage. You can still condemn the landlord for attempting to hide from liability in a maze of fine print. Knowing that your condemnation involves the sacrifice of other compelling values does not rob you of your ability to act; it simply steals your self-righteousness.

Law school deadens your sense of justice in another way, however, a way which cannot be justified. Law school makes justice a matter of abstraction and turns clients into caricatures. Before exploring this, a few words on how law school *enlivens* your sense of justice.

There is no doubt that you will graduate with a heightened sense of *procedural* justice. In the 1960's lawyers working with Legal Services Programs trod where lawyers had not before: representing welfare mothers cut from the rolls, representing high school students expelled from school, representing farm workers evicted from county labor camps. What these lawyers found was a total lack of due process. The importance of due process, the need to have hearings to test fact and the need to have rules to check decisions, is not self-evident. Welfare administrators, high school vice-principals, and county housing officials were not aware they were doing anything wrong; they were not aware that they were denying people important rights. Lawyers, because of law school, were aware and what they found shocked them. Needless to say, the procedures were corrected.

Even if you are to condemn law school for deadening your sense of substantive justice (your sense of when it is fair to cut welfare mothers, expel high school students, and evict farm workers), grant law school its due—it will teach you a whole aspect of Justice generally overlooked.

What then of this allegation that legal education dampens your sense of justice by making jus-

tice abstract and by turning clients into caricatures? What's better proof than a confession?

In my first year Contracts class I wished to review. I put a hypothetical which involved a seller
of widgets who is continually late in making his
deliveries. His buyer finally becomes so incensed
that he cancels the contract. After stating the
problem, I asked:

"If you were the seller, what would you say?"

What I was looking for was a discussion of the
various common law theories which throw the
buyer into breach for cancelling the contract, legal arguments which would allow seller to crush
buyer.

After asking the question, I looked around the
room for a volunteer. As is so often the case
with first year students, I found that they were
all either writing in their notebooks or inspecting
their shoes. There was, however, one eager face,
that of an eight-year-old son of one of my students. He was, it seems, suffering through Contracts due to his mother's sin of failing to find a
sitter. Suddenly he raised his hand. Such behavior, even from an eight-year old, must be reward-
ed.

"Okay," I said, "What would you say if you
were the seller?"

"I'd say 'I'm sorry'."

In casebooks clients are caricatures and not very flattering ones at that. Does anyone, in any of the cases, act decently? Does anyone say "I'm sorry?" A typical law school question is "What else should the plaintiff have argued?" This is an extremely useful teaching technique. Soon, however, the world becomes populated with people whose only interest is in winning. If all we knew came from casebooks, we would conclude that the only interest of defendants (be they civil or criminal) is avoiding responsibility, and, if that's not possible, in gaining as much procedural delay as possible. As for plaintiffs, their only interest is in getting "more."

The caricature stays with us when we enter practice. Criminal defense lawyers are convinced that defendants confess only because they weren't properly warned. Given the standardized ends of criminal defendants, to escape from criminal conviction at all costs, no one confesses voluntarily. Never mind the need to make atonement, the need to relieve tension and the need to communicate. Never mind, in short, *Crime and Punishment*. No wonder, as a young lawyer, I would actually feel betrayed when a client would want to pay a creditor rather than assert all the defenses and counterclaims I had found.

Justice may lie in assuming responsibility rather than escaping it, in compromising claims rather than maximizing them, in saying "I'm sorry" rather than "I got ya!"

And what of this matter of abstraction? Note that Seller doesn't even have a name, much less a life history. Can justice be a matter of the manipulation of abstract rules or must it be the matter of concrete and specific individuals and events?

Writes law professor John Noonan, in *Persons and Masks of the Law:*

> As a law student, I saw, or thought I saw, the great advantage of legal education over the philosophical education I had just received—it dealt with cases. Seavey, [one of Noonan's Law school professors] used to confess an inability to think if confronted by an abstract proposition—"Give me a case," he would demand. Through cases, generalizations were tested. Working with cases, I supposed, was a way of exercising and developing a sense of justice—a sense of what was due to particular individuals in a concrete situation. Law students and *a fortiori* lawyers, I imagined, had a better sense of justice than philosophers or, say, sociologists. Unlike such dealers in abstractions, the lawyers could never forget that their actions affected persons.
>
> After twenty years' experience, I see that I was wrong. The cases are not concrete enough. The characters in them, turning into A or B, P or D, lose personal identity.

As a young lawyer, I don't think I really understood tort law until I had to tell a father whose seven-year-old son had lost an eye during school recess that "there was nothing to be done." I had diligently researched the law and concluded that no one was legally responsible. And I don't think I really understood criminal law until one of my clients, a young mother, was sentenced to two years in the state prison. She had been on bail pending sentencing. The Probation Department was recommending prison but I told her I would do my best before the judge. Holding her small baby, she stood beside me at the hearing. I failed. The judge said:

"I commit the defendant to the California Department of Correction for a period of two years."

The bailiff stepped behind "the defendant," put his hand on her shoulder, and pointed to the door at the back of the courtroom, the door that led to the "holding tank" and, from there, to prison. She was not to leave by the door she came in; she turned and handed me her child.

The realization that we are dealing with persons rather than masks does not necessarily mean our rules and actions would be different. Our concept of justice may require that some kids will go without legal recompense for a lifetime of blindness and that some young mothers will go to prison. However, legal actors must realize their actions affect not sellers and buyers, plaintiffs and defendants; they affect human beings.

————————

During your three years in law school you will hear much debate over legal education. Engage in it as it raises significant issues, not only about legal education but also about the practice of law. The best summary of the debate comes from Bellow and Moulton, *The Lawyering Process:*

Assumption

> The competitive law school environment teaches the independence, aggressiveness and initiative that are required for a lawyer to function well in an adversary system.

Counter Assumption

> The intensely competitive atmosphere in many law schools teaches lawyers: (i) to be exceedingly risk averse—to avoid situations where they might look bad, to hedge all bets, to beware of commitments; (ii) to collaborate with colleagues to avoid the stress and anxiety of intense competition or to "drop out" and "just do enough to make a respectable showing"; (iii) to conform to the requirements and demands of those with the power to decide who will be the winners and losers in the competition.

Assumption

> Students learn to be tough-minded and to "take it" in ways that they need to do well in practice.

Counter Assumption

> Lawyers learn to dominate those who are vulnerable (e.g., clients, third parties or opponents) and to accommodate those who are powerful.

Assumption

> The probing and careful examination of all sides of an issue in terms of consistency, rationality and the interests and policies at stake produces a skepticism and flexibility that is important in client relations and zealous, rigorous advocacy.

[*287*]

Counter Assumption

The emphasis on skepticism and examination of the merits of all positions without confronting the student with the necessity of choosing, acting, and living with consequences often produces a relativism so extreme that many lawyers no longer believe in the possibility of ethical discourse, consensus on values, or moral justification.

Assumption

Emphasis on rationality is needed to produce hard-headed lawyers who will not let emotionalism interfere with their professionalism.

Counter Assumption

Emphasis on rationality prevents understanding of the emotional and moral side of lawyering and cuts the students off from a valuable part of themselves.

Assumption

Recognition of personal inadequacy and the experience of uncertainty are important motivations to work hard and master the complex skills, systems and rules that law practice requires.

Counter Assumption

Inadequacy and uncertainty are experienced as unpleasant and undesirable and students seek to resolve these dilemmas as expeditiously as possible. This often means pursuing some less desirable avenue than developing skill and mastery, e.g., oversimplification; rote learning; redefinition of the task in manageable terms (what do I need to do or know to get by). People are more highly motivated by tasks that are challenging and require stretching one's competencies, but can be achieved.

Assumption

> The rigor of legal education sorts and brings to the top the very best talent and the most excellent minds.

Counter Assumption

> Law schools reinforce existing social and economic advantages and disadvantages with some preference for those with particular kinds of verbal facility and a high tolerance for competition and uncertainty.

And to add one more item to the debate:

Assumption

> Stress on the lawyer's role of defending any and all assures that unpopular people will have legal representation.

Counter Assumption

> The notion that everyone should be represented undercuts student idealism by implying that it makes no difference what side you are on. Given the current distribution of wealth in this country, lawyer neutrality, and that of the law school, favors those who can afford legal services. (The best criminal defenses are those given white collar criminals and perhaps drunk drivers rather than ghetto residents who rob gas stations.)

Return to this debate periodically. You are likely to conclude that there is truth in *both* positions.

———

5. *Haunting First Year Question Number Two:* Can a Decent Human Be a Lawyer?

Many students think the profession sleazy and the adversary system immoral. Why do law students think this? Why is it, as a philosophy professor once pointed out, that law students are much more critical of their profession than are other graduate students of theirs?

I think partly it has to do with the way law is taught. In the cases, the lawyers are not presented as acting particularly nobly; they are presented as making better or worse arguments. Just as their clients seem only interested in winning, so too the lawyers. No reaching the unreachable star here.

Once I met with a group of students for beer. Talking about my experiences as a lawyer, I became animated. My days had been exciting and full; my contributions and accomplishments, I felt, many and significant. Afterwards a student faulted me for not sharing that excitement and those experiences in class. "When I was listening to you, I wanted to be a lawyer. Usually, sitting in class or reading the cases, it seems so boring and pointless. Why don't you spend some time in class about that?" Right on! The faculty must accept partial responsibility for the negative view students have of practice.

Another cause of the view that practice is sleazy stems from the fact that, in the abstract, the

[*290*]

adversary system is just that. I have taught and I have practiced. Teaching, the adversary system makes little sense to me; returning to practice it makes a great deal. Representing a young mother who is about to lose her baby, one does not feel like an immoral "hired gun." In combating the welfare worker who would have the state take the baby, one comes to appreciate the adversary system: It slows up the process of making decisions and challenges the facts upon which they are to be made. In this case the welfare worker wanted to take the baby because the mother had told her she was going to "circumcise him" at home; it developed that the mother did not know what "circumcision" meant and had intended something quite different and quite innocuous in using the word.

My view is that law is an honorable profession. If you are to condemn it, don't condemn it in the abstract. Read biographies of lawyers. Talk with lawyers. Read what lawyers have to say about their jobs in the last chapter of this book. Some, you will find, rush where the brave dare not go. Holmes said that it is possible to "live greatly within the law."

Do it.

CHAPTER 10

THE SECOND AND THIRD YEARS

The rush and intensity of the first year become the calm of the second and third. Gone the fear and anxiety born of uncertainty. You will now know what is expected, both in class and on examinations; you will now know how to read cases and how to engage in Socratic dialogue. You will also know your place in the inevitable scholastic pecking order. Be the news good or bad, it will surely be liberating. Grades no longer will be the ever present concern; you are now free to learn to know rather than to impress.

While some find tranquillity routine and boring, most prosper and grow. The academic pace slackens; there is time to pursue friendships and personal interests. Movies and plays again become something other than study breaks squeezed between Contracts and Torts. This chapter considers second and third year options—law review, courses, clerking. It also suggests some spices—teaching law in high schools, and using the humanities, literature and film, to deepen your understanding of law and lawyering. Making the most of the second and third years, however, is less a question of taking the right courses and more a question of having the *right attitude*. If that sounds a little "Boy Scoutish," so be it. Visualize a campfire, smell the pines, and feel the mug of hot chocolate; we're going to talk the right attitude.

1. The Right Attitude

The last two years of law school are not putting in time, waiting for your career to begin. It has already begun; the last two years of law school are the second and third of your professional life. How to make the most of them?

Your first and primary task is to learn law. Some of it, perhaps even most of it, you will find a chore. That is not the point. Law was not invented to entertain. Realize that in the world of practice things are much different. In practice, the law is vibrant. Cases, statutes and doctrines are no longer things to be studied; they are tools to be used. You have a client and he has a goal. You research the law and all seems well. Then you find the case of *Smedley v. Jones*. First comes consternation, then panic! All is lost—*Smedley* will not allow your client to accomplish his goal. Energy and enthusiasm snap as you reread the heartless prose. A glimmer and then an excitement "Perhaps *Smedley* has been overruled!" Heart pounding you check, but alas, *Smedley* is still good law. *Smedley* smiles smugly. In the darkness comes a flash. "What about that argument we discussed in Torts? Perhaps I can use it to distinguish *Smedley*!" With growing excitement you reread the case. "Yes, yes, it

[*293*]

will work. In fact, reading *Smedley* this way means that it actually supports our position!"

Mark my words: in the quiet of the law library there is much drama, suspense and rejoicing.

Meanwhile, back in law school, *Smedley* just sits there, twenty pages of uninspired prose. Study him closely. Otherwise, he may crush you in practice. Because the inert *Smedley* is hard work, it is easy to fall victim to the myth that what you learn in law school isn't important in practice, that it is all "theoretical junk." Bananas! From my own experience I know this to be false. I met my share of *Smedleys;* those that I tamed, I tamed because I did not tune out those "nice" theoretical discussions in law school. To confess, I did not find those discussions easy and many I did not understand at all. Nonetheless, I stayed awake and kept trying. I was a better lawyer for it; I did a better job representing my clients.

The right attitude, then, is to commit yourself to learn as much law as possible. It is also to realize your unique opportunity: to study with, to argue with, to learn with those intelligent and concerned folk who are your fellows and faculty. Commit yourself to share in the rich intellectual life of the school.

Enough of the attitude, what of the options?

2. Law Review

Law reviews present a mind boggling affront.

During the summer after the first year of law school, the law review student traditionally writes a "Casenote" focusing on a particular recent appellate court decision, usually either that of a U.S. Court of Appeals or a State Supreme Court. The student first states what the court decided and then analyzes that decision on the basis of prior decisions and social policy. Then the student pronounces the decision "wrong" or, with perhaps even greater arrogance, "right." Mind you, for all we know, this student has accomplished absolutely nothing in his or her life except for managing a good grade in Contracts and Civil Procedure, perhaps even one in Torts. Do second year medical students routinely castigate leading surgeons? Routinely congratulate heart specialists with "All things considered, nice job!"?

Holmes wrote:

The life of the law is not logic, it is experience.

The sociology of law reviews suggests, *au contraire*, that the life of the law is not wisdom, it is wit.

This regular affront to the bench, however, does play an institutional role. In our political structure, appellate court judges are generally free of constituency and hence of accountability. Where judges are elected the elections usually are pro forma. Who is to call judges to task for sloppy decisions and opinions? Second year barracuda! To affront the gods, it develops, is perhaps the most religious activity of all.

A vast majority of law schools have law reviews. They provide an outlet for scholarly work (by academics, judges and practitioners) as well as a place for student members to publish. Reviews are run almost exclusively by students with very little help or interference by the faculty. Student editors, who were selected by the out-going group of student editors, decide what to publish and in what form. (Academics, practitioners and undoubtedly Supreme Court Justices have felt the sting of the returned manuscript marked extensively in red; better that, of course, than simply returned.)

Originally membership was offered only to students at the academic top of their first year class. Most reviews today allow for additional students to "write on" by winning a writing contest open to all students irrespective of class rank.

"Law review" is notoriously hard work. Should you accept membership if offered? Yes! You will be involved in the life of the law and you will learn lawyering skills. Additionally, it helps get a job.

Law reviews contribute substantially to the profession; as a member you help make that contribution. The brooding omnipresence of hungry second year writers creates an informal check on judicial abuse. Student writing contributes in positive ways as well. Practitioners rely on student notes as research tools. Occasionally a student note will be cited in a judicial opinion and the contribution to the growth of the law is direct and tangible. Student editors can make a major impact; they decide what will be published. Law reviews, usually through symposium issues, have focused national attention on otherwise neglected areas of the law, such as the law of the poor, the law of mental health, the law of the elderly. These student efforts have made major contributions both to the profession and to society.

Law review work helps your school. The better the Review, the better the image of the school. A good image makes for a better place to be; faculty, students and staff will feel a sense of pride. Better image has more tangible rewards as well. The better the image, the easier it will be for the school to attract good professors; the better the image, the easier it will be for all graduates, not just those on law review, to find jobs.

Law review is a great educational experience. You will write an original piece of work after doing extensive research. Your product will be extensively edited. It is hard and taxing work, make no mistake, but in the end you will have produced a solid piece of legal writing. Beyond the writing and research skills, you will be learning a standard of excellence that you will carry with you into your professional life. You will know when you're being sloppy and, most likely, you won't tolerate it.

Law review also helps come interview time. Although membership is more important to some employers than to others, it helps with all. Simply put, it is easier to get a job if you have been on law review, even if the job is with the public defender or with legal aid. The only downside law review has in terms of employment is that working on the review might cause you to take a job you really don't want. More of that danger in the chapter on careers.

There is one other danger of law review which deserves mention: pomposity. Occasionally the students on law review set themselves apart from the rest of the student body, having their own study groups and outlines. Partly this may be a defensive reaction: many students not on law review simply assume that those that are must be pompous and hence reject them. Whatever the cause, the isolation is quite regrettable. It cripples your education to cut off large groups of your classmates; each person has much to offer.

If you are invited to be on law review, accept. Then read "Goodbye to Law Review," 23 *Virginia Law Review* 38 (1936). Written by then Yale Law Professor Fred Rodell, it has both wisdom and wit.

There are two things wrong with almost all legal writing. One is style. The other is content.

[I]t seems to be a cardinal principle of law review writing and editing that nothing may be said forcefully and nothing may be said amusingly. This, I take it, is in the interest of something called dignity.

It does not matter that most people—and even lawyers come into this category—read either to be convinced or to be entertained. It does not matter that even in the comparatively rare instances when people read to be informed, they like a dash of pepper or a dash of salt along with their information. The won't get any seasoning if the law reviews can help it. The law reviews would rather be dignified and ignored.

The best way to get a laugh out of a law review is to take a couple of drinks and then read an article, any article, aloud. That can be really funny.

Rodell's ultimate point goes, however, to content. And in this he is quite serious. Society faces real and pressing problems. Law may be our only hope.

It seems never to have occurred to most of the studious gents who diddle around in the law reviews with intricacies of contributory negligence, consideration, or covenants running with the land that . . . they might be diddling while Rome burned.

I do not wish to labor the point but perhaps it had best be stated once in dead earnest. With law as the only alternative to force as a means of solving the myriad problems of the world, it seems to me that the articulate among the clan of lawyers might, in their writings, be more pointedly aware of those problems, might recognize that the use of law to help toward their solution is the only excuse for the law's existence, instead of blithely continuing to make mountain after mountain out of tiresome technical molehills.

As a member of law review, realize the seriousness of the mission, that you can, in some small

way, help law solve the problems of the world.
And as a writer for law review, recall the Rodell
Heresy: That in legal writing "it is occasionally
possible to talk out loud or crack a joke."

If you don't make law review, don't lament.
You can get many of its benefits elsewhere.
Most law schools offer courses which require extensive research and writing. Second and third
year Moot Court Programs also offer writing and
editorial experience. As to being involved in the
life of the law, there are other avenues, such as
representing clients in clinical courses and being
involved in outside projects. Contribute also to
the life of the law school: take part in student
government, serve on faculty/student committees
and impersonate Kingsfield in the school play.

3. Course Selection

a. *What Not to Do*

Some students are scared; they take bar
courses. Others are lazy; they take ten o'clocks.
We have all been scared, we have all been lazy;
ours is to understand and to encourage these students to make better use of the short period they
have in law school.

On the other hand, some are simply despicable.
They choose courses in order to protect their high
class standing. There is, I am told, a special
place for these students in the ninth circle of
Dante's Hell. For all time these lost souls gasp

for breath, lungs crushed by dusty piles of diplomas, awards and Order of Coif certificates.

Do not make trivial your legal education by treating it as a bar review. There is no need to take every course that the bar examiners may test you on. Following law school graduation there are bar review courses. These courses consist of intense review of the subjects on the bar. Many can be learned sufficiently for exam purposes in several hours of study. So why waste a semester? (Some students refuse to take bar review courses, insisting that they can pass by reviewing their old notes. These are the same kind of people who wave off the Novocain, often with similar results).

Don't focus exclusively on courses you "know" you will need in practice. If you think you know what kind of law you want to practice, surely take some courses in the field in order to test whether you like it. However it is foolish to over-specialize in law school. Career interests can and often do change. Take courses in many fields to learn if some are more appealing. Avoid painting yourself in the "tax," "business" or even "public interest" corner. Remember, most become *general* practitioners.

b.   What to Do

If you shouldn't be a running dog for bar examiners and if you shouldn't be too concerned about taking all the courses you think you'll need

[*301*]

in practice, how should you go about selecting courses? One criteria is to select courses with an eye to making a more informed career decision. As will be argued in the chapter on career choices, this will most likely mean taking either a clinical or trial advocacy course. Also select courses in order to take interesting professors, to learn writing skills and to put your legal studies in a historical or comparative context.

Select interesting and provocative professors, not just those you agree with or feel comfortable with. Quite likely your faculty is composed of many types, those who see criminal law through the eyes of a cop and those who see it through the eyes of a public defender, those who stick closely to the "law" and those who spin off into the realms of philosophy and social theory, those whose classes are like boot camp and those whose classes are like an encounter group.

There are matters of substance—the gruel of bar exams—and matters of style—the grit of lawyering, indeed, of life. Sitting in class you will be learning more than "Federal Jurisdiction" or "UCC". You will be learning how one lawyer approaches and solves problems, uses and communicates knowledge, treats and reacts to people. Matters of style are at least as important as matters of substance. Think back to the "great" teachers you have had. Images and incidents return, little of what was "learned." The arrogant Professor Kingsfield, in the novel *Paperchase*, greets his first year class with "You will teach

[*302*]

yourself law, I will teach you how to think!" By all means, take Kingsfield. But also seek out those who see their mission as teaching feeling and laughter.

How to know who are the Kingsfields? Talk to second and third year students. This is one area where the rumor mill must be consulted. Talk with many students to get many impressions.

Read through, early on, the catalog of course offerings. Some third year courses may require second year prerequisites. In some courses, such as Remedies, Evidence and Conflicts of Law, you will read cases in many substantive areas, like Contracts, Property and Torts. All things being equal, take these courses in your third year. They are mini-bar reviews and add perspective to your understanding of the law by allowing comparison between substantive areas. (Often Evidence will be an actual or de facto prerequisite to clinical practice and trial advocacy; if so, probably you will take it in the second year).

Essential is at least one course requiring *extensive research and writing* even if (particularly if) you dread it. A good lawyer needs these skills. While it is true that some law practices do not frequently require writing and research skills, without them you will practice with a severe disadvantage. Your credibility as a trial lawyer, for example, will soon vanish if it becomes known that you never appeal; trial judges will begin to impose on you, secure in the knowledge that their decisions will not be reviewed. A trial lawyer must occasionally appeal and this requires writing and research skills. Being afraid of going to court hurts you as a practitioner; so too the fear of going to the library.

There is one kind of course very much to be recommended, the "breadth" or "perspective course": Legal History, Comparative Law, Jurisprudence. Most law schools offer these courses, perhaps still reeling from the sting of Thorstein Veblen's remark that "law school belongs in the modern university no more than a school of fencing or dancing." In a sense legal education does sharpen the mind by narrowing it. All educational enterprises are grounded on implicit world views, assumptions about how the world should and does work. Almost inevitably students come to share those views and assumptions.

A brief illustration. In a third year course, I tell the students that they are employed by a legal services program and Marvin Gardens Tenants' Association has come to them for advice. The Association is comprised of about a third of the fifty families living in Marvin Gardens, a racially mixed lower economic housing development. The struggling Association came together when the landlord, a private development company, decided to evict "trouble makers," the two families who were attempting to organize the tenants. After several meetings and threats of a rent strike, the landlord not only backed off those evictions but is now willing to concede its power to evict to the Association—it will not evict any-one the Association wants to stay (except for non-payment) and will evict anyone the Association wants evicted. Under the applicable state law, the landlord can evict for any reason provided adequate notice is given. The leaders explain that the Association plans to evict families which are disruptive in terms of noise, litter and general tranquility. The Association wants advice on what structure to use to make eviction decisions.

The students work in small groups. Without exception they decide upon what I call the "Due Process Response." They first prepare a code of "evictable offenses," all carefully written to limit the discretion of the fact finder and to give notice to the offending tenants (as if it is a big surprise to discover it isn't nice to blast your stereo at four o'clock in the morning). Next they set up a hearing procedure providing notice, confrontation, and representation. There is usually disagreement on whether lawyers should be allowed. Some student groups even include appeal procedures.

No group has yet to propose that the tenant Association simply select a "wise person" and leave it at that. If a dispute arose, the tenants would go to the "wise person" and have their say. The wise person would then decide "what's right." In many societies, and in many parts of our own, that is precisely the way disputes are settled, without formal rules, without formal procedures and without, alas, lawyers. The issue here is not which system is best; the point is simply that the informal method isn't even considered by the law students. They have been educated by a system of thought that is so committed to the Due Process Model as to take it on faith. Indeed the Model is presented as inevitable. It isn't.

Take this matter of writing down the rules, of defining "evictable offenses." Why not "Families engaging in disruptive behavior shall be evicted" rather than "Families playing stereos between the hours of 10 p.m. and 7 a.m. shall be evicted?"

1. Are precise rules needed to curb arbitrary decision-making? Would our "wise person" use the vague standard "disruptive behavior" simply to punish enemies and reward friends? Perhaps, perhaps not.

2. Deciding controversies by precise rules seems bottomed on the notion that "two cases can be alike." If one family is evicted for playing its stereo late at night, the next family should too. Many cultures reject the notion that two cases can be alike and view each human situation as unique: Without knowing a great deal more about the family, we cannot decide whether it should be evicted for playing its stereo late. If this be so, it is vain to try to resolve disputes by precise rules.

3. Do people need to know the rules in advance to plan their lives? Perhaps. The converse view is that people know proper behavior all along. More sharply, the criticism is that defining and writing the rules causes people to become con-

tentious, to insist upon their "rights" rather than realize their responsibilities: If the rule says "No stereos after 10 p.m." people will tend to blast them until 9:58 and, of course, the rule is silent as to V.C.R.'s.

Take courses that force you out of the traditional worldview, courses like Legal History where you will learn that the rules and even the disputes have not always been the same; courses like Comparative Law which teach you that there are other paths; courses like Jurisprudence which expose the beliefs and values implicit in our legal system. Again this is not to suggest that the values reflected in our legal system are necessarily flawed; it is to suggest that they are controversial and that there are alternatives. Before you represent the good folk of Marvin Gardens be aware of the controversy and of the alternatives. Otherwise you may impose values on your clients which are inappropriate.

4. Clinical Courses

Most law schools offer clinical courses: courses in interviewing and counseling, courses in negotiation and trial practice. In some of these courses you represent real clients; in others you engage in extensive simulation. For law students clinical courses need no justification. The skills taught promise immediate payoff. The opportunity to "practice," rather than merely study, excites. After years and years of arrested adolescence, students are anxious to begin.

Clinical legal education has its academic detractors, however:

Taking clinical courses means taking fewer academic courses. One will learn techniques of interviewing in practice; one can't pick up the substantive knowledge conveyed in an academic course. Why give academic credit to students for learning what they will learn in the first six months of practice?

Before taking clinical courses consider why. Do you think you will learn something you won't learn anyway in the first six months of practice? If so, what? If not, why take the course? The notion is by clarifying your goals and expectations, the more likely they will be achieved.

It is my view that clinical courses offer such a rich potential that every law student should take at least one. Important lawyering skills can be learned. Clinical courses also offer the opportunity to explore what it's like to be a lawyer, to explore the emotional demands and rewards. Ethical tensions come alive. So too issues of jurisprudence: How does the law actually work?

a. The Skill Dimension

Unlike speaking prose, interviewing clients and cross-examining witnesses does not come naturally. Law schools have made great strides in defining and teaching lawyering competencies. While it is true that, in your first six months, you will interview clients, negotiate cases, and perhaps even try lawsuits, this does not mean that you will do these things as well as you might. Clinical courses present models of competent practice, allow for student reflection on those models and offer feedback on student performance. Practice seldom, if ever, allows for reflection or critique. Simply put, you will learn to do it better in law school.

Approach a simulated skills course with reckless abandon. *Don't* "Be Yourself." (Mark Twain once said, "Be Yourself" is terrible advice to give to some people.) Don't "Be Yourself" because maybe you don't know who you are. If you consider yourself shy, try being outgoing and bullish in the role plays—yell at your opponent, pound your shoe on the table. If you are generally aggressive and loud, try being gentle. We are the way we are because we feel safe being that way; trying another way may bring the realization that there are other ways of being safe, some perhaps more fun, others perhaps more humane and effective. Only in simulated courses, where no client is injured, do you have the luxury of experimentation.

b. *The Emotional Dimension*

Performing lawyering tasks allows you to explore the emotional side of law practice. Representing real clients, tensions are often sharp. You may feel inadequate to discharge the real life responsibilities thrust upon you or you may feel delight in making decisions that count. Your

[*309*]

personal like for a client and your own desire to
prevail may tempt you to suggest perjury. Your
dislike of some clients may lead to "dogging"
their cases. Dealing with a real life opponent
frequently causes anger and occasionally tears.
Even in simulated courses emotions are intense.
It is surprising how emotionally involved students become, even knowing that they were arbi-
trarily assigned to one side of a dispute that never really happened.

In many clinical programs, students work under the supervision of lawyers hired by the law
school; in other programs they are supervised by
outside lawyers. In academic circles, the latter
programs are generally suspect in that it is difficult for the law school to assure the quality of
the supervision. For the student, however, there
are benefits in addition to learning skills under
supervision. Here one may closely observe lawyers at work. Are they happy? Perhaps this is
too sophomoric a question; surely it is vague and
abstract. It would seem, however, to be of interest. Do the lawyers seem happy? Seem to enjoy
going to work in the morning? Feel that their
work is meaningful?

c.   *The Jurisprudential Dimension*

Clinical courses, particularly those involving
the representation of real clients, allow you a
first hand look at law in operation. Does the law
school model of the adversary process comport

with the real world? Are the lawyers adverse to
one another or is there more of a "country club"
atmosphere? Do judges follow the legal rules or
do they decide matters on their own gut reactions? Are the individual rights of clients pro-
tected? Does the system actually produce justice? Treat clinical courses as field work in
Jurisprudence.

d. The Ethical Dimension

New lawyers find the ethical side of lawyering
most difficult. When practicing law, ethical dilemmas are not the dry stuff of the law school
hypothetical. They are daily and they are thrown
in your face.

Ethical problems abound even in simulated
courses. Once I was teaching a trial advocacy
course in which practicing lawyers helped instruct. Small groups of students would meet
with these lawyers to work on various trial
skills—direct, cross and so forth. The small
group session was also the place for informal discussions. One student told me that she asked the
lawyer just how much you can "prep" a witness
before trial, just how far you can go in structur-
ing the testimony.

"You can tell your witnesses what to wear. I
don't see any problem with dressing up their testimony."

[*311*]

The student felt the analogy weak and the advice sleazy. Did she confront the lawyer with her misgivings? No. Why?

"I didn't want to be a moral softie."

In the first six months of practice you will experience ethical dilemmas, you will have the opportunity to observe the law in action and question whether it it just, and you will have the opportunity to observe lawyers at work and question their contentment and fulfillment. The question remains: Why do all this in law school? *Because you are still a student;* because you are still in an environment committed to questioning rather than to doing. Once you are in practice the doing overwhelms the questioning; gone is the time for cool reflection and the challenging of assumptions.

In clinical courses, approach lawyering as a student, not as a practitioner. Naturally learn the skills and do a lawyerlike job on tasks assigned. But also step out of role and observe. Question what you see and bring your experiences and insights back into the classroom; discuss your impressions with classmates and faculty. To my mind, the real value of clinical education is allowing you to *reflect upon lawyering before being immersed in it.*

Discussing insights and impressions with classmates can be difficult. One may become vulnerable; one may appear "the moral softie." But it is essential that you be willing to risk. Perhaps the

[*312*]

other students in that small group thought the
advice sleazy; perhaps the lawyer himself was
overstating his position in order to appear "in the
know." Raising the objection the student would
trigger a discussion about ethics and role, about
issues which matter very much to all of us who
call ourselves lawyers. We are all, at least in
part, "moral softies."

Enroll in a clinical course, particularly if you
don't want to. Some students are convinced that
they never want to litigate. Some fear they lack
the skills; others think litigation unseemly. They
may be wrong; during a trial course they may
find they are excellent at it and that they love it.
If not, then they can at least rest assured that
their original assessment was correct—how many
tax planners go through life wondering that perhaps, just perhaps . . . .

Before leaving the subject of clinical education,
a short warning about taking advice, or experience for that matter, all that seriously.

5. On Not Taking Advice (or Experience) Seri-
ously

In clinical courses expect advice.

During negotiation always conceal your actual
goals.

During cross-examination, never allow a witness
to explain.

Arguing before hearing officers, argue the facts;
they aren't interested in social policy arguments.

What to make of advice? Obviously much of education involves the transmission of wisdom, the
giving of advice. But there are dangers.

"I was surprised", sayeth Law Student, "but the
hearing officer did seem interested in the social policy argument. I was sure she wouldn't be."

"So what does that show you?" asketh Law Professor.

"That the hearing officer was an exception."

The first danger of taking advice too seriously
is that likely you won't try out approaches that
may in fact work better. It takes a gutsy student to make an argument he has been told will
not work. Second, even if you try out different
approaches, often you will do so in a way which
will fulfill the prophecy. "I know you're not
much interested in social policy but . . . ."
Third, even if you do disregard advice and do so
successfully, you may not learn from your own
experience; the lesson becomes an "exception" to
what you already know.

Is then experience a better teacher? There are
dangers here as well. Say you argued social policy and won. Is the lesson that you should argue
social policy? Perhaps the lesson is flawed due
to a false correlation between your argument and
your victory. In order to determine whether the
correlation is true, you would need to know:

1. In how many cases was social policy argued and
the case lost?

2. In how many cases was social policy *not* argued
and the case won?

[*314*]

3. In how many cases was social policy *not* argued and the case lost?

Perhaps your social policy argument, rather than being a winner, turned a sure thing into a cliff-hanger.

The dilemma is this. To successfully execute a task, be it a negotiation, witness examination or argument to a hearing officer, you have to have a plan going in; otherwise you will thrash about aimlessly. Necessarily your plan will be based on what you know, either from the advice of others or from the lessons you have drawn from previous experiences. Both can lead you astray. So what are you to do? Plan but be aware that each situation is unique. Be sensitive to this uniqueness and realize that perhaps your plan is in error, that with this particular hearing officer a social policy argument might not work. Plan but don't become so wedded to your plan that you rush ahead blindly.

6. Clerking

a. A Short History of American Legal Education

Was a time when people became lawyers by clerking; there wasn't even LSAT. After working several years as an apprentice to an established lawyer, the novice took the bar and that was that. Originally law schools, or more accurately law courses in universities, supplemented apprenticeship; apprentices gathered to hear lectures on legal principles. Slowly law schools became alternatives to apprenticeship, novices becoming eligible to take the bar by either route. The key year is 1870 when Christopher Columbus Langdell became the first dean of the Harvard Law School. Langdell proclaimed law to be a science and the library to be the laboratory.

> [L]aw is a science [and] all the available materials of that science are contained in books . . . . [T]he library is the proper workshop of professors and students alike; . . . it is to us all that the laboratories of the university are to the chemists and physicists, all that the museum of natural history is to the geologists, all that the botanical garden is to the botanists. (Sutherland, *The Law at Harvard* 175 (1967).

Under Langdell, who remained Dean for 25 years, the contours of modern legal education emerged. The course of study was set at three years. More importantly, the case method came to replace lectures. Langdell himself wrote the very first casebook. (There had to be one and now you know who wrote it.) Professor Grant Gilmore, reviewing Langdell's book, concludes his approach was simply to assert that certain cases were "right" while others were "wrong." It seems, Gilmore concludes, that the origins of the case method had "nothing whatever to do with getting students to think for themselves; it was, on the contrary, a method of indoctrination through brainwashing." Gilmore, *Death of Contract*, 13 (1974).

[*316*]

Soon the Harvard model took hold in other law schools and the American Law school was off to the races at a great clip. Believing that "all the available materials [of law] are contained in books," the new legal academics held little sympathy for the apprenticeship system. Their ensuing victory over it has been almost total—today in very few states can you even take the bar unless you have graduated from an A.B.A. approved law school.

As apprenticeship was being driven from the field, standards were being raised in the law schools. At first anyone could attend law school, then anyone with some college training, then only college graduates and now only college graduates who were at the top of their graduating classes and who did well on the LSAT. Consider the result. Without good academic credentials, no longer is it possible to attend law school; without graduating from law school, no longer possible to take the bar. The circle closes. Without taking the bar . . . .

All of this, of course, in the "public good". Law school trained lawyers will provide better representation than those merely doing an apprenticeship; the more "qualified" the law student, the more able the lawyer. Cynics smile at all this, seeing simply the imperatives of expansionism in the conquest of the apprenticeship system and the more ugly impulses of class and race in "raising standards". There have been no studies showing that law schools produced better lawyers than apprenticeship programs nor that the higher the LSAT, the better the practicing lawyer. These remain acts of faith. This does not mean they are wrong; some acts of faith, but not all, are undoubtedly true. Whatever the truth, woe to all our peoples if the next Abe Lincoln has a bad day on the LSAT.

If you are interested in learning more about the fascinating history of the institution you are inhabiting, see Stevens, "Two cheers for 1870: The American Law School" *Law in American History* 425 (D. Fleming and B. Bailyn, eds., 1971). For the cynical account, see Auerbach, *Unequal Justice* (1976).

b. *Negotiate a Meaningful Clerking Experience*

The history lesson was to introduce the debate about whether law students should clerk. Some professors would take "no prisoners." They argue that students should not clerk as it competes with classwork and diminishes the quality of life in the school. With many law students involved in clerking, there is less energy for law review, interest clubs, speaker programs and school plays. Clerking is a trade-off; you give up other productive opportunities. Yet many must clerk. Even for those who don't need the income, clerking, if limited in time and approached properly, can provide a valuable addition to your law school experience. You can learn lawyering skills, you can observe the operation of the law and ponder its justness, and you can experience one type of legal practice with an eye to your own career decision.

As to learning skills, the ideal clerking job is one where you are closely supervised, with your work being reviewed and evaluated by a supervising lawyer. The tasks would be varied—doing legal research, drafting memorandums and documents, doing investigations, attending client interviews and depositions, and observing trials and hearings. Unfortunately, many clerking jobs offer virtually no educational benefits. Out of the blue comes Research Topic, abstract and without reference to how it fits into a particular case. The research is done, the memorandum is written and turned in. It might as well be dropped into a well; there is no critique of the quality of the work, no disclosure of what ultimately happened in the case. Ripples, nothing more.

Negotiate a meaningful clerking experience. Lawyers who simply employ you, without teaching you, exploit you. They also ignore a paramount professional duty. It has long been recognized that the professional has the duty to pass the torch. The Hippocratic Oath, for example, begins:

I will look upon him who shall have taught me this Art even as one of my parents. I will share my substance with him, and I will supply his necessities, if he be in need. I will regard his offspring even as my own brethren, and I will teach them this Art, if they would learn it, without fee or covenant. I will impart this Art by precept, by lecture and by every mode of teaching, not only to my own sons but to the sons of him who has taught me, and to disciples bound by covenant and oath, according to the Law of Medicine.

As a novice, you have the right to expect counsel and instruction from those more experienced; it is your obligation to become the best you can and it is their obligation to help you do so.

Most employers will not need to be reminded of their duty, indeed most will welcome the opportunity to teach and will be favorably impressed by a demand for training. It may be that some of your activities, such as observing your supervisor at trial, should not be compensated. There is room for discussion. However, if the lawyer or firm simply wants your research skills, seek employment elsewhere, with a professional.

Learning skills from your mentor, be aware that there are many styles of practice. What works for your mentor may not work for you; indeed it may not even work for her. Observe closely but don't be credulous. And do not satisfy yourself with learning of lawyering skills. Remain the student and explore the emotional, jurisprudential and ethical aspects of law practice. For more on this, see the discussion of clinical education.

Finally use your clerking experience as a way to learn about various kinds of practice in order to make a good career decision. Do you think you would find meaning and contentment working in such a job? Consider clerking in various kinds of law practice, firms, agencies and so forth.

If you are to clerk, it should interfere with your classwork as little as possible. It is a *very bad idea* to clerk in the first year and it is best only to clerk in the summers. If you clerk during the school year, don't work over 20 hours a week and arrange your classes so that you will not be forced to miss them to do clerking assignments.

One final point. As a clerk, you will be acting as a professional. Observe the standards of confidentiality and conflict of interest. Before clerking, read, or reread, the *Code of Professional Responsibility*.

7. Fun and Games in the Second and Third Years

a. *High School Teaching*

Some law schools have High School Teaching Programs. If yours does, do it. If yours doesn't, organize it. There are rich payoffs, both for the law student and the high school student.

To give you some feel for the program, I will describe the program at the University of Arizona. The structure of the program is quite simple. Law students, who receive one unit of academic credit, are assigned to specific high school classes—usually senior American Problems classes—where they teach one hour per week for a period of seven to ten weeks. The typical curriculum revolves around a set of materials—or lesson plans—developed for the law students. The basic format is to present a hypothetical fact situation to the high school class and then lead a discussion concerning the legal issues it raises. The hypotheticals involve the following areas—introduction to law (three high school students are trapped in a case, there is enough water only for two, the students decide to draw lots to decide who is to die . . . .), juvenile rights, criminal law, consumer law, family law, torts and First Amendment. There is a trial unit—an incident is staged, high school students are selected to play lawyers, judges and jurors. Robes and gavel are borrowed from Moot Court . . . . Not all of our students stay with the prepared materials. Some create their own hypotheticals and roleplays.

The goal of the program is not to teach law (after all, we want to be invited back). The goal is to introduce high school students to legal decision making. The fascination of the law is that it requires the application of theory to specific problems to reach a result—someone wins, someone loses. Using hypotheticals we attempt to force the high school student through the difficult task of making tough decisions.

The program is a grand success. In fact, its success is almost automatic. For the high school

teacher, the program means one less class to prepare, for the high school student, a new face, and
for the law student, a temporary furlough into
the world-beyond. There are richer payoffs for
the participants.

There are rewarding and moving occurrences.
Once the law student noticed one of the high
school students never said a word. With a stroke
of genius—or blind luck—the law student made
her the judge in the trial unit. The experience
was transforming and the student broke out of
her painful self-conscious shell. She became an
active participant in the classroom.

Law students—even with long hair and ragged
jeans—create a great deal of respect for law.
Two students once gave the program in a custodi-
al institution for juvenile delinquents. At first
the law students were greeted with open hostility; of the many epithets tossed their way, "pigs"
is the only one printable. The students stayed
with it, however, and by the end of ten weeks
something profound had occurred. Each "in-
mate" wrote me a letter and all went something
like this: "I always thought all the police and
lawyers were out to get me—now I know that
some might actually understand me and help
me."

Law students profit from the teaching experience. They become more comfortable speaking
in public and learn how to communicate legal
principles to lay audiences. No easy task, it

seems you must actually understand the principles! On a more jurisprudential level, there is the opportunity to discuss law with people other than law students, law teachers and bored and resentful companions at cocktail parties. Much of our law turns on our assessment of how ordinary folk will react. We actually know very little. For example, a particular tort doctrine is designed by wise judges to discourage certain kinds of activities; it is of sound academic interest to see if any of the potential actors have ever heard of the doctrine. Generally they haven't, and when they do, just as likely they will be outraged.

Finally the teaching program allows law students to experience their own uniqueness and competence. One of the unfortunate aspects of legal education is that it takes a large group of talented and intelligent people and, with a wave of the bluebook, turns most "average." Giving law students responsibility to create their own course turns them back into creative and hardworking individuals.

Hopefully this has convinced you to partake the program. Again, if there isn't a program, agitate. They are quite easy to start. The only difficult part is putting together the materials. West has a book which is widely used, *Street Law*. I'll be very happy to send along the materials we use at the University of Arizona, *Tough Decisions*, for the cost of duplication.

b. *Law and Literature Groups, Law School Film Forums*

Many feel, in their legal education, a sharp break with the Burning Questions of their undergraduate days. Law, they feel, is intellectually tough but not intellectually deep. We are so busy deciding what to do with the decedent's stuff, we have no time to consider the meaning of his life.

Yet the Burning Questions are there. Each legal holding rests on implicit philosophic assumptions concerning the nature of humans and that of the just society; each legal actor must face the tension of role and the anguish of decision. What we decide to do with the decedent's assets reflects at a profound level what we take to be the meaning of his life. Great books, and great movies can contribute vastly to your legal education:

In *Billy Budd*, Captain Vere is caught in the classic conflict; his role dictates one course of action, his heart another. Surely, as a lawyer, you will face this conflict; reading of Vere's decision will inform yours, even though you may decide differently.

Hamlet deals with the anguish of deciding. The problem is not only deciding what to do but, perhaps more difficult, what happened. Can the ghost be believed? Did the uncle and mother really kill the father? *Hamlet* tells us more about decisions than do "Decision Trees."

[*325*]

The *Merchant of Venice* presents the classic contract question: Why shouldn't people be allowed to
agree to what they will? It also presents the
profound conflict between the letter of the law and
notions of natural justice. (At the beginning of the
play, it seems that the letter of the law is villian and
we are moved to disregard it in favor of natural justice; at the end of the play natural justice becomes
the enemy when it is used to justify the most unjust
treatment of Shylock.) The play also presents how
language and rules can be manipulated. If "the devil can cite Scripture for his purpose," what's the
good of Scripture? Does law school simply teach
the effective citation of Scripture, leaving the question of purposes to others?

One way to include the insights of the humanities into your legal education is to take part in
Law and Literature courses (formal or informal),
another is to inaugurate law school film forums.

Law and Literature Groups. If your school
does not offer a formal course, consider organizing an informal one. I'll describe the one at the
University of Arizona to give you some ideas.

The "faculty" is composed of two or three law
school professors and a professor from another
University Department, such as English. (The
professors come and go, talking of Michelangelo.)
There are usually 20 to 30 students, each receiv-
ing two units credit. Meetings occur eight times
over the school year for discussion of the selec-
tions. The meetings are informal and held in the
evenings at someone's home. Prior to the meeting, each student writes a two page paper on the

book to be discussed. The goal is not literary criticism; it is to use literature to better understand the operation of the law and what it is to be a lawyer. Papers focus on issues of justice and issues of role. At the end of the paper, the student proposes one question to be discussed at the evening session. Before the meeting, all the papers are duplicated and read by members of the group.

At the meeting groups of four or five discuss the papers. Each small group selects a "reporter" whose job is to report to the larger group on the discussion. After about 1½ hours, we break and then come together in a large group to hear from the reporters. There are variations on this format. Sometimes we call in outside "ringers" to share their learning and expertise with us. For example, after reading Simon's *Independent Journey*, a biography of Justice William O. Douglas, a law professor who had been one of his clerks discussed experiences and impressions. Similarly, after reading Dostoevski's *Crime and Punishment*, we invited an expert in Russian literature.

The sessions are not heavy academic fare. Indeed, occasionally they more resemble encounter groups—students expressing deep concerns about both the law and lawyering. Even though the faculty gets a little nervous at the looseness of some of the sessions, the students are generally quite enthusiastic.

We meet as a group to select the readings, usually at the end of one year for the next year's group to allow for summer reading. As you will see, we have a rather expansive definition of "law" which means that almost all literature fits into the phrase "and literature." Some of the things we have read:

Bolt, A Man for All Seasons

Bugliosi, Till Death Us Do Part

Camus, The Stranger

Cozzens, The Just and the Unjust

Doctorow, Book of Daniel

Dostoevski, Crime and Punishment

Kafka, The Trial

Kanton, Andersonville

Melville, Billy Budd

Miller, The Crucible

Nichols, The Milagro Beanfield War

Phillips, No Heroes, No Villains

Pirsig, Zen and the Art of Motorcycle Maintenance

Shakespeare, Hamlet, The Merchant of Venice

Solzhenitsyn, One Day in the Life of Ivan Denisovich

Sophocles, Antigone

Stewart, Earth Abides

Tolstoy, Resurrection

Wambaugh, The Onion Field

Wright, Native Son

Film Forums. If law and literature groups bring liberal arts mush into the law school, film forums serve instant mush. The mechanics vary

[*328*]

in complexity. Most simple, rent a film, get a projector and invite your friends. (With video cassettes, the rental of the film will be two or three dollars—the drawbacks are that fewer films are available on cassettes, and those that are must be played on small television screens).

More complex forums involve putting together a panel to discuss the film. Law professors, other academics, practicing lawyers and judges add valuable insights into the themes raised in the film. A panel on the movie *Billy Budd* might include an English Professor who specialized in Melville, a legal philosopher, a psychologist and that jack-of-all-trades, a law professor. A panel after *Anatomy of a Murder* might include a prosecutor, a criminal defense lawyer and a professor of legal ethics.

The crowning touch, of course, would be the traditional black tie Awards Evening.

"For the Award 'Dumbest Thing Said by a Panelist,' the nominees are . . . ."

Movie rental varies, between $30 and $100. Donations or a sympathetic Dean can cover the amount. Stores renting movies have catalogs of available films. Some possibilities:

A Man for All Seasons

Paths of Glory

Twelve Angry Men

Breaker Morant

I Never Sang for My Father

The Informer

Lord of the Flies
Inherit the Wind
To Kill a Mockingbird
The Stranger
Billy Budd
Anatomy of a Murder
Salt of the Earth

Law and Literature groups and film forums provide a context in which to discuss important issues with your classmates and faculty. More broadly, so too the second and third years provide a context in which to explore issues of law and issues of lawyering. Make the most of them.

A Final Word on the Second and Third Years. Space allocations in this chapter may prove misleading. Much space is devoted to clinical practice, clerking, high school teaching, law and literature groups and law school film forums. The space is devoted to these subjects because I think there is more that needs to be said of them, not because I believe that they should be your main diet during your last two years. An overwhelming majority of your time will be, and should be, devoted to traditional courses. Again, the "right attitude" is to learn law even if some is boring, even if some is painful. For in your future somewhere lurks *Smedley!*

CHAPTER 11

CAREER CHOICES

This chapter is the most important of chapters. It is the least helpful of chapters. Most important because it deals with the rest of your life; least helpful because it deals in abstractions and approximations.

It will identify options, both in traditional legal careers and in non-legal careers often pursued by lawyers. Knowing options is necessary but not sufficient. That you might be a criminal defense lawyer or work for a large commercial firm does nothing to tell you which you would find more satisfying. The trick is to move beyond labels, to understand career alternatives in terms of skills and talents, joys and anxieties. To help you do this I will discuss variables that cut across the labels: the degree the work deals with ideas as opposed to people, involves early responsibility, requires aggressiveness, offers training and income, and involves *esprit de corps*. To flesh out career alternatives I have also asked lawyers in various kinds of practice to share with you brief descriptions of what they do. Their responses are found in the next chapter. I will also suggest ways that you can "experience" some of your career options while still a law student.

Career choice involves much more than options and opportunities; it involves aspirations and

dreams. It is easy to forget this in the job rush
that occurs in the second and third years. The
quest too often becomes that of finding a job
rather than of finding meaning. Now, before the
rush, is the time to ask yourself serious questions
about what you want to do and how you want to
live.

1. The Goal: To Thine Own Self Be True

What kind of person do you want to be in ten
or fifteen years? In what ways and for what
purposes do you wish to use your talents? Why
did you come to law school?

Make no mistake: A career is more than a job,
it becomes a worldview. As Tolstoy wrote in
Resurrection:

> No man can play an active part in the world unless
> he believes that his activity is important and good.
> Therefore, whatever position a man may hold, he is
> certain to take that view of life . . . which will
> make his own activity seem important and good
> . . . . To maintain this idea, men instinctively mix
> only with those who accept their view of life
> . . . .

Knowing this, Tolstoy concludes, it should not
surprise us when "thieves boast of their adroitness, prostitutes flaunt their shame, murderers
gloat over their cruelty." He argues that we
mask our own adroitness, shame and cruelty by
adopting consistent views of life and value.

Your career will ultimately shape your concep-
tion of reality. It will also affect greatly who

your friends are, how you relate to your community and even what you do in your spare time. Again the questions: What kind of person do you want to be in ten or fifteen years? In what ways and for what purposes do you wish to use your talents? Why did you come to law school? Obviously here is a place to make use of your Journal.

My premise is that we all have dreams and aspirations but that we often get sidetracked in our pursuit of them. Once a student came to me for an employment reference. He was applying for a job with a large firm in a large city. I asked him if he looked forward to living in the city.

"No, I would prefer working in a small town."

"Well, it must be that you like the kind of law they practice in the firm," I suggested brightly.

"No, I find it boring. Actually I would like to work with juveniles. That's what I did before law school and that's why I came to law school."

"Then why apply to the firm?"

"Because everyone tells me that it is a very good job."

Career decisions should be very much about "reaching the unreachable star." First, realize the star. Second, realize the perils, those attitudes and beliefs that may divert you from your quest.

2. The Perils

a. *Proving You're the "Right Stuff"*

Tom Wolfe, in his marvelous book *The Right Stuff*, argues that America's astronauts were not motivated by money, fame or challenge, but by the desire to prove to their fellows and to themselves that they were made of the "right stuff".

The implicit value system in law school, shared by many faculty and many students, is that the "Right Stuff" is working with ideas rather than with people. The very best students go into teaching or into large firms in a big city. The rest go into "regular" practice. Only academic losers would consider a non-law job. There are variations on the theme. I was a student at Berkeley in the 1960's. Then and there the "right stuff" meant "movement" jobs, working with legal aid or with the public defender. But even in the radicalism of Berkeley the traditional ordering appeared: If legal aid, far better to do "law reform" rather than divorces; if public defender, far better to do appellate work rather than trial work.

This is not to say that law teaching or large firms are inappropriate career choices. It is not to say the value system is flawed. It is simply to suggest that it might not be yours. If you want to work with juveniles in a small town, do it.

[*334*]

Recall one last image. Prince Andre of *War and Peace* is gravely wounded in battle. Awakening on the bloody and smoking field, he reflects on the monstrous curiosity: He is willing to die for the good opinion of people he doesn't even know.

b. Thinking "It Really Doesn't Matter Where I Work"

Many students fail to reach their star because they come to believe that there are no stars. They come to feel that all law jobs are fungible and that it really doesn't matter which one is taken. Professor Liz Dvorkin sees a relationship between this attitude and the adversary process:

> I believe that it is the responsibility of a law student to find the meaning for his or her life. I also believe that much in legal education encourages, whether by design or inadvertence, evasion of the struggle to find meaning in the profession.

> What I find most disturbing is the extent of rationalization and its easy acceptance in the law school. For example, students quickly learn the premise that in our legal system everyone deserves representation. In discussing career choices, they often go on to say that since any person has a valid claim on the services of a lawyer, it does not matter whose ends a lawyer furthers; all ends are legitimate and therefore of equal weight. Since no legal work is more compelling than any other, why not work for those clients who can pay the most? The premise that justifies the representation of the unpopular . . . is transformed into a justification

[*335*]

for believing, in effect, that legal representation is a meaningless business . . . .

There is something wrong when students do not perceive the lawyer's choice of work as critical to the validity of the adversary system. *Becoming a Lawyer: A Humanistic Perspective on Legal Education and Professionalism.*

Again, who are you and what do you want of your career?

c. Fearing Greatness

We wish to succeed. Curiously we fear it. This fear limits what we can become. To reach our full potential is risky—perhaps we will fail. It also requires affront. "Who me? Me reach a star?" Psychologist Abraham Maslow used to ask his students "Which of you will write a great novel? Become President?" The students would stir nervously in their seats. Then he would ask, "If not you, then who else?"

———————

A career decision is of utmost importance. Choose based on your value system, not on that of others. Don't trivialize your decision; what you do matters critically, both to you and to your society.

All of this is not to suggest that your first job will be your last. Most lawyers change jobs after law school. Some move from one firm to another; some go from private practice to government work; others reverse that progression.

Some leave law altogether, some to govern nations, others to make revolutions, still others to broadcast the Dallas Cowboys. So what are your choices?

3. Career Options

When the time comes you have three basic choices:
1. Take a legal job
2. Take a non-legal job
3. Punt

As the last two are least obvious, they will be discussed first.

a. Punt

It is perfectly proper to be indecisive. At least I think it is. The Great Third Year Question generates incredible anxiety: "And what will *you* do next year?" One way to avoid the pressure and the possibility of making an inappropriate decision is to "punt", take a job which by definition is limited to one or two years.

"Punting" can be quite exciting and quite valuable, both in terms of future career choices and in terms of public service. However, there will be pressure not to punt—the feeling that you have deferred reality long enough. The jobs described below, however, involve real work and real responsibility; they are, as it were, in the "real

[*337*]

world". You need not feel guilty in not growing up just yet.

1. *Judicial Clerkships.* Most appellate court judges and many trial court judges hire recent graduates as clerks. Many argue that this is the best way to start practice as you will learn much law and much about lawyering from reviewing briefs and transcripts. You may also get a crack at writing the first draft of an opinion.

2. *Vista and the Peace Corps.* *Vista* places recent law graduates with local Legal Services Programs. The *Peace Corps* has some positions requiring legal training; in many other positions, legal training would be beneficial.

3. *Governmental Internships.* There are many opportunities to work with legislative committees or on the staffs of legislators.

4. *More school.* Perhaps you will decide on a career which will be aided with more schooling. Several law schools offer advanced law degrees in such things as tax. Or you may wish to get another degree in a field which you plan to use in conjunction with law, such as business, finance, real estate, counseling, ventriloquism.

b. *Non-legal Careers—Opportunities for Lawyers*

There are literally hundreds of opportunities for law graduates outside of the traditional practice of law. Why choose one?

- Some dislike the adversarial nature of law practice. While some forms of law practice are less adversarial than others, all sometimes lead into the eye of contention.

[*338*]

- Some find law boring: Careers in business or journalism may be more exciting.

- Some find law confining. Law is not a mobile profession. The idea of taking another Bar Exam reduces most of us to jelly and keeps us close to home. Additionally, after a few years in practice, a move will mean starting over. Even law teaching is not very mobile—professors tend to stay at the school which first hired them.

- Other professions allow for much more movement, not only from one location to another, but also from one employer to another.

It is well that many law students seek non-legal jobs. The sad truth is that law schools are graduating more law students than there are traditional law jobs. I could support that with figures but I do not wish to depress you.

Here my goal is not to list all the possibilities but simply to mention a few by way of illustration.

Business. In most large corporations the number of legally trained persons employed in management and administrative posts far exceeds that employed in legal departments. Consult the pamphlet issued by the American Bar Association, "Non-Legal Careers: New Opportunities for Lawyers," which describes opportunities and suggests ways of locating and obtaining these jobs.

Media. Although Howard appears to have a lock on Monday Night Football, there are other opportunities for lawyers in the media. T.V., magazines and newspapers report on legal developments. Consult with the Journalism School if your university has one.

Teaching. Not to insult my colleagues, I will discuss law school teaching under traditional legal careers. There are, however, other opportunities to teach law in universities and in community colleges, courses such as business law, criminal law, consumer law, and civil rights.

Lobbying. Many lawyers serve as lobbyists for corporations, trade associations, unions and citizen groups.

Administrative. Lawyers serve in supervisory and management positions with businesses, universities, foundations, unions, social service organizations and community groups.

Politics. FDR, Ghandi, Nixon, Castro and Lenin were all lawyers. Many come to law school with politics as an eventual goal. So be it. Politics is a very high form of public service and those engaged in politics should be commended rather than castigated. They do while others complain; they light candles while others curse the darkness.

The list is merely suggestive. Your placement office has more information on non-legal careers. Consult other placement offices on campus as well.

c. *Traditional Law Jobs*

Law jobs can be classified by label: "private practice," "public defender," "corporate counsel," "legal aid," "law teaching." These classifications can be helpful in understanding career options and will be used later in the chapter. There are other ways to classify law jobs. For example, they vary in the kinds of substantive law prac-

ticed. If you have a keen interest in a particular
field of law, likely you can practice it in a variety
of settings—both private and government lawyers practice antitrust, both legal aid and corporate counsel practice labor law.

In addition to kinds of substantive law, there
are other variables that cut across types of law
practice. First, there are the formal, external
differences such as income and security, in-house
training, the opportunity to (or need to) specialize. Second, law jobs vary in terms of internal
psychological pressures and satisfactions—some
are research-oriented, others people-oriented;
some require aggressiveness, others do not;
some thrust grave responsibilities on novices,
others treat them as irresponsible children; some
involve a high degree of *esprit de corps*, others
are merely jobs. I will attempt to flesh out these
variables. The trick is to determine what is important to you and then to find a job which
matches. The difficulty is that there is only a
crude match between "label" and the variables—
large firms generally, but not always, pay more
than small; the public defender generally, but not
always, has a high *esprit de corps*. The broad
strokes of this discussion must be narrowed by
you when you seek employment.

(1) VARIABLES CUTTING ACROSS THE LABELS

Ideas versus people. Some people prefer
working with ideas, others with people. (Robert

Benchley once pointed out that there are two kinds of people, those who think there are two kinds of people and those who don't.) Some kinds of law practice involve almost exclusively legal research and drafting. These jobs offer "nice" theoretical problems, the luxury of extended research and reflection, and the satisfaction that comes in drafting a well written and thorough legal document, be it a brief or contract. Large firms traditionally offer this kind of employment but so too do many smaller "specialized" law firms, "law reform units" of legal aid offices, and "appellate departments" of the public defender and district attorney.

At the other end of the continuum are those law jobs which involve working closely with people. Great satisfaction can come in helping people solve real life problems. One scene always returns when I think about lawyering. I had entered the courtroom to see the judge about a pending case. A jury was filing into the jury box. I sat to wait my turn.

"Have you reached a verdict?" the judge inquired.

"We have your Honor." I looked at the defense table. The lawyer was black, the client, white.

"We find the defendant 'Not Guilty'."

Lawyer and client stood and embraced. Both were crying.

The personal engagements and satisfactions are not often so dramatic. Yet they are frequent and real: helping work out a sensible child custody arrangement, helping two friends set up a partnership, helping a client understand a bureaucratic maze. As a general matter, smaller firms and government agencies offer greater opportunities to work with people. But are "people practices" intellectually challenging? Aren't they boring and routine?

Aside: There are no routine cases. The common myth is that some forms of practice are routine and not intellectually challenging. "Who would want to do divorce work, day after day?"

The first response stresses that routine cases often raise critical issues of legal theory. *Miranda* was, after all, just another kidnap case. That a case is "routine" or "mundane" may mean simply that the lawyer isn't looking closely enough.

The second response concedes that many cases are "routine" at the level of *theory*, but insists that very few are at the level of *fact*. Take the routine custody fight: What kinds of evidence can be introduced to show that the children's "best interests" are to stay with your client? Take the routine drunk driving case: As prosecutor, how do you prove that the driver was "under the influence of alcohol"? Take the routine personal injury case: As plaintiff's lawyer, how do you convince a jury that the defendant did not exercise "due care"? The most routine trial is as

[*343*]

engrossing and as exhausting as a game of chess—there are so many possible moves and so many implications of each. Doing trial work, I slept with a pad and pencil next to my bed to jot down the flashes that would come in the night. Doing appellate work, I slept soundly.

The third response argues that, even if a case is routine as a matter of intellectual interest, it will not be routine as a matter of human drama, aspiration and conflict. There are no routine clients.

Responsibility. The larger the firm or agency, the less responsibility you will likely have. Your work will be constantly reviewed. Whatever you are working on will be a small part of a much larger project or case. The archetype is the new attorney in a large Wall Street firm who spends her considerable talents searching, and searching, old corporate records as a part of one of the numerous discovery techniques employed in a huge, never-ending lawsuit. *Bleak House* revisited!

At the other end of the continuum are jobs that throw the novice directly into the heat of battle. In some small firms and legal aid offices you interview clients the first day; in some district attorney and defender offices, you try cases your first week. Responsibility can be exhilarating; after all those years of studying about the real world you are suddenly immersed in it. You are making decisions that affect, not your grade or even your promotion, but rather people's lives. Decisions count.

Responsibility can be exhilarating; it can be terrifying. Law is quite complex and, as a beginner, you know so little. Add to that the elusive criteria of good practice: "Have I worked hard enough?" "Have I raised all the points?" "Has my client been well represented?" There are many professions which are complex and in which the standards are vague; in law, however, there is a major difference. Only in law is there an adversary ready to leap at your first mistake. More than your training, more than your intelligence, it is the responsibilities and pressures that justify your salary or fee.

Aggressiveness. One of my students once lamented that law practice is "chasing each other around the table!" Some students welcome aggressiveness, others shun it. Many law jobs do not involve aggressiveness. Estate planning is the archetype. Business planning similarly is low on confrontation.

There is a lively debate, both in practice and in the law schools, about how aggressive law practice must be. Can mediation replace litigation? Can problem-solving strategies replace zero-sum solutions (those in which what one side wins, the other must lose)? The debate is important. If you are repelled by the adversary system it suggests that you may be able to practice law in a non-adversarial fashion. Even in traditionally

[*345*]

confrontive law jobs, it may be possible to do
something other than "chase each other around
the table," where the "good" solution leaves both
sides sullen but not yet mutinous.

Esprit de corps. Some law jobs involve a
strong sense of shared purpose. One of the
things I most value about my own days in practice was my relationship with the other lawyers
in the office. We knew about each others' cases,
we talked about them, argued about them and
shared the moments of joy and despair.

I found this sense of shared purpose and involvement in legal aid and in public defending. I
am sure it exists in most prosecuting offices, in
most government jobs, and, I am told, in most
small law offices. The larger the firm or agency,
the less likely the feeling. This lack of *esprit de
corps* will not bother some, those who simply
want a job and look for a sense of community
elsewhere.

Training. It is important to develop your professional skills. Larger firms and agencies generally offer good training. Your work is almost
always reviewed. This is the other side of "lack
of responsibility". Generally you will be given
time to "do it right" and the standards of practice
are quite high.

Many smaller firms and smaller public agencies
also insist on the highest professional standards.
Yet some do not and there is a danger of developing sloppy habits. Some lawyers "fly blind."

"In-depth" research falls to "overview research" which falls to "no" research. These practitioners are sorry jokes. They wound their clients and survive only because their clients are unsuspecting. If your employer doesn't insist on the highest standards, do so yourself: It is your career.

Income. Larger firms start associates at higher salaries than do other law employers; partners in large firms do exceedingly, perhaps embarrassingly, well. Some lawyers in smaller firms undoubtedly overtake their fat-cat brethren and occasionally make "megabucks" by getting into business ventures with their clients. Personal injury lawyers can almost retire if they get "the big one," the happy family on a Sunday drive rearended by a drunken, unshaved interstate trucker causing (Ladies and Gentlemen of the jury, were it not so!) grievous and terrible injury. (It's an ill wind that doesn't blow someone some good.) Lawyers making a career in governmental agencies won't get rich as maximum salaries are set. So too, law teachers, they don't get rich, particularly if you are reading this as a borrowed or used book. Shame on you.

These then are some of the variables that cut across various types of law practice—people versus ideas, the degree of responsibility and aggressiveness, the matter of *esprit de corps* and the very tangible matters of training and income. Without doubt, in reading them, you reacted to each either positively or negatively. Here ask yourself if you have any factual or experiential basis for those reactions. For example, if you reacted, "I could never handle the responsibility," how do you know? As will be suggested later in the chapter, *try out* activities that involve the variables—you may learn to your great surprise that you handle responsibility very well. Don't just assume you can't.

With the variables in mind, now the various kinds of law practices.

(2) THE LABELS

Private Practice

After law school I worked with a legal services program in rural California. Then I worked for the Defenders Program of San Diego and then returned to legal services in San Diego. From there I went into teaching. More of this later. Here I simply want to assure you that I was in private practice as well. For a week.

It may strike you that you can't learn too much about private practice in one week. That's simply not true. I learned several valuable lessons. Such as "get your fee up front!" Had I known that then, my earnings would have been $100 rather than simply $50. Additionally I learned that if you do your own typing your letters become concise and to-the-point:

"My client is not moving!"

"Please don't throw my client in jail!"

"You owe me money!"

And it is quite a time saver to use envelopes that have little plastic windows; that way you only have to type the address once!

So what else is there to know about private practice? There are big firms, small firms, and solo practice.

Big firms. Large firms are a fairly recent phenomenon, their growth paralleling that of the client they serve, Corporate America. Generally they are divided into departments such as "litigation" "labor" "antitrust" "tax". New associates often rotate through these departments, finally coming to rest in one. After several years a decision is made on whether to make the young associate a partner. If the decision is "no" the associate is expected to move on, often to a corporation's law department or to a smaller firm. As the training one receives in large firms is excellent, the passed over associate still has a highly saleable resume.

Despite the fact that the hours are notoriously long and the pressures to "do well" intense, these jobs are relatively "safe". First the large firms tend to clone the law schools (or vice versa)— what you will be asked to do is what you have already done, research law and write memorandums. Second these jobs are safe because they involve no real responsibility—there is little client contact (how does one ever have contact with the corporate bond division of G.M.?) and decisions are reviewed by superiors.

The monetary rewards are obvious; associates start at high salaries and senior partners do much better. As large firms hire only students who have done well in school, an additional satisfaction is in matching wits with top legal talent, running on the fastest of tracks even though that track might be something of a circle. So too the satisfaction from "being there", in the hub of things, where "big decisions" and "big deals" are made. In large firms it's leather briefcases and lunch at the finest restaurants.

Aside: Is big firm practice a sell-out? Many law students view working with a large firm tantamount to working with the Devil. Some vow never to work for one; others shrug their shoulders, firmly set their jaws and steel themselves to evict widows and to pollute the countryside with toxic waste.

To the first group of students, two rejoinders. First, as legal adviser to Corporate America, you help it cut transaction costs. In theory this will make more goods and services available to more people at lower costs. Surely this counts as a public, as opposed to private, good. Second, once you have the ear of Corporate America, your opportunity to "do good" is that much increased.

The second group of students plan to work for large firms even though they are convinced it will

[*350*]

involve the forfeiture of their souls. Professor Duncan Kennedy, who teaches at the lush vineyard of the large firms, Harvard, gives his first year torts class the horrible hypothetical.

> You are asked to defend a personal injury suit; your client was grossly negligent and the plaintiff was substantially and permanently injured. There is a highly technical defense that you can assert which will bar the suit. The plaintiff will hence spend his days in pain and agony, all without compensation. What do you do?

Most students, Kennedy finds, assume that they will be fired, not only if they refuse to raise the technicality, but even if they express misgivings in doing so. The students *assume* this; perhaps it is not true. Perhaps the senior partner might respond, "You know, I always thought that was a sleazy defense. Maybe we should discuss it with the client and if he insists, maybe we should withdraw."

Don't assume your employer is the Devil. If you think something stinks, say so. Otherwise, you may become a devil by forfeit. This advice, of course, applies no matter where you practice—the temptation to be sleazy is present, perhaps more so, in the most noble of causes.

Small firms. With a small firm you will come into contact with clients and take responsibility early. Most likely there will be a feeling of shared purpose among the lawyers and staff. Although some small firms specialize, most do not. As the clients usually cannot afford large fees, generally there will be less possibility to do "in-depth" research.

One definite drawback to *some* small firms is the matter of money. In some firms you will be expected to bring in clients. For most hustling clients is distasteful, so too the fear that the monthly overhead may not be met. Also in smaller firms you will have the unpleasant task of discussing fees with clients. Try explaining to someone who makes $8 per hour that you charge $80 or that, even though they have a valid claim, it would cost more to bring it than would be recovered. In larger firms, associates do not discuss fees with clients. Even if they did, the clients can well afford them. (Attorney fees can be a "necessary business expense" and at a corporate tax rate of 46%, it can be argued that the general taxpayer foots 46% of those fabulous Wall Street salaries. Now compared to the subsidy for legal services for the poor . . . . But I digress).

Solo practice is more than a law job, it is a vision. So too the decision of two or three graduates to form their own firm. The vision offers the freedom to be your own boss, to practice law the way you think proper. There is the excitement of creating a new institution. Where should the office be? What books should be in the library? What filing system should be used? What hours? What kind of clients and cases? "Reinventing the wheel" is an activity often ridiculed, mostly, I suspect, by people who have

[*352*]

neither invented one nor reinvented one. Creation supplies energy, excitement, and accomplishment—so what if the folks in the next cave had the wheel two weeks ago, so what if they already had leased the same word processor?

There are, however, two major problems with going out on your own or starting a small firm with classmates: lack of clients and lack of experience. Renting space in an on-going law office is a partial solution to both. Being in an office with more experienced lawyers leads to client referrals; it also allows the novice to ask questions and discuss cases as he might with a senior partner.

There are several books on how to reinvent the wheel. Anyone seriously considering this option should read them *before* taking the step.

"Public Practice": Legal Aid, Government Work, Prosecuting and Defending Criminals

A curious category, one which includes legal aid, government work, and prosecuting and defending criminals. Surely I have confused the bad guys and the good guys. Not so. I have put them together because these lawyers have a vision of the public good and believe, quite rightly, that their jobs make the world a better place. It is the sense of social involvement that makes up for lower salaries. It is the vision that supplies the excitement.

Legal Aid. I worked with California Rural Legal Assistance in the San Joaquin Valley, mostly with farm workers and their families. I did both individual cases—divorce, landlord/tenant, consumer problems—as well as "law reform" or "impact litigation"—such as challenging a state statute which had the effect of discriminating against Spanish speaking citizens, and filing a class action on behalf of a group of poor families to enjoin the operation of a cattle feedlot next to their homes. I also worked with community groups, one trying to improve neighborhood roads, another running a program for children. There were four other lawyers in the office who were doing similar things. The intensity was constant and intoxicating. We talked law at lunch and over beer; we worked early, late, and on weekends. After explaining legal points to a meeting of the farm workers' union, we would hold hands to sing "We Shall Overcome."

We were brash; surely we did stupid and hurtful things in our enthusiasm and energy. Yet we made a lasting contribution to many. I am proud of those years.

Government Jobs. The jobs are varied:
- Working as house counsel to a local school district
- Working for a state legislature drafting statutes
- Working as a hearing officer for a state welfare agency
- Working in the investigation division of the I.R.S.

- Working as a counsel to a legislative committee
- Working for the Attorney General advising the states' mental hospitals
- Working for the U.S. Attorney on the organized crime taskforce
- Working for the Civil Rights Division of Justice enforcing voting rights
- Working for a City Council, advising and drafting ordinances

These jobs run the gamut from those requiring adversary skills to those requiring planning skills. They vary in terms of salary, training, *esprit de corps*, working with people or working with ideas. Government jobs are alike in that usually you assume substantial and early responsibility. They also share the excitement and fulfillment that comes from using one's talents for the public good.

Prosecuting and Defending Criminals. Jobs with the District Attorney and Public Defender are similar in many respects. First, you litigate. There are no better places to refine your trial skills. Second, you meet the local bench (judges, clerks, bailiffs) and the local trial bar. Interesting folks. Third, you will likely be working in an office with a high *esprit de corps*. Fourth, many of your friends will stop talking to you. This last concern I wish to address.

"How can you *defend* those people?" My experience in the Public Defender's Office was that most of my clients, while guilty, surely did not

[*355*]

deserve what the prosecutor had in store. As a defense lawyer you come to know the defendant; no longer is he a "burglar", he is someone you have sat with, someone you know. Justice cannot demand he be confined in the horror of prison for five years. You conclude this, not because you are a bleeding heart, but because you know the individual rather than the label.

Seldom, if ever, are you greeted by a defendant who says "I did it, I'm proud of it, and I want you to get me off so I can do it again!" Most who admit guilt want to enter a plea; as defense counsel you try to get a "deal" in proportion to your client's "crime". If you do a good job, even if it results in a prison term for your defendant, you contribute. If your client believes that you worked hard and did your best, a step towards rehabilitation has been taken. He cannot blame his incarceration on his lawyer and, for perhaps the first time in his life, he can believe that someone in the "establishment" went to bat for him.

Finally there is something real in the notion that by defending the guilty one protects the innocent. Raising "technicalities" (such as the Bill of Rights) is one obvious example. So too insisting that the State prove its case "beyond a reasonable doubt." This routine response by the defense bar forces police to be very sure before invoking the awesome power of the state against the individual.

[*356*]

What then of prosecution? Sometimes the debate is staged as if the only thing prosecutors did was extract long sentences for those who smoke pot. The sad truth is that there is much more to it than that. There are people who are dangerous, who prey on the weak and who would, if able, destroy our hard won civilization. Surely it is a noble use of one's talents to seek punishment in such cases.

A prosecutor can also soften the fury of the criminal law. Many are caught up in the criminal justice system who are neither vicious nor hardened, yet the cold language of the Penal Code allows for few distinctions. Whereas defense counsel can only ask for a reduction of charges, it is the prosecutor who answers.

Other Traditional Law Jobs

Teaching Law. What can I say? Admit to the whole world I made a terrible mistake? Law teaching is great. Mostly it's the freedom. There is no "correct" way to teach Contracts (at least I hope there isn't) and so you're free to try your own. And after you have taught a course a few times, you have time to pursue your academic interests. No one tells you to explore this or that particular aspect of the law, you can pretty much roam where you will.

Freedom has its downsides. As most "do their own thing" there is little sense of shared purpose with your colleagues. I also miss the immediacy of practice, the telephone calls to be returned, the letters to be answered, the briefs to be written. Academics work for months on an article, finally get it published and then . . . nothing. Maybe a letter or two from a Professor far away saying she read your article and found it "interesting." Interesting? Six months of blood, sweat and tears—interesting?

But there is the rush of teaching, the challenge of discussing difficult concepts with intelligent people. After a good class session, I don't do much of anything for at least an hour.

Most law teachers went to prestigious schools and did well. Students at less prestigious schools often find it necessary to make their credentials "respectable" by getting a Masters at a major law school. However the old route of "Harvard Law, Supreme Court Clerk, Assistant Professor" is giving way as law schools are hiring more people with "practice experience", not only for clinical courses but for others as well. If you're interested in teaching, your professors will be quite happy to discuss this with you.

Corporate Counsel. Several corporations maintain their own law departments rather than retaining an outside firm. Often these jobs "mix" other duties, such as management.

Law Publishing Companies. Lawyers serve as editors, writers and salespeople. New areas are being opened with computers.

[*358*]

Law Libraries. Law schools, courts, bar associations, government agencies and large firms often hire full-time personnel. Sometimes a library science degree is also required.

4. Choosing: Turning Labels Into Experiences

What's it *really* like to practice law? You won't really know until you do but here are some ways to learn more about your career options.

a. Courses in Law School

Most law schools offer courses in trial practice and in clinical practice, usually involving representing real clients either in a law school clinic or in a field placement. I feel that these courses are very important (only partly because I wrote a book on trial and practice skills).

"Law review types," those students who are doing very well academically, often shun "practice courses." These students may need them more than others. As they do well academically, likely they enjoy academics and are hence drawn toward those jobs which clone the law school experience, big firm or agency practice, where one works in a library rather than in court. But perhaps these very same students would enjoy the hurly-burly of trial more than cool reflection of the stacks, enjoy helping people solve real life problems more than solving "nice" theoretical quandries. Drink at the well of practice even if you conclude, as did one of my trial advocacy stu-

dents, "Good course. Now I *know* I never want
to go to court."

Clinical courses are needed by those students
planning to work for small firms or on their own.
There is the danger of developing sloppy work
habits. Law school courses will instill a sense of
excellence in practice.

If you are considering a specialty, obviously
you should take the courses in law school that relate to it. Similarly there may be courses in other departments of the university which will expose you to the "nuts and bolts" of a particular
career. For example, if you are considering
something in the media, check the catalogue of
the Journalism Department. Better yet, go over
and chat with the people there. Another obvious
example is Business School. However, as career
goals often change it is a mistake to focus too exclusively in the area of law you think you'll practice.

b. *Clerking*

A good way to experience practice is to clerk.
Law firms and agencies often hire second and
third year students to do legal research. Doing
the research, hanging out at the office, talking to
attorneys and staff can give you a good feel for
that particular kind of law practice.

Many law professors advise against clerking,
arguing that students will learn more by sticking
to the books. I disagree and believe that clerking

can be, if approached from the proper perspective, a valuable learning experience, both in terms of legal doctrine and in terms of career choice. For more about clerking, consult Chapter 10.

If you are to clerk, what kind of clerking job should you take? Should you take one with the kind of firm or agency you "think" you would like to eventually work for? Or should you take a job with one of those "I-could-never-work-with-them" firms? There are pros and cons for each. Some students find permanent employment out of their clerking. On the other hand, much can be said for testing as many alternatives as possible. Even if you confirm your suspicion that you could never do insurance defense, having clerked with such a firm will make you a better personal injury lawyer.

c. Asking Lawyers and Professors

Most of us like to give advice (me, apparently, more than others). If you are considering prosecuting, why not go to the prosecutor's office and ask to see one of the attorneys.

> I'm not here looking for a job. I'm here because I want some advice. I am thinking about prosecuting when I graduate but I really don't know much about it. Perhaps you can tell me about it, perhaps I could sit in and watch what you do.

Note: This can be turned into a very clever job getting ploy.

Now, Ms. Banker, I'm not looking for a job working in your legal department. I realize you are probably full. What I would like is some advice on how to go about getting a job in the legal department of a bank.

Of course *I* would never be bold enough to simply show up at a law office, unannounced. The problem is meeting lawyers. One possibility is to get together with some classmates, ask a friendly professor for some names of recent graduates, and throw a party.

We're first year students and we want to meet some lawyers so we can get some feel for what it's like. Want to come to a party?

Another device is to try to get your professor talking about her practice experiences. Most likely they will be more interesting than the Rule in Shelley's Case. I sincerely hope so, for her sake as well as yours.

d. *Go to Court*

It takes absolutely no courage to quietly walk into the back of a courtroom and sit through a trial. Again this experience is probably most needed by those who will "never" step into a courtroom—who knows, perhaps they'll never leave.

e. Read Books

There are several books about practice. I recommend, as openers:

The Associates, Jay Osborne (author of *Paper Chase*) deals with life in a Wall Street firm.

Trial and Error, D. Michael Tomkins, story of a young lawyer starting off in solo practice.

Confessions of a Criminal Lawyer, Seymour Wishman, a criminal defense lawyer reflects on several years of practice.

These books are relatively short, quite candid, and at places, humorous. They are excellent introductions to various kinds of practice.

For other books on Lawyering, see the discussion of Law and Literature groups in Chapter 10.

A final word on careers. Once you have finally embarked on a career and begun to settle in, be aware the danger:

The horrible thing about all legal officials, even the best, about all judges, magistrates, barristers, detectives, and policemen, is not that they are wicked (some of them are good), not that they are stupid (some of them are quite intelligent), it is simply that they have got used to it.

G. K. Chesterton

CHAPTER 12

LAWYERS TALK ABOUT THEIR JOBS

My thinking about this chapter has changed. The original intent was to have lawyers write about what they do in order to provide career information. Reading what they have written it strikes me that the real value of the chapter lies elsewhere, in combating cynicism concerning the practice of law. My sense is that law students quickly lose idealism and enthusiasm for their chosen profession. I think this happens because in law school, law practice is presented as something abstract and lifeless, as intellectual game-playing without emotional or ethical content. My hope is that, in reading what these lawyers do, you will realize that yours was a wise decision. The practice of law is neither abstract nor amoral; it is alive, fulfilling, and caring.

The lawyers who write on the following pages are friends, not statistical abstracts. I selected them because they are reflective and insightful. Although I selected lawyers doing different kinds of law jobs, no attempt was made for "balance", either in terms of "type" of practice, age of practitioner, or geography. In describing to them their task I again rejected the goal of balance. I prescribed no format. I simply told them that I was writing a book for first-year law students, students who likely knew little about various legal careers and who likely knew little about what lawyers actually do. Write, I advised, what you think might prove useful.

Some focused on questions of career: how they made their own career decisions, the pros and cons of various kinds of practices, things you might do as a law student to help you prepare. Others focused on what they do as lawyers, describing either a typical day or a typical task. A quick disclaimer. These are *individual statements*. I told the lawyers that they were not writing as "representatives" of their kind of practice and not to worry if what they wrote might be atypical. People experience things differently.

This then is not an encyclopedia of the types of law practice. It is rather a collage of what some lawyers thought important to share with you. I have learned from them; so will you.

ANDY SILVERMAN

Legal Aid

[Currently Andy Silverman teaches law.]

It is 9 a.m. I arrived at work awhile ago. The waiting room is filling up and it is my day to be "on".

Being "on" in the legal services parlance signifies your day to do intake interviews. It is the first time the client talks to a lawyer. Such days generally amount to 10 to 15 of these encounters . . . the real guts of a legal services practice. I know it is a day that I will get no other work done but seeing clients.

The phone rings . . . it is the intake worker informing me that my first client is ready. I am now officially "on" and the stream of clients may go on all day . . . one right after another.

A young woman with a three-year-old tagging along walks into my office. After the introductions, I go for the extra legal pad and colored pens I always have ready and hand them to the child. I know that if the

[*365*]

interview is going to be at all meaningful I have to keep the child happy and busy.

The woman tells me that she is two months behind in rent and the landlord has sent her an eviction notice. She has been out-of-work for the past four months and her ex-husband who she cannot find has not paid child support for the past year. Her problems sound overwhelming . . . where do I start . . . is there anything legally I can do?

Well, being a lawyer, my initial reaction is to think of legal remedies . . . the law school approach to the problem. Is there a violation of the landlord-tenant law? Is the eviction notice proper? Will she have any defenses to a possible unlawful detainer action? I start going down this road and quickly realize she can no longer afford this apartment and all she wants is time to find suitable but cheaper housing for her and her child. A phone call to the landlord from me, the lawyer, might do it. She tried the day before and failed. I call and the landlord reluctantly agrees. And another call to a friend in the public housing office helps her cut through the bureaucratic maze to find new housing. She leaves a bit relieved.

Before my next client I think about whether I am a lawyer or a social worker. Did my last client need a lawyer? Or did I do for her just what a corporate attorney does for the corporation president: identify the true problem and find the easiest and fastest way to resolve it. Well, it does not matter, I helped someone and that's all that really counts.

No more time to reflect, the next client is standing at the door. He is a man in his 50's who works part-time as a laborer. He had purchased an insurance policy because of a newspaper advertisement that had made generous promises. But when he became ill, the company said his claim was not covered. Sounds like a legal problem and one that another lawyer in the office may be interested in pursuing. She has handled similar problems and is looking for "the" case to litigate. This may be the one. I get the facts and tell the client we will be in contact. I will talk to the other lawyer tomorrow when I am "off" intake.

Legal problems keep flowing in all day. Food stamp cutoffs, car repossessions, housing foreclosures, there is no end. They have one common ingredient: a person in trouble that needs help. That personal side of legal services keeps me going. It is frustrating . . . it is gratifying . . . it is being a legal services attorney.

At the end of the day an older woman walks into my office as my final intake of the day. She does not speak English well but gets across that her son is in the county jail. My first reaction is that she has a criminal problem which legal aid lawyers do not handle. In my tired state I think that I may be able to get rid of this problem quickly. But I hear her out and become fascinated. I remain after closing hours talking to her about her son's complaints about the conditions in the jail. I have heard about that "awful jail" for years but now may have a real, live client that wants to do something about it. She tells me that her son and others in the jail would like to talk to a lawyer about such a suit. I promise her I will see her son tomorrow. It all seems worth it.

RITA A. MEISER

Large Firm

The practice of law in a "large" law firm varies dramatically depending upon the firm and the city. In many, people hate briefcases and consider lunch at Mc-

Donald's a gourmet delight. Each firm has its own personality, which is reflected in many ways, especially the manner in which it deals with associates. As a result, I describe my practice to you as a person who, while content in my role as a practitioner in my particular law firm, might also not be content in a different large law firm. I also write as a person whose initial perception envisioned a happier legal life in a small firm, and who has been pleasantly surprised at where I have ended up.

My primary orientation in becoming an attorney was to maximize my involvement with people. The areas of law in which I am mostly involved reflect this goal. Mostly I practice hospital law. This is one of those areas that you do not know exists when you are in law school. Hospital law encompasses a broad range of legal problems: removing from a hospital staff a physician who does not perform at the proper standard of care; determining what procedures must be followed when a physician decides that life support systems should be removed, and working through the administrative procedures necessary to have a hospital add a department or beds. The work appeals to me because it involves effecting positive, tangible change in a way that is often lacking in the practice of law.

My second area of practice is employment discrimination, primarily from a defense perspective. I find this work intriguing because of the variety of people and areas to which it exposes me. Processing a discrimination charge, I learn the business operations of the client, as well as meet and work with people involved in the world of business. It has not been my experience that practice from the defense posture necessarily mandates advocacy of personally offensive legal positions. Business people are generally fairly practical. If they recognize that a policy or practice is unlawful and will cause them continuing economic harm, they are generally receptive to changing it. The lawyer plays a role in advancing this recognition.

Finally, I represent two adoption agencies on a pro bono basis. The gratifications are obvious and the ability to participate in this type of activity is often a luxury less easily available in a small firm.

As can be seen, there is little correlation among my major areas of practice. Also, my practice in these areas is not to the exclusion of occasional work in other areas. This is an example of a difference in the personality of my law firm as opposed to some others. Large firms place differing emphasis upon the importance of an attorney specializing, how quickly specialization should occur, and how much pressure is placed upon the associate to specialize in a given area. My specialties evolved over the course of three years of exploring numerous legal areas.

A large firm offers a new lawyer diversity, not only in terms of the type of legal practice offered, but the in people themselves. I initially perceived this to be an advantage of a small firm, but I now find it to be one of the greatest attributes of a large firm. I assumed that I would have closer personal relationships and find the working atmosphere more pleasant and intimate in a small firm. I now believe that a large law firm incorporates numerous types of personalities, and its size permits this diversification not to generate conflict. In a small firm, a personality conflict between two members can create tension for the remaining members in a way which does not occur when 70 lawyers are involved. Also, to the extent one specializes, the pool of working relationships narrows, thereby promoting the more intimate working relationships.

There are advantages and disadvantages to large firm practice, and what those factors are is the func-

tion of the given firm. The emphasis upon time com-
mitments, responsibility, and client contact are all variables which must be assessed in evaluating the
personality of any firm. In my particular firm, client
responsibility and contact came quickly; however, this
is not true in every large firm. If you are considering
work in a large firm, interview carefully, particularly
for second year clerkships, and try to select the firm
which you think has the personality with which you
are most compatible. Use your second year clerkship
at that firm not only to verify whether your percep-
tions were correct, but to develop your ability to analyze the makeup of other firms, so that if you interview at another firm, you will more quickly be able to
assess whether it's for you.

GRACE WILLIAMS

Mid-Size Firm

When I decided to become a lawyer, it was not because I thought the law would be exciting. I thought
it would be boring. I did not expect to like the law, let
alone love it the way one is supposed to. I wanted a
job that would give me responsibility, a chance to use
my brain, a good salary, and a chance to advance, none
of which I had as a secretary. Those were my sole
reasons for applying to law school.

It is amusing to recall what I expected the practice
of law to be like when I was in law school. I expected
it to be boring and tedious, so tedious that the hours in
the office would drag by. Nothing could be further
from the truth. I enjoy at least 90% of the things I
must do. Filling out time sheets and preparing bills to
send to clients are no fun at all, but working on my
cases is so interesting that I find I can think of noth-

ing else. I think about my cases all my waking hours and often most of the night. I even dream about them. When I am at a social gathering where I am supposed to be having a good time, I find myself wishing I were at work because it is more exciting.

The responsibilities and time pressures are, however, very stressful. The matters one handles are extremely important to the clients, and they place a great deal of trust in you. Because of that, and for many other more selfish reasons, there is great pressure to achieve an excellent result in every single case which is, of course, impossible. You never have enough time to be as thoroughly prepared as you would like to be. No matter how well organized and self-disciplined you are, every day is a struggle against time. There are never enough hours in the day. In that respect, law school is good preparation for practice.

In law school there is so much emphasis on legal theories that you begin to feel that legal knowledge and skill in legal analysis are all you need to be a good attorney. Law school doesn't prepare you for the psychological aspects of practicing law. You must build a good relationship with your client and make him or her have confidence in you. You must make the opposing attorney at least respect you, and it is to your advantage to convince him that you are tough, that you know the law, and that you will persevere no matter what. It is to your advantage to make him afraid of you. Yet sometimes you need his cooperation, so you must know when to be nice to him and when to apply pressure. (I use "him" when referring to the opposing attorney because, in litigation, nine times out of ten your opponent is male. If you are a woman, the difficulties of dealing with him are multiplied because even before he meets you, he has probably decided that you

[*371*]

are either a pushover or a bitch, and that whichever you are, you are not very bright.)

You need to convince the judges before whom you appear that you know the law, that there is a good reason behind every statement you make, and that you would never mislead them. You must pull out of witnesses the answers you want and need. You must convince juries that you are credible and that your client deserves their verdict.

There is always room to grow. There are always ways you could have handled a case better, which is one of the reasons you are always most excited about your newest case.

RANDY STEVENS

Prosecutor

It took just a little more than a year after my graduation from law school for me to realize that private practice wasn't for me—at least not at that time in my life. I wanted more variety, more action, more excitement. I also wanted to be handling cases that had greater significance than just importance to the client. Having watched several excellent trial attorneys perform in court, I knew that courtroom practice was something I had to try, but I also realized it would take years to get any meaningful experience if I stayed in private practice. Telling the people I worked with that I'd be back in a year or two, I left and joined the local prosecutor's office. That was fourteen years ago.

From my perspective, the *total* experience available in prosecution cannot be duplicated elsewhere, especially for an attorney in the first four or five years. It isn't just the legal experience; it is the broader awareness of life, people and society, awareness of aspects of our society that most of us never dreamed existed. While at the same time, prosecution is an accelerated course in all aspects of trial practice.

Prosecution is the perfect opportunity for you to find out if you really want to be a trial attorney. Almost every young attorney experiences some degree of trial resistance—a hesitancy to try a case in front of a jury. There is a fear of making mistakes, of embarrassing oneself, of "freezing up" and not knowing what to do next. In a busy prosecutor's office, this resistance is usually overcome simply because there isn't time to dwell upon it. A heavy caseload doesn't allow for it. It isn't unusual for new prosecutors to find themselves trying several cases a week. If he or she begins to enjoy what they are doing, and are comfortable in court, it is only a matter of time before they want to begin trying more complicated and more serious cases. But not all attorneys experience this. After six months to a year, and sometimes even sooner, some realize that they aren't enjoying courtroom work, that they don't like the pressure and the demands of trial work, something no one can really know before they've given it a try. Most prosecutor's offices expect this to happen with a percentage of the young attorneys they hire.

It is usually during the fourth and fifth years when trial skills begin to reach a plateau, which means the attorney can try any type of criminal case with a high level of competency. Most trial attorneys will agree: if a person can competently prosecute a lengthy, difficult criminal case, that person can probably try most any type of civil case. Law firms recruit heavily from prosecuting offices.

Most attorneys who prosecute do so for five to ten years, then they move on to something else. Looking back, asking myself why I've stayed so long in prosecution, the answer really isn't that hard to determine: I've thoroughly enjoyed myself. I've actually looked forward to going to work each morning. The constant flow of different types of cases, the interchange with victims and witnesses; working with every level of law enforcement; all go together to constitute a level of excitement that makes the job more than just enjoyable. It's experiencing life three or four times more than the average person. Along with this is the additional feeling that in some small way, you are doing something positive for society.

DAN COOPER

Public Defender

The most satisfying part of being a public defender is representing people who are despised by the public, the press and the prosecutors. Most cases remain obscure and create no reaction. On occasion, however, a defendant comes along who stirs the conscience of the community into moral outrage. It is defending this person that makes me proud to be a lawyer.

I recently represented a man who, along with his wife, was charged with child abuse. The facts were grisly. When I first met my client I was somewhat taken aback by his absolute and total lack of guilt. I try not to prejudge my cases. I was, however, aware when I received this case that the evidence was overwhelming against my client. I was perplexed at his total lack of emotion. Throughout the duration of the case he remained stoic in the face of constant hostility. The prosecutor called my client "a monster." The newspapers covered the case extensively and without objectivity. Even some close friends of mine asked

[*374*]

how I could represent this man. The trial lasted nearly two weeks and, although I could not honestly say
that I had fun, it was an experience I would not trade.
The victim in the case, a nine-year-old girl, was found
hog-tied in a motel room. She weighed thirty-two
pounds and had been beaten. She had a chipped front
tooth, bruises on her face and at least twenty scars on
the top of her head which, the State alleged, came
from a blunt object. A psychiatrist testified that she
had never seen a worse case of psychological and emotional child abuse. A pediatrician testified that the
child had been systematically starved for at least four
years. A radiologist testified that the child's growth
would, in all likelihood, be permanently stunted. And
the most damaging witness of all was the little girl,—
tiny, charming, precocious. She broke down in tears
as she turned to look at her mother and stepfather.
My client stared at her impassively.

Against the advice of some very skilled trial lawyers, I put my client on the stand. The other lawyers
felt that my client's testimony would only enrage an
already upset jury. But I wanted the jury to see how
narrow and rigid was my client's view of the world.
His testimony was stilted, rigid, unsmiling and, I felt,
demonstrated a myopic, inadequate personality perfectly capable of being unaware that his nine-year-old
stepdaughter had been systematically starved and
abused. Certainly his testimony would not prove his
innocence. But there was an outside chance that the
jury would convict of the lesser, non-intentional child
abuse charge if they felt my client was rigid, myopic
and pathetic. It was a slim chance in an unpopular,
highly publicized case. My closing argument to the jury was emotional. I had convinced myself, if no one
else, that the lesser offense would be the appropriate
verdict. That the jury convicted my client of the

greater offense has not changed my mind. But perhaps my feelings today about that child abuse case typify the nature of this job. I am proud that, in the face of overwhelming adverse publicity, against insurmountable evidence, while not able to convince a jury of my client's innocence, that jury knew that the defendant had a lawyer who believed in him.

MARY DOYLE

Federal Agency Practice

[Currently Mary Doyle teaches law.]

President Jimmy Carter admonished an uninterested nation: The Energy Crisis is the "moral equivalent of war" (later tagged "meow"). Invoking his statutory authority, the President decreed that we would save oil by turning down the thermostats and air conditioners in every commercial building in the United States. With another staff lawyer at the U.S. Department of Energy (DOE) I was called to the boss' office in May 1979 and assigned the task of drafting the President's "Emergency Building Temperature Restrictions." Here are a few snapshots from the memory album of a government lawyer at work creating regulations.

Meeting with the Engineers. The White House is eager to follow up the President's announcement pronto. Within four weeks, Peter (the other lawyer) and I must produce a set of draft regs for the bosses' review and publication for public comment in the *Federal Register*. So we sit down with four guys who look like they just arrived from Bulgaria; they are the heating, ventilating and air conditioning boys. How is a consistent and uniform air temperature maintained in every room in a thirty-story office building? Did any of you ever consider that question before this moment? The answer is far from simple. The windowed tier of offices on the outside must run hotter or cooler than the spaces located around the building's core. How can that result be achieved with a centralized heating and cooling system? Everything's more complicated than you thought before you thought about it.

Rather large policy questions loom out of the haze. What about exemptions or waivers? Should commercial establishments where people undress in winter—meaning such innocent enterprises as exercise spas or the Y—be allowed to run warmer than 65°F? What about hospitals? Nursery schools? To each of these questions we come up with nonarbitrary and capricious answers. For instance, since Peter has a child in nursery school, we give the toddlers a break on heating.

Public Participation. The proposed regulations are published for the nation to consider in the *Federal Register* in June. My name is listed as the person to direct your comments to. I got more than fifty phone calls a day for several weeks thereafter:

"I run a funeral parlor in Savannah: The bodies are bloating and the floral tributes are wilting."

"I own a bar here in Akron. My girls won't be able to wear their hotpants to wait tables in December."

"I'm a bank manager in Reno. I can't work with women when it's hotter than 78°." (I never understood the bank manager, though I thought long and hard.)

Enforcement. The program includes no funds for enforcement. But we are curious. So I deputize myself and Fred, one of the heating engineers, as the Enforcement Squad. Fred packs a device called a "sling psychrometer," which measures ambient temperatures, and we set off to measure compliance around Washington. At the suggestions of our co-workers,

[*377*]

we pick our targets: the *Washington Post* and the federal Office of Management and Budget top our list. What we find in two afternoons' work is massive compliance. Every building engineer we visit has made real efforts to comply and most are very complimentary about the technical aspects of the regulations. The only violator we find is a fancy candy store on Connecticut Avenue, which is running very cold, "preserving the integrity of the chocolates."

The work of the regulatory lawyer is work of the most responsible kind because it affects the health, comfort and welfare of many Americans and carries important consequences for the nation's economy. The responsibility factor alone is enough challenge and reward. But there's more. Every legal issue that lands on the desk of the regulatory lawyer brings with it a shadowy political issue that must be dealt with too. (Every regulated entity is in a Congressional district.) If you care about the country, you like politics. And if you like politics, consider a career with a regulatory agency.

DON B. OVERALL

U.S. Attorney–Civil

"There, it's ready to file." The lawyer signs off on an over-thick pleading, opposing summary judgment in a $3 million case. But this government defense lawyer can't stop there, for other files are piling up.

Those who have chosen to work with a large government agency quickly find themselves enmeshed in significant cases. The issues seem important and the dollars involved are staggering. "But this is what it's really about in the lawyering business, isn't it?"

The next file slides from the upper heights of the growing stack on the desk. Medical malpractice is the allegation in this one, a back operation where a government employee, a medical doctor, performed a procedure which did not give the hoped-for relief. It's a very expensive claim, and we can't just settle all of them, even for nuisance value. Better pick up the telephone, line up some consultants and send out the medical records for review. "Let's get working on this one" the lawyer barks to the paralegal, really a secretary now doing paralegal work. They learn fast in this business, they have to.

Some files are simply auto accidents—cases where agency employees driving their vehicles have run into litigious opposing drivers. Their lawyers are on the contingency; they win if the plaintiffs win. They are hungry, and won't let up. It's a battle, but then that's litigation.

The lights of the office usually dim somewhere between 5:30 and 6:30. Last night was a later one, about 7, as comrades in the civil division offered their theories on how to defend a death by drowning on public recreation land. Does assumption of the risk or contributory negligence apply? Should public land be posted as a "dangerous instrumentality"? Reasonable minds may differ, but some feel that many injuries on public land, such as by lighting, or harm to a camper from a wild animal in a wilderness area, are simply acts of God—can't be prevented, but the cases get filed anyway and we defend. What's the government to do, we can't put neon warning signs every hundred yards in the virgin forest. We'll give legal advice later, but defending suits is the work to be done first.

Before the next file is reviewed, witnesses begin to stack up in the waiting room. Today we go to court,

defending what is basically an alleged "police brutali-
ty" case.

On the other hand many files are routine. After
your seventeenth traffic accident case or eighth slip-
and-fall suit, the adrenalin simply doesn't pump as
high anymore. But other factors make it interesting.
The lawyers across the hall, those doing the criminal
cases in the government's law office, have given me
the file on an appeal coming up next week at the Cir-
cuit Court. It's a real bonus, because it means travel-
ing to the big city and appearing before what has
sometimes been called "the best and the brightest."
You never know who's on the panel, and last time it
was even the famous Judge Bazelon from the D.C. Cir-
cuit, a real treat. It's interesting to take these cases
once in a while, field the questions from the Court,
sharpen the appellate skills and hopefully see justice
done for the client.

The pay is less than the large firm private-practice
attorneys for sure, but lawyering in the government
does have its bonuses. The work seems significant.
Here, at our shop, turnover doesn't seem to be much
of a factor anymore. Lawyers are staying longer, and
some genuinely consider it a career slot. There's com-
radery and a sense of shared duty. We generally get
along. The other lawyers in the office are willing to
help do the job or cover a deposition or hearing when
you need it. You'll be doing the same for them. One
does need some time to do other than just lawyering.
Some time away—whether a real "vacation" or simply
"R and R," life is simply too short to pass it by.

"Back from court already?" the secretary asks.
"Continued until tomorrow." The court had to finish
off a criminal calendar that simply couldn't get completed. Speedy trial for criminal cases may delay

some civil suits, but ultimately we *will* get to court. Perhaps tomorrow.

WILLIAM C. CANBY, JR.

Federal Appeals Judge

My work cycle is monthly, not daily. One week a month I travel to another city to hear appellate arguments. The other three weeks I am home in chambers dealing with the results of those arguments.

An Argument Day

I arrive at the courthouse where I am supplied with a desk. I have read the briefs for today's arguments during the past week, and now review bench memos prepared by my law clerks. The bench memos summarize the facts and analyze the legal issues.

After half an hour I leave for the robing room, where I meet the other two judges assigned to hear cases with me that day. We enter the courtroom and the presiding judge calls the calendar. The first case is a criminal appeal. Was there probable cause for the search that revealed the cocaine? That determination is highly factual, and all three of us ask questions about the evidence presented at the suppression hearing.

The next case came from the National Labor Relations Board. Was there substantial evidence to support the Board's determination that a union steward was fired for union activity? He had been guilty of some unrelated discipline infractions. When there are mixed motives for firing, what is the test to determine whether the firing was permissible?

We continue through the calendar, hearing either 15 or 30 minutes argument per side in each case. I find that I am on edge during the arguments, both because I find arguments exciting and because I don't want to miss what is said or pass up the opportunity to inject my own questions. We continue through the calendar, without stopping to rule or recess. We hear an admiralty case (man overboard), a diversity case (breach of contract), and an antitrust case (vertical conspiracy).

We return to the robing room to discuss the cases. Because I have least seniority, I give my views first. Some cases are quickly disposed of; the search was legal and the conviction can be affirmed in a short memorandum. We disagree about the antitrust case; that one will take a long time, require an opinion, and I may dissent. The presiding judge makes the writing assignments and we all go to lunch. As I relax I am reminded that arguments are the most satisfying but tiring part of my job. I will spend the rest of the afternoon dictating notes of this morning's cases and getting ready for tomorrow's calendar.

A Day in Chambers

I begin by going through the morning mail, good and bad. Some are memos from other judges concurring in opinions I have drafted and circulated, almost invariably with minor suggestions or corrections. One memo from another judge suggests that one of my proposed opinions is seriously off track. I will have to go back through the opinion, read the cases the other judge cites, and either make changes or risk his dissent. Next I review two proposed opinions by judges in cases where I was a member of the panel; they were heard six weeks ago. I assign each to one of my three law clerks for review. Each will come back to me with a memorandum commenting on the draft.

I next work on the pile of proposed opinions that have come back from my clerks with such memoranda. I go through each opinion, read a case or two if crucial, and check my notes from argument against the opinion. I review my clerks' comments. I then draft a memorandum to the other judge, perhaps concurring, including suggestions for change and noting possible problems.

I meet with my secretary and law clerks together to go over the work in the office. How many opinions are in the mill, and how late they are? Clerks are making initial drafts of almost all of them; I am working on one or two from scratch. We review assignments of bench memos for next month's arguments, and set deadlines for them.

Finally, I get to work on an opinion I am writing. Indian law. I have been working on it off and on for six weeks, and find it difficult and challenging. Ideas for it keep coming up when I am doing other things, and I use some of them. Soon I will float it to my colleagues; eventually it will come down, I hope the way I want it to. *The result matters to a lot of people.* Sometimes it is hard to see that fact behind all the paper in the office, but it comes to the surface every so often. And that makes all the matter to me.

BILL BOYD

Law Professor

It's just after noon. The bluebooks will be delivered shortly. I wonder how the students have done. Was the exam too difficult? Too easy? Was it fair? If not, it wasn't for lack of effort.

I don't look forward to grading exams. Not many of us do. As the Dean is fond of quipping, "Exam grading is what we get paid for. The rest is fun." In any event, most of us worry about the grading. We know the process is far from scientific. The goal is to reduce the margin for error—to design a test that measures a student's command of the subject matter as comprehensively as time permits. This is no modest goal.

The exam today is in bankruptcy. Bankruptcy is a two-hour course. Frankly, that is not enough time to cover such a complicated body of substantive law and procedure. But this can be said about most courses. Perhaps I tried to cover too much. I continually ask myself what it is that students need to know so they can begin to deal intelligently with the range of bankruptcy issues they are likely to confront in practice. Realistically, how many of them will have to worry about the role of a 1111(b)(2) election in a "cram down" of a Chapter 11 plan? But then, can any self-respecting course in bankruptcy not expose students to such mystifying concepts?

It's a difficult line to draw. A well-conceived course is one that accommodates the realities of the limits of time and the needs of most students with the crush of information contained in most areas of the law.

Most of us strive to make our exams reflect this accommodation. The exam should test what we have judged to be important. Obviously, it isn't feasible or necessary to test for everything we cover. But a fair cross-section of the material should be implicated. The trick is to weigh the questions commensurately with the time and attention given the particular point or points in class.

Contrary to what students are inclined to believe, the exam isn't intended to "do in" a certain percentage of students. There are no "traps" aimed at tripping up the unwary. Nothing would please us more if all the students did well. After all, their level of performance reflects upon the quality of our teaching.

We are sensitive to the imperfections in the examination process. We labor hard to compensate. We look for clues that reinforce what the "raw scores" suggest is a good, or a bad, performance. We tend to resolve doubts in a student's favor. It isn't unusual for a teacher to overlook an important omission, or even significant mistake, and to assign an A or B grade to an exam that otherwise is exceptionally good. In such cases we attribute the omission or error to test design or exam pressure.

We don't want students to do poorly. Poor performances present perhaps the greatest difficulty. What accounts for the poor performance? Was it the test? Most of us reread the "bad" exams. We don't want to "ding" a student. We examine carefully for "clues." Is there a problem with completeness? Does it appear that the student seriously misallocated his or her time? Is the deficiency in the depth or accuracy of analysis? Has the student missed or mistreated even the most fundamental of issues? Is the performance truly unsatisfactory?

We agonize a good deal in assigning a grade below a C. Some teachers simply refuse to give bad grades. They don't want to defend them. It's easier to pass all the students. Such behavior is unfair. It's unfair to the students who worked hard and earned a passing grade. It's also unfair to those of us who feel that making the hard decisions "goes with the territory."

Well, here they are. Let's see how they've done. Hmm. OK. Not bad. What? You didn't learn that in my class. Oh, that's better. What explains the earlier blunder? Hey, this is not bad at all. Good point.

[*385*]

I hadn't thought about it quite that way myself. Whoops. You can't mean that. Did you misread the question? I see what you did. You were assuming the creditor was only partially secured. Too bad. But the analysis is correct given your assumption. Let's see now. You were clearly wrong on the conversion issue. And you misread one part of the question. But you've hit most of the major points. Some interesting analysis. Very respectable bluebook . . . .

MICHAEL SACKEN

Large Firm

[Currently Michael Sacken is a Professor of Education.]

Like many students who wander into law schools I was uncertain of my goals, beyond delaying my separation from the university environment and finding some meaningful occupation. At orientation, an old friend and I pledged our joint *non*-goal: Never to work in a big, corporate law firm—not for political reasons ("selling out"), but because it sounded so distasteful and mercenary. Ultimately, we both abandoned our pledges, at least initially, and joined our destinies to large, institutional firms.

The first step on the primrose path was succeeding in law school, which is not a goal to be consequently jettisoned. After my first year, I was elected to the law review. After anointment, I was courted by various law firms, which always approached new review members. My circle of acquaintances during the second and third year included more review colleagues, because we worked together and were thrown or chose to join together in social activities.

There was an intoxicating and delusive sense of being the "best" of our class. Whatever diversity of goals originally existed among us, we experienced a coalescence. New mythologies were introduced regarding big firm practice. The really complex and challenging issues were encountered there; you worked in a collegial atmosphere, surrounded by individuals of comparable intellect and ambition ("your kind"); and you were proximate to and advisors of the powerful. Even the sweat-shop working hours were translated into a reasonable expectation. After all, *you* were used to interminable work for the review.

Even so, I retained enough skepticism to work with a small litigation firm during the key second summer, rather than accept the traditional big firm clerkship. This experience provided an unintended consequence: I returned for my third year irrevocably committed to a big firm, for new reasons. The lead attorney in this small stable was a superior trial lawyer (and, perhaps inevitably, an indifferent law student). Measuring my potential against his realized abilities, I feared that I would never be a "successful" litigator. For one who had the "right stuff," a lesser standard than excellence seemed inconceivable. I developed a disabling "won't" category: I won't litigate. Big firms offered specialized practices without litigation, and an ego assuagement as well (I am still among the best). It was absolutely the wrong decision for me.

My *worst* decision was to exclude advocacy categorically, because that narrowed extraordinarily my range of options. Unfortunately, in those antediluvian days, my school offered few trial practice or clinical courses, and I was too intimidated to take what was available. The single critical decision to make prior to seeking employment is to litigate or not to litigate. That decision defines your career alternatives as no other.

[*387*]

Take trial practice or a clinical experience. For reluctant litigators the dread of the unknown is far worse than pedestrian reality.

My second poorest decision was to choose a large prestigious law firm, in part because I believed that it was expected of me and the only worthy choice. That practice turned out to be exactly what I suspected (and indeed somehow previously knew before I "learned" otherwise in law school): What I did not want to spend my life doing. Unfortunately, reviving that self-knowledge required an unfulfilling couple of years.

This is an idiosyncratic account, not a generalized indictment of big firms. What I experienced has a lot to do with me, and perhaps the firm that I chose, and perhaps little to do with you. At least, be cautious about rejecting such an opportunity because you see yourself as too idealistic, introspective or humanistic. The information system at law schools is riddled with explicit and implicit biases. Pursue these questions vigorously and extensively; then react on your own biases. And, a final bit of Polonian wisdom, never be afraid to admit your first decision was a mistake and move onto a preferable pasture.

DAVID KAPLEY
Solo Practice

I want to emphasize to you that your life in the law will be uncertain and fast.

I say "uncertain" because many of you will be surprised when you discover your eventual place in the law. What you do in the law will likely depend on accident and chance.

When you can only find a job in a medium-size firm that has a business office practice, that is where you will be, at least for a while. You might get a job in some high-powered law factory, where beehive-like specialization is the order of the partners. Of course, you will specialize. You might become a sole practitioner whose practice will, for one reason or another, drift in the direction of, say, criminal defense work. Even if you prefer civil litigation, you will probably do criminal defense—if that will put bread into your mouth.

Do not believe that you are certain of the type of law that you will practice when you leave law school. You need to have a broad survey of the law.

There are uncertainties no matter what type of law you will do. Something in the law is always changing. There are so many new cases, and so many new statutes, and so many new rules and regulations. There are changes in what you learned in law school. The law is so large that the general practitioner is facing what might become an intolerable roadblock. You will find that it is difficult to keep up.

I say that you will likely find the practice of law "fast" because of the dizzying pace at which many lawyers work. Things must be done in a hurry.

Today you are a law student and, perhaps, a law clerk. You have a distorted idea of what constitutes the practice of law.

A lawyer must solve many legal problems with moderate, little, or no research. There is a want of time and money. Many of your clients will not be able to afford a law clerk who can spend 10 or 15 hours on a project.

I knew of a professor of basic civil procedure who required his students to memorize large parts of the rules of civil procedure in his state. Many of his students protested the requirement of memorization. A lawyer does not need to memorize rules that are within the reach of an arm in an office, was a comment made by those students. They were wrong.

You will not have time to meander through the rules whenever you confront a problem concerning civil procedure. You must know those rules well to spot issues, even though you will rely heavily on reading the rules when the need arises.

The rules of civil procedure are only an example. I want to impress this upon you: study and learn thoroughly the substance of the law. You must have a good knowledge of law to do efficient research. You will not have the same, excellent opportunity to learn that substance once you are out of law school. Remember, your student days are nearly at an end.

I do not direct my plea primarily to first year students. Many of those are still driven by a fear of failing and a lust to succeed in law school. They will study.

But how unhappy are those second and third year students who take pride in their neglect of their school work. So many of those will grow up to be bad lawyers.

Study your law books! You need to know the law when you practice it.

JIM WEBB

Government Work/Private Practice

The Revolving Door. The first time I saw one—at age five—I knew that the revolving door was an inherently dangerous instrumentality. Nevertheless, I quickly learned the manipulation of the several variables involved in getting in the door and safely out the

[*390*]

other side. By the time all the vectors of the problem were resolved: coincidence of speed, angle of attack, heavy-lady-heavily-laden approaching on conflicting courses, I began to forget my instinctive response to the contraption. When years later I heard of the "revolving door" as metaphor for the shift from private to public practice and out again, I had lost my youthful wariness.

The Federal government occasionally publishes a document known, in the vernacular, as the "Plum Book." It lists all the many appointed positions in the executive branch of the government; many acceptable, without great corruption of standards, to lawyers. The Book is full of jobs which are, in turn, full of challenge, power and prestige. It's easy to imagine, in reading that book and thinking about your place in an incoming administration, that the public, honoring your Glorious Leader and your stunning performance as administrative assistant to the assistant administrator for administration, will repeal the twenty-second amendment, and that you and your President will go on indefinitely from triumph to triumph. At worst, it appears that you can, following your government service, slip gracefully into a fine job with a firm or industry that is crying out for your important experience and important contacts.

It doesn't always work that way. A revolving door is a good place to get hung out and dried.

Government jobs are often highly specialized and highly special to government. No matter how much you know about the Endangered Species Act, you are not going to get a job with the Snail Darter Trust or the Furbish Lousewort Corporation.

The ground also shifts rapidly in politically oriented work. The significance of your experience and your contacts can evaporate as easily as an electoral plurali-

[*391*]

ty. Air Force procurement policies, for instance, may
provide fodder for a hundred good practices. You,
poor turkey, may find after you leave government service in that area that there are a hundred and twenty
good practitioners already in the field, and that Jane
Fonda is the new Secretary of Defense.

A lawyer's highest distinction and greatest solace is
competence. The most reliable way to gain competence is to stick to place and to a defined progression
of skills and responsibilities. The revolving door
breaks progression.

After a few years away from my home jurisdiction
my most confident recollection of the State's law was
the color of the annotated statutes. A rather torpid
legislature and a stately judiciary had somehow managed to change a lot of that collections' contents and I
had somehow managed to forget a lot of what they
hadn't changed. Four years of great decisions made
on the Potomac had not done a thing for the simple
and vital skills of private practice like effective calen-
daring and timekeeping. Being less apt at some of
those skills than a junior associate or, worse, produc-
ing less income for the firm than that junior, doesn't
do a thing for the ego.

My view now is that every new start in the practice
of law is a start from well behind the line of scrim-
mage.

One who is a thin-ice-skater and an abyss-skirter,
one who ardently wishes to benefit, or, at least, to
meddle with others on the broadest possible scale, one
who can walk with Assistant Secretaries of Commerce
and not lose touch with himself or the kids, one who is
an exceptionally quick *and* thorough study and is curs-
ed with nomadic instincts, may find a home for his neu-
roses in the revolving door.

Today, I find that I am not so constituted. Today, I find myself struggling uphill against the problems of the new start and the envy I often feel for my classmate who found a place and stayed in it, quietly honing his skills, peaceably nurturing his friendships, his practice and his portfolio.

RICHARD DAVIS

Private Practice, Mid-Size Firm

I arrive in my office at 7:30 a.m. I look at my calendar and realize that I have to travel to a hospital which our firm represents to meet with the Administrator and Risk Manager. Others will be present. A few days ago a 20-day-old premature baby died at the hospital while on a ventilator. The original account suggests that the machine malfunctioned preventing the baby from breathing normally.

Immediately after the accident, the Director of the Medical Lab at the hospital wanted to test the ventilator. I advised a delay long enough to notify each of the interested parties and to give them an opportunity to be present. The manufacturer of the ventilator and the parents of the baby were notified.

The test is scheduled to begin at 9:00 but I get there early. This will allow me to become familiar with the machine and interview the hospital's personnel who were on duty when the incident occurred. Arriving at 8:15, I talk to the respiratory technician, the nurse on duty and the medical lab technician who will do the testing. By 8:45 I have a general idea of how the machine works, of the suspected problem and of what happened the day in question. I also learn that the hospital coffee gets old after the second cup.

The first person to arrive for the meeting is an investigator from the County Medical Examiner's Office. The family asked that office to be present and to determine the cause of the baby's death. We exchange pleasantries. I am a little anxious and apprehensive because I really do not know what the tests will reveal. My hidden hope is that the tests will prove my client blameless.

The manufacturer is sending someone from its national headquarters in Texas. It is now 9:00 and we receive a call advising us that the manufacturer's rep will be late. The small talk and anxiousness continue. At 9:30, the manufacturer's representative arrives. There is an immediate disagreement over the tests that should be run and who should run them. After discussion, ground rules are laid and pictures are taken to verify and preserve settings on dowels and pressure gauges. Each test is run carefully and meticulously. The pressure gauge is saved for last because it is the suspected culprit. It proves faulty.

Further tests are necessary to determine why the system failed but that necessitates a breakdown of the unit. Moreover, the necessary equipment is not available. The manufacturer's representative wants to take the machine back to the factory for further testing. I disagree. I feel that the machine should be stored in a place where no one can get to it without my knowledge and prior approval. Besides, there should be no destructive testing without giving every interested party an opportunity to be present along with an expert. I suggest that since the Medical Examiner's Office is involved, it should store the machine at its facility. The Medical Examiner's investigator nixes that idea but recommends that it be placed in the Police Department's storage room. We agree and the police are called.

When I arrive in my office around 3:30, I find thirteen telephone messages, most of which require a return call. I learn that two cases were settled and a person with a 2:30 appointment showed up and left after waiting about one-half hour. My secretary says that she was very angry.

I dictate a memo to the file concerning the test because I am certain that a lawsuit will be filed. I sort through the telephone messages and mail so I can arrange them according to some priority.

At 4:30 I receive a telephone call from a friend who is being investigated by the FBI. We wants my advice. I make an appointment for the next day. Next I receive a call from a representative of Farmers Insurance Group. He has a question concerning the value of a case and what should be paid to settle it. I recommend a figure. I answer a few letters and review tomorrow's schedule. I realize that I have a deposition scheduled at the same time that I set the appointment for my friend. I call him back but there is no answer. My calendar indicates that I have a trial next week and there are some things that I must do to be ready for it. I make a list. It is now 6:10 and it is dark outside. There is still a lot of work to be done but it will have to wait until tomorrow.

TOM MAUET

Prosecutor

[Currently Tom Mauet teaches law.]

My partner, Patti Bobb, and I are the two prosecutors assigned to a busy trial courtroom in the Chicago Criminal Courts Building. This day begins like any other. We arrive at work at approximately 8:30. As usual, we are in the middle of a jury trial. There are

[*395*]

100 things to think of that very moment. First, we decide I will go to court and handle that morning's motion call; Patti will stay in the office and prepare witnesses for the trial.

At 9:30 court commences. I have four cases—a murder, armed robbery, burglary and heroin possession—set for "conferencing". That is, they've been specially set for the lawyers to get together to work out possible plea agreements. After the initial call, the court takes a one-half hour recess so I can talk to each of the lawyers. The burglary and the heroin cases are the easiest to dispose of, since neither defendant has a prior conviction. Given the realities of overcrowding in the jails and prisons, these cases are routinely "pled out" to probation. I agree to plead both cases for 3 years probation.

The murder and armed robbery are more difficult. In the murder case the defendant has a prior robbery conviction. The defense attorney knows that because of this he will not be able to call his client as a witness at trial. Unless the client testifies the state would not be allowed to bring out his prior conviction; if he does, then we can impeach him with it. In any event, the possibility of beating the rap is small. I offer to reduce the case to voluntary manslaughter if the defendant will take 6 years pen time. The lawyer conveys the offer to his client, but predictably he doesn't want to "do time." The lawyer and I agree to continue the case for a few days so that he can soften his client up to reality: No one walks after a murder. This case should plead out the next time it appears on the call. On the armed robbery case the defense lawyer and I are miles apart, so the case will have to be tried.

When the judge comes back on the bench, he takes the guilty pleas to the drug and burglary charges. It is now 11:30 a.m. It is obviously too late to start the jury trial before lunch, so court is adjourned until 1:00 p.m.

I go downstairs to our office, which is packed with seven witnesses who we expect to call during the day. Those witnesses that Patti has already interviewed are sent out to lunch and told to be back by 12:30. Patti and I split up the remaining ones and interview each of them. Around 12:30 I run down to the cafeteria and bring back 2 sandwiches and coffee, which Patti and I wolf down. Another typical lunch in the county attorney's office.

At 1:00 o'clock, the trial begins. The armed robbery on trial is typical. Two 19-year old unemployed high school drop-outs are charged with robbing a Church's Chicken store at closing time. The indictment alleges that the defendants, armed with sawed off shotguns, forced the store employees into a storage room while they rifled the cash register, and fled with several hundred dollars cash. One defendant was picked out from a mug book, and this led to the co-defendant's arrest. Since there is no corroborating evidence, our case depends on the ability of the employees to make credible identifications of the two defendants in court. This is simply another "who do you believe" case, the store employees, or the defendants.

All afternoon we parade the eyewitnesses and each recounts the terror of the crime and identifies the defendants. The defense attorney, a public defender of three years, does a good job at undermining the credibility of those identifications.

The case is unfolding pretty much as planned. No surprises. But then, when you've tried several routine stick-ups like this, you get to be a pro at figuring out what will happen in court. At 5:00 o'clock, after having heard from 5 of the 7 witnesses, court adjourns. We have to tell the 2 witnesses that did not get to testify to come back the next morning. Here's hoping they will. Losing a day's pay is a great incentive not to come back—another thing no one told you about in law school.

At 6:00, Patti and I pull the files for the next morning. This time she'll take the morning call. She will take the files home and work on them that night. I'll worry about the trial and prepare my closing argument. At 7:00 we leave.

It was a great job, one I wouldn't have traded for any other.

JOHN G. BALENTINE
Legal Services

When asked to write a few pages on my career in Legal Services I hesitated; it is inevitably an emotional and unsettling experience to reflect on what you have done with the last 10 years of your life. I have spent my time with Legal Aid. On reflection, it has been time spent well.

I began in a neighborhood office with three other "rookie" attorneys. Our office was something out of a Tom Robbins novel—we shared a building with a tavern, had to fix the cooler and heater ourselves, and were flooded every time it rained. It was a wonderful way to learn about the practice of law; I think we sank more than we swam. (Today, thankfully, there is more of an emphasis in Legal Services on proper training and supervision for new attorneys.)

After two years as a staff attorney I spent another two years as a Managing Attorney working primarily on consumer and landlord tenant cases. I then became Litigation Director for our office and supervised the 20 to 25 other attorneys in the program. This was an especially enjoyable period for me. I handled only five to ten cases at a time but they were all complex cases, mostly class actions or appeals in federal or state court, usually on issues of importance to the poverty community. For the last three years I have been the Executive Director of the office. It is a whole new world: personnel decisions, budgets, dealing with the private bar, complaints from clients and those occasional odd complaints from a staff member.

Legal Services is famous for posing inscrutable choices: Do I represent the client whose house is being foreclosed, the senior citizen whose Social Security benefits have been cutoff, or the client whose husband is being deported in the morning. Our office currently has only 10 attorneys for a client population of over 80,000. There is simply no way that everything can be done—we are constantly attempting to allocate insufficient resources in the most effective manner.

Our work involves problems which are critical: loss of housing, jobs, public benefits, children. The problems are seldom easy to solve. I recently finished a class action involving access to statutorily mandated free health care for indigents. One of our plaintiffs, separated from her husband, and out of work with no income, was six months pregnant when she was denied free care by the county. Untreated she suffered a miscarriage. After three years of litigation, one appeal and three special actions to the state appellate courts, the county was ordered to do what the statute had required since its adoption in the 1920s—provide free health care to all eligible indigents.

In my view, the law is primarily an instrumentality used by those with wealth and power to retain those two coveted commodities. Legal Services practice offers an opportunity to attempt to balance the scales.

ROBERT J. HOOKER

Judge, Superior Court

We place too much emphasis upon occupation—it becomes an end rather than a means. This isn't anything new; we have all studied this phenomenon in sociology classes. Now, however, it is real for me. A person's status, ego gratification, the perception that others have, are based upon what he does, rather than what he is.

It is a struggle to maintain perspective, to realize that a job is something to do to enjoy life and what it has to offer. Law is particularly perilous. It is easy to get a distorted, overinflated view of one's own importance. It is easy to take one's self too seriously. Take my own present occupation, that of a Superior Court Judge. Everyone goes out of the way to be respectful, to refrain from offending, to kow-tow, to laugh at jokes, to invite to parties and events I would not otherwise be invited to, to introduce me as "Judge." Indeed, I am not referred to by name anymore, even in off-work hours, but rather referred to by title.

Litigants tell me that the case I am deciding is critically important to their clients and often tell me that my decision will have ramifications beyond. The fact is that many, many times, the case isn't that important, even to the parties involved. But it's easy to forget this.

Practicing law and being a judge are extremely confining for those who want to get things done or see changes made. The lawyer has the job of convincing the judge to make that change but it is the judge's job to follow precedent, maintain continuity, dependability, and reliability. In law creativity scares the hell out of

[*400*]

people. A creative lawyer scares the judge; a creative judge scares lawyers and the court of appeals; and the creative court of appeals scares everyone.

If there is anything that intimidates a lawyer, it is having his case assigned to a judge that he cannot predict. To combat this, the legal community has adopted a plethora of restrictions: precedent, guidelines, codes, statutes, local rules, uniform rules, civil rules, criminal rules, administrative rules, informal rules of practice for a particular judge, justice court rules, city court rules, state supreme court rules, federal district court rules, federal court of appeals rules, United States Supreme Court rules, rules of evidence, rules for domestic relations cases, codes of conduct, traffic case rules, rules of appellate procedure, rules for special action, mandatory sentencing. And, don't forget local custom or what I like to refer to as the "good ole' boy" rule. That's the rule that transcends all others. Regardless of what the applicable court rule or statute might provide, the "good ole' boy" rule can completely circumvent it and the violator goes unpunished. The "good ole' boy" rule is never written, but holds that this is the way we do things around here and the hell with what the Legislature or Supreme Court has said, and God help the lawyer or judge who doesn't know or respect that rule.

All these rules, laws, and statutes, are designed to guarantee one thing—uniformity and thus predictability. Uniformity and predictability stifle creativity. I may attempt to effect change but only within the confines of all of those restrictions. Mavericks are not appreciated.

MO UDALL

Member, U.S. House of Representatives

I had a passion to become a lawyer since my boyhood days. World War II slowed me down some. I practiced law privately after my graduation in 1949 until my election to the U.S. House of Representatives in 1961. I started law practice trying personal injury cases. I suspect I would have continued down that road and made a bundle of money. But I do not regret my decision to get into what my dad used to call "public service."

It's difficult for anybody in public life to plan their career. I've observed a number of bright young people who come into politics with a master plan: the legislature in 1950, the state senate in 1954, the governorship, then on to the congress and the White House on a track that's all figured out in advance. My whole career has been a bunch of disappointments followed by struggling on with what looks best and eventually reaching some goals that I had thought I might not reach.

In 1954 a congressional seat opened up in Arizona and I wanted to go, but I was convinced by some people in my family that I was too young. In restrospect, age 32, which I was at the time, is about the best age to come here so you can get some seniority before you get too old. Anyway, I declined to run and my brother Stewart sought the seat. I thought that avenue was closed because my brother would stay there a very long time. So I thought maybe of succeeding my father as Supreme Court Justice. I worked very hard in the Arizona State Bar Association and my father indicated that he was getting ready to retire at a fairly early time and that maybe I could move in and run with considerable popularity among lawyers. Well, about the year my father and I were going to maybe work out a retirement for him and race for me, he unexpectedly died of a stroke. The Republicans had control of the Governor's office and were looking for someone to appoint to the Supreme Court who would hold my father's seat in the election. A very obvious candidate was picked, my favorite uncle Jessie A. Udall. This was in 1960 and he was elected to a full term in the fall of that year and went on with a long and distinguished career on the court.

At that point I decided that public life was never going to come my way and that I might as well be a good lawyer and enjoy life and have some inputs in public policy in other ways.

As it turned out, a year later I was sitting in Congress. My brother, Stewart, went to work with John Kennedy as a member of his cabinet and in a special election I went to Congress where I've been ever since. My party has been in the majority for the 22 years I have served. I helped lead the fight to dismantle the most undesirable aspects of the seniority system, and I therefore take pride in having been chosen Chairman of the House Interior and Insular Affairs Committee for the past 3 terms.

During my service in the Congress, I've been instrumental in doubling the land in our national parks, in establishing the Land and Water Conservation Fund to expand and acquire local, state and national parks, in creating a series of wild and scenic rivers that will remain untouched, and in requiring strip mining scars to be covered.

It has been an exhilarating 22 years and, I'm sure, as satisfying as a good trial practice. The training I got in trial preparation and courtroom persuasion dur-

ing my years of private and public practice have
served me well in the Congress.

My father told me something many years ago about
what he called public service and others call politics.
He said that I probably won't leave you any money,
but I think I'll leave you a good name and a good family reputation.   And he really did.

CHARLES E. ARES

Law Professor

Teaching law is hard work.   I've been at it since
1961 and keeping up with movements in the law and
getting prepared for class seem to take me about as
long now as when I started.

But there is another way in which law teaching is
hard.   The longer I'm in the academic world the more I
worry about just what it is that we teach our students.
I don't mean "the law" and "the legal method"—we do
that better and better all the time.   I mean what we
teach, mostly implicitly, about the role lawyers are
supposed to play.   We teach students from the very
outset, as we should, that they are to be highly skilled
partisans, that they are to be analytical and very skep-
tical of factual and legal propositions.   They learn under our prodding to state the case as strongly in their
clients' favor as the credulity of their audience will
permit.   They may, in fact, learn not only that truth
takes many elusive forms but that sometimes it
doesn't really exist.   Only zealous representation of
our client really counts.

I wonder how many students think that the "legal
method" involves lying, or at least "massaging" the
truth.   Many of us who have been in the profession a

while don't realize that we may, at least unconsciously, convey the wrong message to neophytes. One of the most heart warming and yet depressing statements I've heard from a law student was recently uttered at the end of my course in Professional Responsibility. On the way out of the classroom, this good and conscientious student said, "I had almost decided I didn't want to be a lawyer because I don't want to lie for people. But now that I've learned we're not supposed to lie for clients, I feel a lot better."

Good people can be good lawyers. It isn't easy, but then preserving one's integrity never is.

*

INDEX

References are to Pages.
How to use this book, 7–8

INDEX
References are to Pages

†